March 1981.

EDWARD VIII

The Road to Abdication

FRANCES DONALDSON

EDWARD VIII

The Road to Abdication

Weidenfeld and Nicolson London

Designer Charles Elton

ISBN 0 297 77523 5

Printed in Great Britain by
Butler and Tanner Ltd, Frome and London

Contents

Acknowledgments

The illustrations in this book are supplied or reproduced by kind permission of the following:

Aerofilms 75;
Associated Newspapers 96;
Camera Press 172, 179;
Central Press 38, 67 (below), 74, 95, 107 (below), 121;
John Frost Historical Newspaper Service 110, 164;
Keystone Press 10, 63 (left), 80, 106–7, 132, 145, 149, 160–1 (above), 173, 181;
Mansell Collection 25, 85, 89, 92, 148 (above), 151;
National Portrait Gallery 13;
Popperfoto 20, 21, 22, 27, 30, 31, 32, 37, 40, 43, 47, 48–9, 51, 54 (bottom), 54–5 (above), 56, 59, 66–7 (above), 73, 78, 82, 83, 87, 97, 100, 101, 105 (above), 105 (below), 111 (below), 122, 133, 142, 148 (below), 156, 160–1 (below), 166 (above), 166 (below), 175, 176, 178 (above), 178 (below), 180;
Punch Publications 150;
Radio Times Hulton Picture Library 28–29, 34, 42, 52, 61 (above), 61 (below), 68, 69, 111 (above), 113, 115, 120, 128, 131;
Reuters Photos 177;
Sunday Times 170.

Picture research by Caroline Lucas

Introduction

The life of a king is usually the life of his times, and, although the best official biographers make every attempt to present the person and even some of the warts, it is the place of the man in the political and social history of his reign which gives these volumes their solid importance. The history of Edward VIII, however, is the history of an abdication.

The facts of the Abdication have been told again and again from every point of view and in the greatest possible detail. It is unlikely that a great deal will ever now be added or much fresh light thrown on a story which by constant repetition has been rammed into immutable shape. It seemed to me when I first thought about these things that what no one had yet attempted was a serious explanation of what happened, how these things came to be. How did the beautiful, eager English boy turn into the sad-faced man living between Paris and New York; the most popular Prince of Wales in history into the Duke of Windsor?

It is obvious that there is no easy answer. Only by learning as much as one can of the developing character, by adding detail to detail until one has the man, or something of the man, can one get anywhere near it. This is the task of the biographer – not ignoring the field of the psychologist but not usurping it – to seek out and represent as faithfully as possible the human being behind the history. A desperate enterprise at the best of times, it is a hundred times worse when the subject is a member of the Royal Family. I cannot claim to have completely understood the character of this man who, whatever one may think about it, performed an act unique in the history of kings, nor to have presented a picture finished in detail. Far from it. I claim only to have rescued a great deal that would otherwise be lost, in recording the recollections of people who actually knew him, and to have strewn the ground with clues for others to pick up. I have tried to be impartial in presenting the evidence, but books are not written without emotion and I cannot claim not to have formed my likes and dislikes. I have not tried very hard to disguise these prejudices, but, as far as possible, to show the evidence which might be cited in support of views different from my own.

Many of the friends and contemporaries of Edward VIII do not wish to go into print. Sometimes this is for reasons which can be easily understood, at others merely from preference. One of them said to me: 'Having avoided publication all my life, I don't want to begin now.' Nevertheless the reader will wish to have some proof of good faith, and so I have observed the following rules: (1) I have not stated anything as a fact unless the source for it is unimpeachable or independently corroborated; (2) where I use 'it is said' or other phrases of that sort, it means that I believe it and have evidence for it, but have been unable to get corroboration.

I must acknowledge my debt to professional historians and writers. I have experienced the most kind help wherever I have sought it and wish particularly to record my gratitude to: Mr Keith Middlemas and Mr John Barnes, Professor Donald Watt, Mr Brian Inglis, Mr H. Montgomery Hyde, Mr Ladislas Farago and Mr David Irving. I must also acknowledge a particular indebtedness to *Abdication* by Brian Inglis, *Baldwin* by Middlemas & Barnes, and *Baldwin: The Unexpected Prime Minister* by H. Montgomery Hyde. Finally, I have to thank the executors of the late Lord Monckton and Sir Edward Peacock for permission to quote from their notes made at the time of the Abdication and afterwards, and A. D. Peters, for their permission to include the extract from *The Memoirs of Lord Chandos* which appears on p. 39.

PART I

1
Childhood

King George V had been married for seventeen years when he came to the throne in 1910, and, because of this and because he and Queen Mary were so well suited to each other, their life together has come to be regarded in twentieth-century terms. Wars and revolutions have swept crowned heads from their thrones and reduced the number of marriageable princes and princesses, and the effect has been to widen the choice of the Royal Family, so that the arranged marriage has become a thing of the past. But in 1891 Queen Victoria surveyed the eligible princesses with an expert eye and chose Princess May of Teck as the one most suitable to be Queen. Prince Albert Victor (Prince Eddy), the Queen's grandson and, in succession to his father, the future King Edward VII, her heir, thereupon proposed marriage to Princess May and was joyfully accepted. Soon after he died of pneumonia and a wife had then to be chosen for his brother. Rather to the embarrassment of the Royal Family, it quickly became apparent that Princess May was still unrivalled as a candidate for the hand of the heir to the throne. It was a matter of chance, though a happy one, that the Duke of York was, by character and temperament, the more suitable both for the crown and to the tastes and affections of his future wife.

Princess May, a girl of serious and purposeful character and reliable disposition, was steeped in the history and traditions of the British Royal Family and trained from her earliest days to revere them. She was cut out to be Queen, and the Duke of York found no difficulty in falling in love with her. 'I adore you, sweet May,' he wrote to her quite early in their married life, while she, more self-contained, wrote to her old governess, Madame Bricka, 'Georgie is a dear ... he adores me which is touching,' and added, 'I feel as if I had been married for years and quite settled down.'

For the first seventeen years the Duke and Duchess made their home at York Cottage, Sandringham, which had been given to the Duke by his father. 'Until you have seen York Cottage, you will never understand my father,' the Duke of Windsor told Sir Harold Nicolson, who, in his biography of George V, described it as 'a glum little villa'. 'The rooms inside, with their fumed oak surrounds, their white overmantels framing oval mirrors, their Doulton tiles and stained glass fanlights, are indistinguishable from those of any Surbiton or Upper Norwood home.' At the time of the Duke's marriage the plumbing was primitive, the bedrooms like cubicles, while the lady-in-waiting slept in a cell above the pantry 'separated from it by the thinnest of flooring through which every sound penetrated'. As

(Opposite) Edward VIII's parents, Princess Mary and Prince George (then Duke and Duchess of York), in fancy dress, 1897.

The Duchess of York's little sitting-room at York Cottage where Edward spent his earliest years. This 'glum little villa', in the words of Sir Harold Nicolson, was so cramped that the Duke of York himself said he supposed the servants slept in the trees.

for the servants, the Duke of York himself said he supposed they slept in the trees. When his family increased he constantly added on to the house until outside it was 'all gables and hexagonal turrets and beams and tiny balconies', while inside it 'became a rabbit-warren of tiny rooms connected by narrow passages, in which royal pages and tall footmen would sit or stand, blocking the way'. The bathrooms were insufficient and before meals 'the whole house reeked of food'.

In the course of time the Duchess of York gave birth to five sons and a daughter. Five of them were born at York Cottage, but the eldest was born at White Lodge, in Richmond Park, at that time the home of the Duke and Duchess of Teck. (The younger children were born at York Cottage for the endearingly human reason that the Duke of York could not a second time stand the long association with his mother-in-law.)

With the birth of their eldest son in 1894, the Duke and Duchess of York immediately became involved in a covert struggle with Queen Victoria as to the name he should bear. It was the Queen's wish that her own son should be known as Albert Edward when he became King and that all his male descendants should bear the name Albert to the end of time. In turn each of her children can be seen determined to avert the name of Albert. On this occasion the Duke of York expressed to his grandmother his wish to name his son Edward, after his dead brother, Prince Eddy, to which the Queen replied that the real name of 'dear Eddy' had been not Edward but Albert Victor. There is therefore a fine inconsequence in the fact that, although the baby was finally christened Edward Albert Christian George Andrew Patrick David, he was always known to his family as David.

To mark his birth telegrams were received from all the royal families of Europe and from every public body in England, while crowds lined the roads from the station when Queen Victoria travelled to Richmond to see her great-grandson. *The Times* remarked that never before in the history of these islands had the sovereign seen three male descendants in the direct line of inheritance. And in the House of Commons, speaking on a motion congratulating the Queen on the birth of her great-grandson, Mr Keir Hardie made a speech which is so eminently quotable that it is unlikely anyone will ever write about this Prince without reference to it. Having remarked that the motion sought to 'elevate to an importance it does not deserve an event of everyday occurrence', he said:

From his childhood onward this boy will be surrounded by sycophants and flatterers by the score and will be taught to believe himself as of a superior creation. A line will be drawn between him and the people he is to be called upon some day to reign over. In due course, following the precedent which has already been set he will be sent on a tour round the world, and probably rumours of a morganatic alliance will follow (loud cries of Oh! Oh! and Order!) and the end of it all will be the country will be called upon to pay the bill.

During the early years of their married life the Duke and Duchess of York were not called upon to perform many public duties and until 1901, when, after the death of Queen Victoria, they went on tour in Australia, they lived lives that were not immensely different from those of a country squire and his wife. The upbringing of their young children might have been expected to be much the same and certainly not less propitious than that of hundreds of other upper-class children of the day.

All upper-class children were reared in isolation from their parents whom in many families they saw once, at most twice, a day when they had been specially dressed and prepared to meet them, and it was quite common for their parents to be uneducated in child care and subject to the conventions of the time. The only obvious difference between the routine arrangements for the royal children and those of hundreds of others throughout the land was that, when they were taken to the drawing-room to meet their mother, she was normally attended by a lady-in-waiting. There were, however, other differences and these were for the most part unlucky.

At this time there reigned in the nurseries of England, in complete charge of the children and in respectful control of the parents as far as anything affecting their children was concerned, that historical character, the English nanny. The nanny at her best had a vocation – a generous vocation to give her charges the mother-love which is all-important to the early years of the human child, to ensure them a stable and secure background, a nursery fire and an aproned lap; to teach them a moral sense and a satisfying, if sometimes oddly conceived, sense of right and wrong; to supply in fact all the things that are necessary to children but which through the conventions of the day were often withheld by their parents.

The nurse who had charge of the children at York Cottage drew attention to herself after she had been with the family three years by having a nervous breakdown, when it was discovered among other things that she had not had a day off during all this time. This nurse, who was 'sadistic and incompetent', was totally unfitted for her job. She adored Prince Edward and, when she took him to the drawing-room to see his parents, indulged a strangely perverted love for him by pinching him or twisting his arm, so that he bawled and screamed on entering the room and was speedily returned to her. Her feeling for him, although distorted by her insane possessiveness, was, nevertheless, one of love. Prince Albert she ignored and neglected, and fed so badly that he developed a chronic stomach trouble. No one has attempted to explain how these things could have happened in this over-

Keir Hardie in a sketch by the top political cartoonist of the time, 'Spy'. His speech in the House of Commons on the birth of Prince Edward included a strangely prophetic reference to a future morganatic alliance.

filled house with its ladies-in-waiting and its thinly partitioned walls, nor
how such an unsuitable nurse came to enter the service of the Duke and
Duchess of York in the first place.

There is no doubt that King George V and Queen Mary failed in their
relationships with their children and were for different reasons temperamentally unsuited to parenthood. It is more common for parents to be lacking in deep affection for young children than is sometimes believed, and
it is noticeable that in societies where married couples hand their babies
over to the care of servants they tend to check the development of their
own parental love. In addition the King and Queen suffered the handicap
of majesty, which was bound to increase both the awe in which it was proper
for their sons to hold them and their own mortification in the face of an
inability to predict or control the behaviour of very young children. The
King particularly was afflicted with that kind of irrational pride which causes
people to see themselves in a permanently superior relationship to their
children and this affliction would, as Prince Edward and Prince Albert grew
to maturity, become very pronounced and in a large measure be responsible
for the breakdown in trust and affection which occurred between himself
and his eldest son.

Yet the King was affectionate and fond of children and when his own
children were born he was unaffectedly happy as a family man, bathing the
babies and playing with them. He was by nature a disciplinarian and a martinet. He was tidy, punctual, hard-working and a stickler for tradition. He
believed that the customs and fashions of his youth were immutable and
he attached a moral significance to such things as dress or speech. (A new
kind of haircut or the wrong pair of shoes were quite strong evidence of
going downhill, and might earn the final term of condemnation, a cad.) He
was also very excitable. 'Since he was impetuous by nature,' Mr John Gore
says in his biography of the King, 'he gave vent to his feelings instantly and
without reserve.' And Sir John Wheeler-Bennett in his biography of George
VI adds that the Queen found it difficult 'to stand between them [the children] and the sudden gusts of their father's wrath'. These two sentences alone
make it plain that in moments of stress the King, like his father before him,
exercised little restraint with his Household or with his children. But
whereas his servants and courtiers understood him and were equipped to
deal with him, his children were not.

The King's temperamental qualities were distorted in his relations with
his own children by anxiety, and this was particularly so in his dealings with
his eldest son. Here he found himself in the uncharted realm of the education
proper to the heir to the throne. Prince Albert and Queen Victoria had once
attempted to devise the ideal upbringing for the future sovereign and had
reduced Edward VII as a child to a physical and nervous exhaustion which
used to bring on screaming fits. King Edward in his turn had been determined that his own children should never suffer anything of the sort, and
he and Queen Alexandra were by nature affectionate and indulgent parents.
Far less tolerant than his father, George V was oppressed by the necessity
to inculcate in his children good character and seriousness of purpose, and
there were some branches of their education in which he would have liked
to see them excel. What in another man might have been a rather low desire
for self-glorification through his children, must be credited in him as a very
real understanding of the importance to the monarchy of the qualities he
tried to instil.

Consequently, he was too often harsh and fault-finding, while his anxiety

spoiled even his most genial characteristics. The children were nearly always uneasy in his presence and sometimes reduced to what Sir Harold Nicolson had described, in words that clearly have been carefully chosen, as 'nervous trepidation'. In his autobiography the Duke of Windsor, speaking of his childhood, tells us that nothing would ever be so 'disconcerting to the spirit' as a message delivered by a footman that the King wished to see him in the library. Yet his description of what followed at the interviews in the library is no worse nor more frightening than was probably normal in any Victorian library and in fact comes as an anti-climax. Sometimes his father merely wished to show him something, although usually he wished to scold him for being dirty or late or making too much noise, or to deliver one of the vast number of 'don'ts' which were an intrinsic part of the educational system of the time. The truth seems to be that the King was unimaginative, very opinionated and over-anxious, and maintained an attitude of hectoring disciplinarianism to his sons long after it ceased to be appropriate. But all who knew him are genuinely horrified at the suggestion that has been made in some quarters that he was deliberately cruel or threatening to his children in any way which might by itself induce 'nervous trepidation'. Such charges are too crude an explanation of the far more ordinary and at the same time more subtly tragic situation caused by the almost total inability of this family to communicate with one another. Both the King and Queen wrote charming letters to each other and to their children, but the King as well as the Queen was almost completely inhibited from any more personal expression of affection or any intimate exchange of ideas. In addition it seems probable that the distance and hostility that grew between the King and his eldest son were due in part, as family hostility so often is, as much to the qualities they shared as to those in which they differed. As his children grew to manhood the King's desire to dominate them and to hold them captive to his

Three future British monarchs appear, one in front of the other, in this otherwise typically Victorian family photograph. (Standing) Louise, Duchess of Fife; Edward, Prince of Wales; Duchess of York; Princess Maud of Wales; Prince Charles of Denmark; (seated) Alexander, Duke of Fife; Duke of York, holding Edward; Alexandra, Princess of Wales; Princess Victoria of Wales.

authority certainly became excessive and had undoubtedly damaging effects, but it seems likely that in their childhood his shortcomings were not so very different from, or so much greater than, those of many another Victorian papa.

In households where there is some warm and stable influence that supports them, children become acclimatized to grumbling and hectoring, just as they do to the east wind and having their hair combed. Without it they are prey to fear. In childhood the princes surely suffered less from the failings of their father than from their almost total estrangement from their mother, and the coldness with which she rejected them. After all, the curious story of the possessive, pinching nurse rests on the assumption by everyone concerned that if, over a period of time, her eldest son, not yet three, screamed with pain in her presence, he would instantly be removed from it.

The earliest years are the most formative and during these years the most necessary part of a child's environment is his mother's love. Given the security of mother-love, the child will gradually and naturally be weaned from his dependence on it, whereas denied it, he may seek it in one form or another for the rest of his life. Queen Mary's exceptionally reserved and undemonstrative temperament made it impossible for her to give her children the love and affection which is taken for granted in happier homes. From the first she disliked the period of pregnancy and the physical aspects of childbirth and held herself aloof from the demonstrations of intimacy and affection these were apt to provoke. The Empress Frederick of Germany (Queen Victoria's daughter) described her as 'very cold and stiff and very unmaternal', while someone who knew her in later life summed up what dozens of people bear witness to by saying: 'Queen Mary had nothing of the mother at all.'

The Queen's inability to communicate with other people extended to almost all human relationships. Thus she could not deal with her own staff or correct or dismiss the people who served her, so that if the arrangements for the children were unsatisfactory it was the King who altered them. With her children she reminds one of a very shy person in enforced contact with someone else's. Speaking of her first child she wrote to his father in terms in which the note of humour does not disguise a genuine difficulty: 'I really believe he begins to like me at last, he is most civil to me.' And, although as her family grew up she began to feel more at ease with them and to perform many of the normal maternal functions such as reading aloud or teaching them little things, she never had the slightest doubt where her first duty lay. 'I have always to remember', she said of her children, 'that their father is also their King.'

When Prince Edward was three years old and his nurse's mental instability was discovered, her place was taken by the under-nurse Mrs Bill, who came to be known to the family as 'Lala'. For a few years she seems to have provided a stable presence, yet there is no evidence to suggest that she had the exceptional character that would have been necessary to replace all that was lacking in this nursery. Certainly Prince Edward was aware of the coldness of the climate in which he was nurtured. As a young man he was very much devoted to the two little daughters of Mrs Dudley Ward and one day, scolding one of them for some reckless act, he said: 'You see, you are so much loved you are spoilt. You have no idea of the lives of many children.' And he told her that in his own childhood he had never known love. There were servants, he explained, who seemed to love him, but he could never forget that this might be because he was heir to the throne.

However, it should not be overlooked that, with his three eldest sons at least, George v was dealing with children of a highly nervous temperament. Prince Albert stammered from an early age and gave other signs of a nervous disposition; but the half-controlled physical indications that the heir to the throne was at least equally highly strung have attracted less attention. People find it so difficult to believe in the vulnerability of princes that the constant tie-pulling and cigarette-smoking of Prince Edward as he grew to manhood passed as an extra charm, an unexpected and delightful human modesty, instead of being understood for what they were, the outward signs of an extreme inner tension.

When they were children Prince Edward and Prince Albert were also terrified in the presence of their great-grandmother, although it is not certain whether their terror was caused by Queen Victoria herself or by her Indian servants. In any case, they would frequently burst into tears in her presence for no obvious reason, which 'both saddened and annoyed the Queen, who would ask, with the petulance of old age, what she had done wrong now. It also mortified the children's parents.' If one remembers the prevailing attitudes to children at that time, it is not surprising that this mortification led the anxious parents to believe that what was needed was more 'character-building', rather than less.

Nevertheless, much has been made of the mishandling of these boys in

Queen Victoria in 1899 with her grandchildren (left to right) Prince Albert, Princess Mary, Prince Edward, and Prince Henry.

their childhood, and it should never be forgotten that in their family environment they had the benefit of noble ideals and a strong sense of purpose,
and that their parents and grandparents were all people of a very high and,
in the circumstances, surprising degree of natural goodness. And, if their
parents were excessively strict and had temperamental difficulties in communication, their grandparents suffered no such constraints, but adored
them openly and spoiled them considerably. There are several charming
stories of Prince Edward as a child, of which the following is both amusing
and revealing. It is said that a tailor's assistant had called with a suit for
Prince Edward to try on and was waiting in the passage outside the nursery
when the little Prince rushed out to her. 'Come in,' he said, 'there's nobody
here.' She replied that she thought she had better wait, the time might not
be convenient. 'There's nobody here,' he persisted. 'Nobody that matters,
only Grandpapa!'

As soon as the children were old enough to start lessons their nurse, Mrs
Bill, was joined by Madame Bricka, their mother's old governess. In 1901,
when the Duke and Duchess of York were on tour in Australia, King Edward
and Queen Alexandra took charge of their grandchildren, and took them
with them wherever the court went. They liked children to be 'romps' and
their own boys had been very wild as children. Now they had their grand-

*While the Duke and Duchess of
York toured Australia in 1901, the
York children stayed with their
affectionate and indulgent
grandparents, Alexandra and
Edward. Their aunt, Princess
Victoria, is on the left of this
picture taken at the time.*

Sandringham 1901.

children constantly with them, and encouraged them to run about and show off even in the dining-room, and mix freely with the guests. On one occasion 'Grandpapa' dodged the disciplinary presence of Madame Bricka for two whole weeks at Sandringham by the simple expedient of leaving her in London. The Duchess of York, who had obediently accepted the complete authority of her parents-in-law, even on such matters as the planting of her own garden at Sandringham, nevertheless felt so strongly about her children being spoiled that she wrote to complain.

One of the strangest aspects of these children's lives is that they were seldom in the company of other children. Consequently the little walled-in family grew very close together, sharing jokes, family conventions, punishments, treats; and in this closed society the eldest child established a dominance over the others which seems to have owed as much to his own qualities as to their awareness of his unique and exalted destiny. Psychologists and sociologists have lately cast doubt on the long-held belief that a large family is of itself a good thing, but these children owed most of their happiness to the companionship of one another. And, if they were 'walled-in', they were walled into unusually splendid places. When King Edward moved to Buckingham Palace after his mother died, he gave his son Marlborough House in London, Frogmore House in Windsor Home Park and the little castle of Abergeldie in Scotland. From this time, although the children still spent most of the year at York Cottage, they were in London in the spring, from where their mother often took them to Frogmore, and they spent August at Abergeldie.

On the Sandringham estate the children spent much of their time on bicycles and they were allowed to cycle to the nearby village of Dersingham to buy sweets or to the station at Wolferton to watch the trains. They were all physically courageous and, crouched over their handlebars, they would race about, the eldest in front, his brother and sister tearing along behind. At Frogmore, the wide drives cut through the great lawns were an enormous attraction from the cyclist's point of view, although the nurseries at the top of the house were so hot in summer that water had to be sprayed on to the roof to cool them off. The little castle of Abergeldie was 'in the matter of creature comforts' no improvement, but in the early days here there were picnics with their mother in the wild Highland country, and later, when they were old enough, grouse-shooting and deer-shooting.

Yet if the family life of the princes was in some ways more propitious than it is often represented to be, the same cannot be said for their early education. At York Cottage the cultural environment was no richer, the vitality of the intellectual life no greater, than in the villas of Upper Norwood and Surbiton. As biographer Sir Harold Nicolson would complain to his diary many years later,

I fear that I am getting a down on George v. He is all right as a gay young midshipman. He may be all right as a wise old King. But the intervening period when he was Duke of York, just shooting at Sandringham, is hard to swallow. For seventeen years he did nothing at all but kill animals and stick in stamps.

George v was quite without what Henry James has termed 'the deeper sense', and his children were conditioned to disregard, if not to disapprove of, matters of the intellect or the spirit, which one suspects, like many another Englishman, he believed prejudicial to the development of character and a moral sense, as well as boring to himself. Sticking in his stamps he managed to indulge the instincts of the collector and remain absolutely pure of any trace

Sandringham, 1905: Prince Edward (known in the family as David) and his brother Albert ('Bertie'), in a photograph from Edward VIII's personal albums. The Princes are 'helping' to build a new reservoir.

of aestheticism. Queen Mary, on the other hand, was to acquire a reputation as a collector of furniture and *objets d'art*, but this was a hobby that developed late in life, primarily as a result of her interest in the history of the British Royal Family.

In these circumstances it is hardly a surprise to find that, when Mr Hansell was engaged as tutor to the boys, the choice fell on him not for his intellectual attainments but for his keenness as a yachtsman and a golfer. According to Sir John Wheeler-Bennett, Mr Hansell was fully conscious of his inadequacy for his task and often said that the princes would be far better off at a good preparatory school. Since this suggestion was always vetoed out of hand, he tried to do his best.

In his own strange way Mr Hansell endeavoured to create at York Cottage as much of this school atmosphere as possible. He fitted up a classroom with two standard desks, a blackboard, bookshelves, etc., in a corner room of the first floor; here from 7.30 till 8.15 the boys would do their preparation before breakfast; and from 9 till 1 and between tea and supper they did their lessons. On some occasions … Mr Hansell would organize immature football matches in pick-up sides in which the Princes joined with the boys of the village school, but it is doubtful whether these games gave very much enjoyment to anyone.

The trouble was that, having easily achieved the dull and ugly appearance of an Edwardian school and the dreary routine that went with it, Mr Hansell was unable to supply even the uninspired but technically competent education which should have accompanied them. He starved his pupils of any stimulus to the imagination and it was left to the Sandringham village schoolmaster, a self-taught naturalist who used to take the boys on long rambles in the woods, to introduce them to the only genuine enthusiasm for knowledge they met. Extra tutors were brought in to teach French and German and, when King George discovered that his two eldest sons, aged about twelve and ten, could not strike the average weight of the stags he had shot at Abergeldie from the game record, a master was engaged to teach mathematics. Unless one counts the performance of a pipe major from the Scots Guards or the childish singing of folk songs, no attempt seems to have been made to teach music or any appreciation of the arts. The princes were not taken to concerts, nor, until they were nearly grown up, to the theatre, and none of the people who surrounded them seriously attempted to interest them in the arts.

In the palaces of the sovereigns of England these children were brought up with their backs to one of the finest collections of pictures in the world, with their ears attuned only to the bagpipes and in almost total ignorance of the vast inheritance of English literature. If this feat seems almost incredible, one can only say that it was easily achieved by the heirs to other great builders and collectors. There was much philistinism in the British upper class at the time and children who grew up with a background of genuine culture were correspondingly rare.

What qualities can one begin to discern in the little boy who would one day be King of England? From the time when his nurse carried him into the room where his mother sat with her lady-in-waiting, he had learned that he and his family were the objects of homage from the rest of mankind. As soon as they could walk, he and his brothers went first behind their parents or grandparents as they entered a room and the subservience of the courtiers and the reality of the power was unquestioned. Both his grandfather and his father bawled at their courtiers if crossed, and their lightest

Mr Hansell, the tutor employed by the Duke of York for his children for his sporting rather than his academic abilities, takes his two royal pupils for a walk.

words brought the noblest in the land scurrying to attention. Prince Edward seems to have understood at a very early date that on him devolved both great honour and some special responsibility. While still a child, he instructed his brother to 'Smile' while listening to a dull story, and, when told at a children's party to thank his hostess for the sword she had given him, he mounted a chair and said: 'Thank you for giving me such a beautiful sword. I shall always keep it and remember this night.'

For many years of his life the Prince would be the object of a close and affectionate regard from Lord Esher, and the fact that he took an almost entirely favourable view of the Prince's character does not diminish the revelatory nature of some of his earliest comments. Of these, one of the most remarkable is the first. On 25 May 1904, staying at Windsor Castle, Lord Esher wrote in his diary:

I have been walked off my legs, and pulled off them by the children. The youngest is the most riotous. The eldest a sort of head nurse. It was queer looking through a weekly paper, and coming to a picture of the eldest with the label 'our future King'. Prince Albert at once drew attention to it – but the elder hastily brushed his brother's finger away and turned the page.

On 24 January 1906, again at Windsor Castle, he noted:

Prince Edward develops every day fresh qualities, and is a most charming boy; very direct, dignified and clever. His memory is remarkable – a family tradition; but the look of *Weltschmerz* in his eyes I cannot trace to any ancestor of the House of Hanover.

From all of which one must assume that Prince Edward was alert and clever and, most remarkable of all, that even at this early age some element of embarrassment entered into his feelings about his exalted position. We know that he was shy, frightened of his father and kept at a distance by his mother, but that he was not lacking in physical courage. From what Lord Esher tells us, although he had the fairest looks, he acquired quite early an air of wistfulness, as though something in the view from his elevated position had permanently blighted his hopes.

(Opposite) George, Mary and five of their children in 1906 (their youngest child, John, born the previous year, is not in this photograph).

2

The Education of a Prince

At the age of thirteen Prince Edward was sent to Osborne Naval College on the Isle of Wight, where he was later joined by his brother Prince Albert. King George himself had received a similar education and, according to John Gore, 'He was well aware that his education as a sailor had ill fitted him for many of his new responsibilities.' Gore goes on: 'It had been only during his father's reign, nine swiftly moving years, that he had done something to repair the gaps in his knowledge of English and Constitutional History and to attain to the normal educational standard of the average public schoolboy at the leaving age.' One would have been grateful in the circumstance for some explanation of why, while the King was engaged in repairing the deficiencies of his own education, he should have chosen for his two eldest sons the very schooling which had made his task necessary. Few people would care to dogmatize on the proper education for the heir to the throne, but on the surface it seems fairly obvious that some knowledge of languages (almost every crowned head in Europe was a close relation of the Prince's at the time), of history and of the classics was more suitable for the future King of England than the specialized training of a naval officer. And, if the King was intent on character-building, one would have thought that the rigours of an English public school would have been great enough for two little boys who had never been away from home and scarcely ever met other children of their own age.

Nevertheless, the King was not neglectful of his sons' interests and happiness in the upper-class way exemplified by Lord and Lady Randolph Churchill's treatment of their son, Winston, and, when the Prince went to Osborne for the first time, his father accompanied him, travelling from Portsmouth to Cowes in the Admiralty yacht. Before leaving his son the King told him that he must always remember that he was his best friend, advice the Prince would always find impossible to follow, although it was sincerely meant. King George visited his children at school when he was able, and had a normal father's pride in their accomplishments and pleasure in their company. 'Dear David,' he recorded in his diary, while staying at Goodwood, 'looking thinner but wonderfully well, came from Osborne, his holidays having just begun.' And on a different occasion: 'Darling May's birthday ... children all recited their poems. David did it quite extra-ordinarily well. He said Wolseley's farewell (Sheakespeare) without a mistake.' [*sic*]

Mr Hansell's incompetent and uninspired régime had ensured that in turn

Prince Edward and Prince Albert would find it hard to keep up with his class at Osborne. In the specialized curriculum of the naval colleges, priority was given to mathematics, navigation, science and engineering. Much time was spent in learning how to tie knots, splice rope, sail a cutter, read and make signals, box the compass and master all the intricacies of seamanship. Prince Albert once achieved the feat of being sixty-eighth out of sixty-eight and Prince Edward wrote of being forty-six in the order, or thirty-second, which, he said bravely, he thought quite good for him. At the end of each term at Osborne every boy was given an envelope to take home. Prince Edward's first report passed without comment but his second produced the dreaded summons to the library. Mathematics 'in all its hideous aspects' had been his undoing and his report, which his father gave him to read, seemed curt and cruel and bearing no resemblance to what he thought he had achieved. When, therefore, after his third term he was once more sent for to the library, he burst into tears before the King had time to speak. Yet here again his father is shown as behaving not unkindly, and, after saying that this was no way for a naval cadet to behave, he added: 'Besides, you have quite a good report this time; and I am pleased with the progress you have made.' On another occasion the King wrote to the Prince: 'I am sorry that ... you ... lost several places in the last order, that is a pity and I am afraid you didn't pay as much attention as you ought to have done, but perhaps the questions were harder.'

The King's decision that his sons should attend the naval colleges of Osborne and later Dartmouth rather than one of the public schools, while ensuring that the Prince would grow up at least as ill-educated as himself, seems to have had two more immediate effects. The first is that the physical conditions he encountered were much harder and the impact unnecessarily cruel. It may be argued that in 1907 life at many of the public schools was fairly barbaric, particularly in that so little attempt was made to control the bullying of younger boys. The difference was that in the naval and army schools a harsh philosophy behind the strict discipline made a virtue of physical discomfort and led to an attitude which, if it did not exactly condone bullying, inevitably encouraged it. If the Prince had been sent, for instance, to Eton (Prince Henry, the King's third son, went to this school, for reasons equally unexplained) he would have had a room of his own. At Osborne, this boy, to whom a village football match had presented an unusual opportunity to meet children of his own age, lived in a dormitory with thirty others. He was called by a bugle blowing reveille at six o'clock in the summer and at 6.30 in the winter and then, in answer to a series of gongs, he was expected to jump out of bed, say his prayers, brush his teeth and run to the end of the dormitory and plunge, shivering, into a green-tiled pool. This, like everything else at Osborne, had to be done at the double. All day long the boys were expected to run from pillar to post, a system that may have done less to stimulate the desired alertness than was believed. The food was so bad that the Prince was often hungry, and on one occasion was caught malingering, having pleaded sick in the hope of getting a square meal out of the friendly matron in the sick bay. He had no freedom to follow his own pursuits or to develop those personal tastes and preferences which are the reserves most people fall back upon in times of loneliness or trouble. Everywhere outside the college grounds was out of bounds, and every hour of every day, except Sunday afternoon, was filled.

When he first arrived at Osborne he was faced with the barrage of questions customarily fired at new boys. Here again, if one may once more make the comparison with Eton, in the relatively sophisticated atmosphere of that school he would have been merely one, even if the most exalted, of the sons of a great English family, and he would have found it easier to achieve that anonymity which is so essential to the happiness of the very young. He was alone in never having been to school before, and he was embarrassed by questions about his father and his home. For these and similar unorthodoxies he received, if we are to believe what we are told, punishments to fit the crime. On one occasion his head was thrust through a window, the sash let down on his neck, and he was left to reflect on the fate of Charles I and the treatment England gave to kings who did not please her, until someone heard his cries. However, it is difficult to believe he had to submit to a great deal of individual bullying and he seems to have achieved a reasonable

degree of popularity and the nickname 'Sardine'.

The second effect of the Prince being sent to the naval colleges was that, since so many of his companions were to spend most of their lives at sea, he made few friends at school whom he would meet later in life. At first sight this appears a further major disadvantage of the naval colleges, but, as one speculates on these things, one begins to believe that here on the contrary might be one of the clues to the King's decision. Of an earlier generation Sir Philip Magnus wrote:

Excessive anxiety caused the Queen [Victoria] and her husband to draw an arbitrary distinction between companions and friends, and to hold that the latter were a luxury which princes were bound to deny themselves. They warned their children often that they were no better than other children, while hesitating even to admit companions to Buckingham Palace and Windsor Castle because they considered that ingenuous youth would seek inevitably to convert companionship into friendship, and friendship into an impermissible relationship of equality.

And the Duke of Windsor tells us that, much as he dreaded his father's summons to the library, he had reason to be grateful to him because he had always taught him not to think he was either different from or better than other people. To which the Duke adds the rider: 'To be sure by *other people* he meant the children of the well-born.' These sentences are manifestations of more than one hidden attitude which, if understood, might throw light on the King's choice of school for his sons.

When the King told Prince Edward that he must never get the idea that he was different from or better than other people, he clearly meant that the boy should not confuse his person with his position. But it was itself a confused and confusing statement to make to a child who must have noted every minute of every day that he and his family were treated as very different

During his time at Osborne, the Russian royal family came to visit their British cousins (Tsar Nicholas II was Queen Alexandra's nephew). (Left to right, standing) Prince Edward, Queen Alexandra, Princess Mary, Princess Victoria, two of the Tsar's daughters, (seated) Princess of Wales, Prince of Wales, the Tsarevich, King Edward VII, the Tsarina, the Tsar, and another of his daughters.

from and certainly superior to other people. The difference between a person and his position is a concept easily understood when applied to anyone but the sovereign and his heir, but in their case it ignores the most important aspect of modern monarchy – the metaphysical one. No longer the leader in the field, nor even the holder of much political power, the sovereign today owes his very existence to the desire of the people for a transcendent figure. There is a sense in which the king must be 'better than other people', and it is the difficulty of reconciling this with the Christian belief that all men are equal in the sight of God which gives royal utterances on the subject a naïve, even disingenuous, air.

George V laboured under a further difficulty, which is implicit in the Duke of Windsor's statement that by other people he meant the well-born. The King paid lip service to Christian ideals by teaching them to his children but he did not entirely believe what he said himself. In the world over which he reigned he would have been very unusual if he had not made this division between the well-born and everyone else. One of the aspects of the aristocratic and hierarchical society which existed in England before the First World War, really until after the Second, is that the nobility, upper and middle classes were alike in regarding the working population as a different and inferior type of human being. Concepts such as 'blue blood' and 'well-born' were understood to have a real meaning.

George V's anxiety that his children should not make friends was possibly no less than his grandmother's, but progress towards democracy forced him to adopt a double standard when speaking to his children. It is probably not therefore too much to suggest that the dangers of friendship influenced his choice of school. Trotting about at the double with only Sunday afternoon free, and meeting only men who looked forward to a career at sea, the risk at the naval colleges was not great. If Prince Edward had been sent to one of the leading public schools – Eton or Harrow – he would have met the children of the 'well-born', that class with whom the taboos were at their weakest. Some of these boys might have been the over-confident, rather raffish type often met among the well-born, who exert so much charm over the minds of the very young. There are children of a phlegmatic and unresponsive nature who might survive these dangers, but, for the little, alert heir to the throne, far better to grow up unable to spell the name of the national poet than run such risks as these.

At the beginning of May 1910, while Prince Edward and Prince Albert were preparing to return to Dartmouth and Osborne after the Easter holidays, their grandfather King Edward VII was taken seriously ill. On the evening of 6 May, at a little before midnight, he died. Two weeks later he was buried in St George's Chapel, Windsor. The princes Edward and Albert, in the uniform of naval cadets, marched in the funeral procession behind their father, the new King George V, with all the crowned heads of Europe.

On the accession of his father Prince Edward automatically became the Duke of Cornwall and inherited vast estates and properties in the west of England and at Kennington in London. After the funeral of his grandfather, however, the new Duke of Cornwall proceeded back to Dartmouth and continued to receive the pocket money of a naval cadet. On his sixteenth birthday King George conferred the title Prince of Wales upon him.

1911 was a year of great public ceremonies for the young Prince. While convalescing from an illness, he received a letter from his father telling him that, as he would play a prominent part in the Coronation ceremonies, his

Caernarvon Castle on 13 July 1911, the day of Edward's investiture as Prince of Wales. The castle was partially rebuilt for the occasion.

time at Dartmouth must be cut short. It was the custom for cadets in their last term to embark on a final cruise before graduation as a midshipman, and the Prince, who had inherited his father's real love of the sea, regarded this cruise as the goal of his present ambition and was naturally very much disappointed.

The Coronation of the new King took place on 22 June 1911. As Prince of Wales, Prince Edward was among the first to pay homage. Kneeling before his father he recited the words: 'I, Edward Prince of Wales, do become your liege man of life and limb and of earthly worship; and faith and truth I will bear unto you, to live and die against all manner of folks. So help me God.' Then he kissed his father's cheek and the King kissed his. That night in his dairy the King recorded: 'I nearly broke down when dear David came to do homage to me, as it reminded me so much of when I did the same thing to beloved Papa, he did it so well.' And other observers spoke of the dignity with which the young Prince played his part, 'in his face the bashfulness of youth and the serious thought of a man called to a great destiny'.

But the great ceremonial for the Prince of Wales was his own investiture at Caernarvon. For the ceremony the Prince of Wales wore white satin breeches and a mantle and surcoat of purple velvet edged with ermine. When he first saw this 'preposterous rig' there ensued what he has described as a 'family blow-up'. However, he was persuaded to wear it, and so on a sweltering summer day he appeared in this costume at Caernarvon Castle where, after Winston Churchill as Home Secretary had proclaimed his titles, he was invested by his father as Prince of Wales. Then, leading him by the hand through an archway to one of the towers of the battlements, the King presented the Prince to the people of Wales. That night the King wrote in his dairy: 'The dear boy did it all remarkably well and looked so nice.' But the Prince tells us that when the commotion was over he made a discovery about himself; whereas he was willing to play his role in the pomp and ceremony, he recoiled from personal homage, and he realized that even the association he had been allowed with the village boys at Sandringham and the naval cadets had made him 'desperately anxious to be treated exactly like any other boy of my age'.

A few months later the Prince was informed that the time had come for him to leave the Navy, and that the King had decided to send him to Oxford. This decision was very surprising to the Prince who knew that basically his father distrusted scholarship and, like many other Englishmen, regarded intellectual capacity and attainments almost as a handicap to sound judgment. However, we have been told of the difficulties the King struggled with himself, and, although it is said that it was Mr Hansell's idea to send the Prince to Oxford, the King probably did not need much persuasion that a year or so spent on languages, history and political economy might benefit his son. The Prince, however, was upset and angry. He told the King he had no interest in learning, and that if he was sent to Oxford his years there would be wasted; and he told Mr Hansell what he thought about it in very much stronger terms. Nevertheless arrangements were made for the Prince to go up to Magdalen College as an ordinary undergraduate. He was to be spared the entrance examinations, for which he was so ill-equipped, and to be accompanied by Mr Hansell and an equerry, Major the Hon. William Cadogan.

In September 1912, just before he went up to Oxford, the Prince was staying at Balmoral where Lord Esher again recorded his impressions of

King George V and Queen Mary present Edward as Prince of Wales to the cheering crowds. Edward considered the ceremonial robes 'a preposterous rig', and there had been a 'family blow-up' about them.

him. In a letter written on 19 September, he wrote: 'I have had two walks alone with the Prince of Wales. He is a most captivating, strange, intelligent boy, with a remarkable vocabulary. He is sad – with the sadness of the world's burdens.' And on 20 September he wrote in his diary:

A very long talk with the Prince of Wales ... I let him have his say about the Navy; he is devoted to his old profession. His memory is excellent ... and above all things he thinks his own thoughts. They are long thoughts too. He has opinions, and strong ones on naval matters, and he aired them all in grave fashion – views on types of ships, on a sailor's education, on strategy and naval policy.

He told me of his friendly relations with the officers and men with whom he had served, how he loved to talk with the men of their homes and their pleasures and their troubles. He was full of the 'responsibility' of midshipmen and young lieutenants, and eloquent on the merits of such a training.

Looking very much the eldest, and now allowed a pipe, Edward stands in a Scottish loch with brothers (left to right) George, Bertie and Henry.

I asked him how, if he were charged with the education of a Prince of Wales, he would plan it. This riddle he is going to think over. He said, 'I am not clever, not a bit above the average.' I asked him how he knew that. He replied by the test of examination. But he sees that this test is only half a test.

It is a charming mind – grave, thoughtful, restrained, gentle, kindly, perhaps a trifle obstinate and sombre for so young a lad.

As the Prince of Wales grew to manhood his relationship with his father suffered the strain inevitable between two strongly obstinate characters with widely differing tastes. It was when he went to Oxford that the Prince first gave a demonstration of that stubbornness which had been a characteristic of every generation of his family since Queen Victoria, about whom Sir Charles Dilke once said: 'Her obstinacy constitutes power of a kind.' Silently the Prince rejected his father's right to choose his friends. Lord Derby's son, Lord Stanley, had been sent to Magdalen at the same time at the King's request but, although the two young men spent two years together, they did not become close friends there, for the Prince was always unwilling to give his confidence to anyone who owed his introduction to him to the King. The Prince believed that the disposition to please majesty is limitless and he regarded everyone who was a friend or appointment of his father's as a potential spy. At this time he was merely a young man who intended to enjoy himself without encouraging the advent of a footman with a summons to the library. Later in life his distrust of his father's friends was to have more positive effects.

Another of the Prince's personal qualities which emerged at this time was his extraordinary interest in clothes, an interest far deeper and more extensive than a mere desire to dress himself up. This aspect made a great appeal to him, however, and it was in his own clothes that his fascination first declared itself. His personal tastes were for informal clothes and he liked bright colours and large patterns. Some people thought his taste very vulgar and first among those to whom it made little appeal was the King.

It was not so much that George V was indifferent to the question of men's clothes as that he also was deeply interested in it. He had a conservative taste in clothes but they were to him, too, an absorbing topic of conversation. Belonging, as has been said, to a generation who were apt to judge people's morals by the cut or the fit of their suits, he had, nevertheless, a certain weakness for colour, which showed itself in his country tweeds and his kilts. But these were the King's only departures from the conventional, and the Prince has remarked that his childhood was 'buttoned-up' in every sense. He and his brothers invariably wore starched Eton collars and were never permitted to take off their coats. Even with shorts they wore long stockings right up to their thighs, the sight of the knees being acceptable only with kilts. When one of them as a small child went into the King's presence with his hands in his pockets, orders were immediately given to 'Lala' for the pockets to be sewn up. The King and all his generation always wore boiled shirts with a frock coat by day in London, and, when the Prince of Wales

Another snapshot from Edward's own album – with Queen Mary, Bertie and Mary outside Mar Lodge.

Self. Mama. Bertie. Mary.

visited his father, he was expected to wear a morning coat, while, when he dined with him, he wore a tail coat with a white tie and the Star of the Garter.

It is not therefore surprising that at Oxford the Prince was enthusiastic about the fashion for more informal clothes, appearing in flannel trousers with sports coats and early versions of the garment called 'plus-fours', nor that he wore trousers with 'turn-ups' which were then the latest thing. He tells us that he disliked ceremonial dress and cared nothing for uniforms, but this is probably untrue. All his life he took great pleasure in his own clothes, and, so unscholarly in other ways, he made a serious study of the history and evolution of dress. It has sometimes been suggested that his choice of dress was influenced by a desire to provoke his father, and, if this is true, he was certainly successful, but, in fact, long afterwards when the clothes he wore were no longer of much interest to anyone but himself, Diana Hood reports him in the garden of his house in the south of France wearing crimson trousers one day with a light blue shirt and red and white shoes, and another day bright blue trousers with a canary yellow shirt and blue shoes.

When the Prince first arrived in Oxford he was diffident and lonely. He tells us that, surrounded by young men who had come up with friends they had made at Eton, Harrow, Winchester or some other public school, he felt nostalgic for the Navy. He was not however alone in having very little learning, nor in the fact that he need not rely on an honours degree for his future career. Most young men enjoy university life, and once he had settled down the Prince was no exception. Steering clear at first of the public school boys, he earned a reputation for modesty in his choice of friends, but he soon disclosed where his real tastes lay. While the dons exerted all their brilliance and charm in an attempt to interest their royal pupil, Major Cadogan had no difficulty in captivating his full attention. Major Cadogan had orders from the King to teach the Prince to ride and he undertook this task with patience and skill. The King had repeatedly stressed the necessity of learning to ride, and wrote:

In your position it is absolutely necessary that you should ride well as you will continually have to do so at parades, reviews, etc., and so the sooner you make up your mind to it the better. The English people like riding and it would make you very unpopular if you couldn't do so. If you can't ride, you know, I am afraid people will call you a duffer.

Soon the Prince, who had begun by complaining that riding was very dull and only necessary to please Papa, was hunting with the South Oxfordshire hounds and appearing on the polo fields. He would never make a first-class horseman but he had unflinching physical courage and boundless enthusiasm. In fact even before he left university his father began to find his energy and love of hard exercise excessive, and wrote to him: 'You certainly have been doing a great deal, hunting two days, out with the beagles twice, golf and shooting one day, besides all your work, which seems a good deal for one week. I only hope you are not overdoing it in the way of exercise.'

In his second year the Prince entered very fully into the life of his fellow undergraduates, wining and dining as well as participating, if sometimes only as a spectator, in the various sports. In June 1914 in an article in *The Times* a fellow undergraduate wrote of him as follows:

He plunged at once into a catholicity of interests and amusements. He was entertained and gave entertainments in return; and those present found that, though he was at first rather shy, he was a delightful addition to a dinner party, most

attractive in the quiet and humble part he took in the conversation, but full of humour and with opinions at once decided and sane. His laugh and smile are, perhaps, particularly attractive. . . .

He played football eagerly and perseveringly for the second eleven; he played golf and ran with the beagles. He was a zealous spectator of college competitions and in Eights week there was no more untiring follower of the boat from the tow path. . . .

In November 1914, after the Prince of Wales had left Oxford and joined the Army, Sir Herbert Warren, the President of Magdalen, wrote a report of his sojourn at the college. In this he said:

From the first he took his own line, with equal modesty and firmness, determined in his own mind that he would be really *par inter pares*, that he would seek and accept no tribute except on his merits, that he would take as habitual and as assiduous trouble to avoid deference and preference as others to cultivate it, desiring as the old Roman poet put it, 'that men should give what he wanted, but that they should be free to deny'. His natural dignity and charm and, it should be added, the good sense and feeling of his college companions, and of Oxford generally, that democratic aristocracy, enabled him to go far in this resolve without mishap or untoward result. Once having started on it he pursued this narrow, nice line with increased confidence until it seemed the most easy and natural and unconscious thing in the world. . . . He did not want to spend any time at all, even a little, in being treated *en prince*.

Warren successfully attempted to define for the contemporary reader the quality which enabled the Prince to conduct himself so easily in his unique and uniquely delicate position. We owe to him the first impressions of the very real talent this Prince had for natural feeling and natural behaviour in an impossibly artificial situation, of the 'narrow, nice line' that, pursued with increasing confidence, would soon carry him to amazing heights of popularity almost all round the world.

(Opposite) Edward's first taste of comparative freedom came when he went up to Oxford University. He is seen here, in the more informal clothes he preferred to those approved of by his father, at the Magdalen College point-to-point races.

3

The War Years

By the time war broke out in August 1914, the Prince had persuaded his parents that he had had enough of Oxford and had won their agreement to a programme of travel for the rest of the year, after which he was to have joined the 2nd Battalion of Grenadier Guards in January 1915. In July he was attached to the 1st Life Guards for a short period because his father, still disapproving of his seat on a horse, wished him to learn from the riding master. Every morning from nine to eleven he paraded in the riding school with the recruits, a system which left him free to experience the pleasures of the London season.

From the very first he showed an uninhibited zest for night life, and very soon conquered his natural diffidence. On 7 July he attended his first ball, by 9 July he is recording in his diary that he has become fond of dancing and loves going out, and, by 10 July, that he has had no more than eight hours' sleep in the last seventy-two. In common with all his contemporaries he was soon to have his natural development distorted, his environment blasted, and his sight accustomed to scenes of tragedy and horror which in the whole history of the world have hardly been equalled.

His first reaction to the holocaust was to try and get into it, and it must be accepted that no emotion in his whole life was more sincere than his desire to serve and to suffer, if necessary to die, as every young man in the land might do except himself. On the outbreak of war the instructions he received from his father were to wait in London until suitable employment could be found for him, a situation he found quite intolerable. He wrote to his father telling him of his distress at not being allowed to serve his country and asking him for a commission in the Grenadier Guards. 'And dear Papa', he wrote in his diary, 'never hesitated for a moment and immediately instructed Lord Stamfordham to notify this to the War Office.'

On being gazetted to the Grenadier Guards he was posted to the 1st Battalion and detailed to the King's Company. In mid-September forty-eight hours' leave was granted as a preliminary to the 1st Battalion being sent overseas and, to his intense chagrin, the Prince was immediately transferred to the 3rd Battalion, stationed at the same barracks. He determined then to call on Lord Kitchener. Dressed in the uniform of a subaltern he ran up the marble steps of the War Office where he asked if he might see the Secretary of State for War. When Lord Kitchener received him, the Prince sat at the great table in the famous oak-panelled room that looks out on to Whitehall and pleaded to be allowed to go to France. 'What does it matter

Like many young men of his generation, Edward was eager to join up on the outbreak of war in 1914 and serve his country. 'What does it matter if I am killed?' he asked Lord Kitchener. 'I have four brothers.' He is seen here at the Officers' Training Camp at Farnborough.

if I am killed?' he asked. 'I have four brothers.' But Lord Kitchener explained to him that the danger was not that he might be killed but that, until there was a settled line, he might be taken prisoner, a chance he was not prepared to let him take.

The Prince persisted in his attempts to be allowed to go to France until in November 1914 he was attached to the staff of Field-Marshal Sir John French, Commander-in-Chief of the British Expeditionary Force. Sir Dighton Probyn, writing to Sir George Arthur, said:

I saw the dear ... Prince of Wales yesterday. He came to wish me goodbye – and it was really delightful to see the change that had come over him since he had last been in this room. On the last occasion he really *cried* with sorrow at the idea of 'being disgraced', and he said he was not being allowed to go to the war. Yesterday his face beamed with joy.

When the Prince arrived in France he was employed on paperwork and tasks such as the carrying of despatches, designed, as he was quick to see, to conceal from him his non-combatant role. And soon he was complaining that his only real job was that of being Prince of Wales. This job he already performed with a natural distinction and in January 1915 Lord Esher noted in his journal: 'The King sent for me in the afternoon: he had just heard from the Prince of Wales, who has been motoring all through the French lines in Alsace. He has seen all the French generals and was extraordinarily well received. This must have done a great deal of good.'

But the Prince would never rest content with the life the authorities had chosen for him, and he steadily opposed their plans by his determination to see more active service. In May 1915 his efforts were partially rewarded and he was attached to the General Staff of the 1st Army Corps near Béthune. From Béthune the Prince made a practice of slipping up to the front to visit the Guards and other regiments. His energy was as usual extraordi-

Most of Edward's wartime duties were public relations exercises designed to keep him away from the front line. Despite this, he overcame his frustrations and showed a genuine flair on occasions such as this meeting with Italian and French officers in Italy.

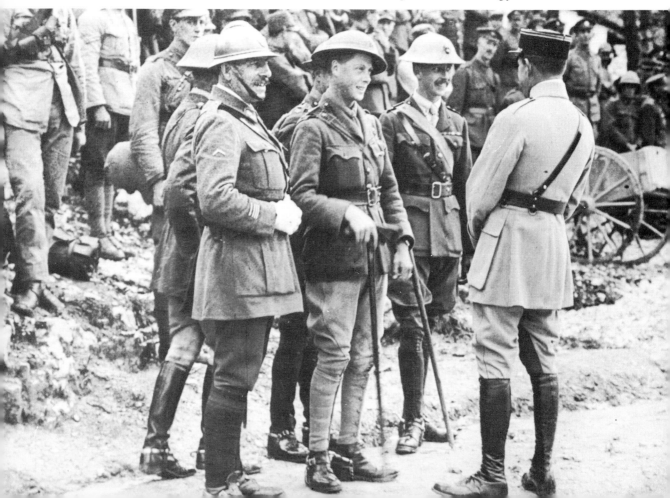

nary and he thought nothing of walking six miles before breakfast. 'The Prince eats little and walks much: we eat much and walk little,' Oliver Lyttelton, a brother officer, wrote. This same officer has given us one of the most convincing pictures of the Prince of Wales ever written:

By the beginning of August 1915, though still an ADC, I was back amongst my brother officers of the Guards division. I found that the Prince of Wales was an extra ADC. He was the most charming and delightful human being that I had ever known. He, too, chafed at being at HQ, and all the more because he recognized that he was unlikely ever to be allowed to serve in a battalion. He never stopped trying.

It was a hot and sunny month and our duties at HQ were light. One morning, HRH came into the divisional staff office and asked whether I was also dining with Desmond FitzGerald, his great friend, then commanding the 1st Battalion Irish Guards. 'If so, we will go together.' I said, 'Yes, Sir, I am the other guest,' and was delighted because Desmond lived three or four miles away, and the road was nearly all up hill. The Prince's car would get us there in under ten minutes.

About 6.30 he arrived again in the staff office and said, 'By the way, you have got a bicycle, I suppose? If you haven't you had better get one, because we ought to start. Dinner is at 7.30. . . .'

It was still very hot when we set out. 'I never get off,' said HRH as we faced a mile or two of hilly road. 'It is one of the ways that I keep fit.' I was in good training, but after a mile I had sweated through my Sam Browne belt and had begun to entertain some republican inclinations. However, we had a gay and delightful evening: the Prince was happy, and in the highest spirits; we had replaced our lost tissue with some old brandy, and free-wheeled home to our cage like schoolboys.

It is rarely that I am given a chance to pay my respects to him these days, but for me his spell has never been broken.

He used to lend his large grey Daimler car to any brother officer who could find the courage to ask for it. After I had returned to duty, I later got some leave and asked to borrow the car to get to Boulogne, because by this means you could get an extra day in England. He sent me a slip of paper agreeing at once, but asking me whether I would take a letter to 'my people' at home. This was how he described the King and Queen.

As I reached the quay the leave boat had just cast off, but I was not the Prince's messenger for nothing and, waving his letter to the King, I persuaded the embarkation officer to order the ship to put back. I swept up the gangway in triumph, and delivered the letter at Buckingham Palace in a few hours.

It was true that the Prince never ceased to try to get into the trenches. He kept up a steady pressure on everyone he thought might help him, and in September 1915 he got his desire. He was appointed to the staff of Major-General Lord Cavan in command of the Guards Division. Almost immediately his new position was endangered, however, by a narrow shave in which his driver was killed while the Prince was touring a front-line sector. Soon afterwards Lord Esher wrote to the Prince as follows:

You can imagine that I had rather a cold shiver when I heard of your escape, and the disaster to your poor chauffeur. But in future, which may be full of unforeseen difficulties in the years far ahead, your gallantry and determination to live the life of a soldier and run the risks will never be forgotten. If it ever is, then our people will have lost all their noble traditions of regard for what is best in their princes and in the youth of our country.

About the same time Lord Esher visited the Queen and recorded: 'I had two hours with the Queen. I told her everything that had been going on in France. She is proud of the Prince of Wales. I tried to make her see that after the war thrones might be at a discount, and that the Prince of Wales's popularity might be a great asset.'

King George V's children had been brought up out of the public eye, and the Prince of Wales first became known to the British people through the quality of his courage, energy and enthusiasm during the war. He soon became a byword. 'A bad shelling will always produce the Prince of Wales,' the officers of his regiment said, and the private soldiers wrote home of his courage and keenness. 'The Prince complained that his employment was artificial,' Kitchener's biographer, Philip Magnus, summed up laconically, 'and it proved impossible to keep him out of the front line whenever he had the opportunity to go anywhere near it.'

His eagerness was in no sense a covert craving for popularity, nor, as has been suggested, did it stem from a compulsion to test himself. One of the greatest contradictions of the Prince's strangely contradictory nature was that he was both diffident and self-assured. He was often shy and uncertain in his relationships with other people (although never when he wanted something badly), but he had unusual confidence in his own opinions and no apprehensions about his physical courage. The British ruling classes have often failed in the liberal virtues but seldom in the heroic, and the Prince's reaction was the simple one of a brave and ardent young man.

In the spring of 1916 the Prince of Wales paid a six weeks' visit to the Middle East to inspect and report on the defences of the Suez Canal. Here he met Australian and New Zealand troops recently evacuated from Gallipoli. Then he reported for duty to the XIV Army Corps which took part in the Battle of Passchendaele. And watching this great offensive, begun with so much enthusiasm, achieve nothing but death and exhaustion, the Prince of Wales shared the weariness and cynicism of the combatant troops and learned from his own experiences to fear and hate war.

Edward and his father examine gas bombs in France, 1917.

During the war a story went the rounds of two soldiers detailed to accompany the Prince. 'It's all very well for him,' one of them said to the other, 'but if he gets killed, we shall get the blame.' This story, at first sight merely amusing, pinpoints in a dozen words the quality of ruthless singlemindedness which carried the Prince to the centre of the war, a singlemindedness which in this situation operated almost entirely to the general good. There can be no pretence that his war was the same as that of other young officers in the British Army or that he ever ran the risks they ran. But, owing to his exceptional keenness and determination, he understood what the survivors had endured, saw with his own eyes the horrors that afflicted them, and shared the overwhelming and indescribable experience which divided them from the civilians at home; and because of his naturalness and modesty he made an unforgettable impression on the suffering and disillusioned armies in France. He took to riding a green army bicycle and he pedalled hundreds of miles inspecting camps or ammunition dumps and home again to write his reports. 'Even now,' he wrote forty years later, 'after three decades, I still meet men who will suddenly turn to me and say, "The last time I saw you, you were on your bicycle on the road to Poperinghe" – or Montauban, or any one of a hundred French villages.'

In the First World War the Army was granted fairly regular leave from France, and the Prince had in addition duties which brought him home more often than his fellows. In spite of his war service he spent a certain amount of time in England, and in 1915, when he was twenty-one, he fell in love for the first time.

The Prince was deeply in love three times in his life. His first romance was to last for three years. Lord Leicester's daughter-in-law, Lady Coke, was twelve years older than the Prince of Wales when she became the object of his affections. He saw much of her when he was in England and when he was away poured out his love in letters to her. It is not known to what extent she returned his love, but certainly she was pleased and flattered by it. In societies in which chastity is imposed on young girls, love affairs between young men and older women are not exceptional, but in this case, small, lively, with an individual humour, above all married, Lady Coke was a portent.

Then on an evening in February or early March 1918 a young married woman named Freda Dudley Ward walked through Belgrave Square with an escort known to her as Buster Dominguez. Dudley Ward, a relation of Lord Dudley, was a Liberal Whip and he spent so much of his time in the House of Commons that his wife was accustomed to going out in the evening without him. On this particular evening, as she and Dominguez strolled through Belgrave Square, the maroons that, like the sirens in the Second World War, sent civilians running for cover, proclaimed the imminence of an air raid. No obvious shelter offered itself except the open door of a nearby house where a party was obviously in progress. Mrs Dudley Ward and her escort ran into the hall of the house as the people at the party came streaming down the stairs, and their hostess, who later identified herself as Mrs Kerr-Smiley, realizing what had happened, called her two uninvited guests to accompany her down to the cellar. Thus they presently found themselves standing rather isolated in the cellar of a strange house among a large group of people they did not know. It was at this moment that in the semi-darkness a young man appeared at Mrs Dudley Ward's side and started an animated conversation with her. When the air raid was over Mrs Dudley Ward and

Edward and a fellow-officer leave the War Office in 1917. Despite the horrors of the war, the good-looking Prince still looks more of a boy than a young man of twenty-three – although he had already had one love affair with a married woman, Lady Coke, and was about to start another.

her escort tried to leave, but Mrs Kerr-Smiley came over to her and invited her and her escort to come upstairs and join the party. 'His Royal Highness is so anxious that you should do so,' she said. So Mrs Dudley Ward went upstairs and danced with the Prince of Wales until the early hours of the morning, when he took her home, Buster Dominguez having at some time disappeared forever into the night. The next day the Prince of Wales called on Mrs Dudley Ward and there began a relationship which was to last for sixteen years.

The improbable circumstance of their meeting is matched by an equally strange coincidence: the Mrs Kerr-Smiley in whose house this meeting occurred was the sister of that same Ernest Simpson who would figure so largely in the life of Edward VIII.

There was never any secret about the Prince's relationship with Mrs Dudley Ward, although it was conducted with complete discretion. It was known to hundreds of people, not merely to the friends of her friends and friends of their friends, but to everyone who went about in London Society and saw this young couple together at the Embassy Club, or at private parties, or on golf courses, at the races, or in country houses. Mrs Dudley Ward is as ineradicable a part of British royal history as Mrs Fitzherbert or Mrs Keppel.

There have been few published references to Mrs Dudley Ward. One of the first was by Lady Cynthia Asquith, who wrote in her diary on 12 March 1918: 'Saw the Prince of Wales dancing round with Mrs Dudley Ward, a pretty little fluff with whom he is said to be rather in love. He is a dapper little fellow – too small – but really a pretty face. He looked as pleased as Punch and chatted away the whole time. . . . He obviously means to have fun.'

There are two imperceptive statements in this account. In the first place the Prince of Wales was not a little in love with Mrs Dudley Ward, he was madly, passionately, *abjectly* in love with her. If this is not understood, nothing about his whole life can be understood and it is thrown so much out of balance that people contemplating it have found it necessary to invent explanations – a certain immaturity, for instance, which prevented him falling in love or wishing to marry. From 1919, when he returned from the Army, to 1934, the whole of his life has to be set against the background of the fact that when he was in London he went every day to see her, usually at five o'clock, often staying to dine or to take her out to dinner, but, if this was impossible because of his public engagements, returning to her house later in the evening. He telephoned her regularly every morning and wherever she was he followed her, physically whenever possible, when not possible with his extreme devotion. Occasionally he had brief affairs with other women, but he was never more than superficially faithless, and Mrs Dudley Ward was during all this time the strongest influence in his life.

Lady Cynthia Asquith is imperceptive once more in describing Mrs Dudley Ward as 'a pretty little fluff'. She was, in fact, one of the most attractive women of her generation, being gifted with charm as some people are gifted with a talent for music or acting. It is notoriously difficult to analyse charm but one of the concomitants often present is an almost innocent candour which prevents any trimming of the personality to match the conventional attitudes of the day. In the 1920s, when these attitudes were conspicuously arrogant, speech was clipped, and strangers complained that in English society no one ever introduced anyone to anyone else, except occasionally and vaguely by a Christian name, Mrs Dudley Ward had an unpretentiously friendly manner and original opinions to which she habitually gave a droll expression. Very small, she matched the Prince in physical attributes and, although she was not beautiful, her looks were very pretty and delightful. In a pleasure-loving age, she was pleasure-loving, but she was not superficial. Her influence on the Prince was said to be entirely for his good in all ways except one. But that, after all, was a fairly important one. It was for Mrs Simpson that King Edward VIII renounced the Crown, but it was because of Mrs Dudley Ward that he was free to do so.

The Prince of Wales was in middle life to perform an act which, however one regards it, must be admitted to be without parallel in the history of the Crown. Even the most amateur of psychologists may surely be allowed to see significance in the fact that he began at the earliest age the process which led to regal suicide by depriving himself of the opportunity to marry and have children. For this Prince, who declared that he would not marry except for love, would never again find attractions in anyone who was not already a married woman.

One of the strangest aspects of his history is the extent to which his personality apparently changed as he progressed through life. But some things remained constant throughout: confidence in his own opinions in dealing with the world in general; in personal matters an unshakeable determination to have his own way, combined with an unusual certainty about what he wanted; above all, a capacity beyond what is often found in a man to become engaged with and dependent on a woman. During almost all the years he was Prince of Wales he was attached to Freda Dudley Ward.

Mrs Freda Dudley Ward (seen here in a later photograph) first met the Prince of Wales during an air raid in 1918. She was to become his closest friend and the strongest influence on his life for the next sixteen years.

4

The Prince Abroad

The Prince of Wales was nearly twenty-five when he returned from the war, and it needed no great perspicacity to see that he was miraculously fitted for the job to which he had been born and bred. The fact that he had original views on how to behave when carrying out his public duties, and an ability quite unusual in royal personages to project a personality on to the world stage, had not yet emerged; but, with the looks of a wistful choirboy and a small, slight figure on which his army greatcoat swung with the grace of *haute couture*, he would have been seized upon for the role of Prince Charming even in the idealized world of dramatic art. This, and the reputation which followed him home from the war, was enough to make him a national hero; while, for those who met him at close quarters, he had subtler charms. Probably the most winning of these was his ability suddenly to dispel the natural sadness of his face with a smile which lit it brilliantly from within. In his public appearances, speaking in a strong, clear voice, he seemed always enthusiastic and friendly and moved by an intense desire to please.

The only problem to be decided was where to make the best use of him. At home there was much discontent and disillusion among ex-servicemen, too many of whom were on inadequate pensions and unable to find either a job or a home, and it was believed – not unnaturally in view of the fate of the Romanovs, the Hapsburgs and the Hohenzollerns – that the British monarchy was less stable than it had been at the beginning of the war. As the King's representative, there was much that the Prince might do in his own country. However, the Prime Minister, Lloyd George, had a plan for him to undertake immediately a series of tours in the Commonwealth countries to thank them for their contribution to victory and to strengthen their ties with Britain.

The Prince's own most immediate concern was to gain his parents' permission to leave the family home. 'I don't want to marry for a long time,' he told the Countess of Airlie, lady-in-waiting to Queen Mary, 'but at twenty-five I can't live under the same roof as my parents. I must be free to lead my own life.' His choice for himself fell on York House, St James's Palace, which had been one of the homes of his family in his childhood. York House was old and rambling and the furniture was largely Victorian. Here and there were some very fine pieces, however, and with the aid of these and of Mrs Dudley Ward the Prince made it all that he wanted. A reasonably large room on the first floor became his sitting-room, off which he had a bedroom and bathroom. On the ground floor there was a large dining-room, but, when he was alone or had intimates with him, the Prince had his meals on a table brought up in front of the fire in the sitting-room.

In the early part of 1919, while he was in England, the Prince of Wales embarked on the strenuous programme of public duties which fell to him as the King's heir. The natural ease, good humour and genuine concern he displayed in the performance of these duties assured his popularity wherever he went. However, he did not satisfy everyone. Sir Frederick Ponsonby, the King's Secretary, warned him that there were risks in becoming too accessible, and the King, who so often warned him not to think himself better than anyone else, now adjured him to remember his position. The war, the King said, had made it possible for the Prince to mix freely, but he should not believe he could behave as other people.

At the time the Prince of Wales left for Canada and the first of his Empire tours, it had already become plain that the most important function of modern royalty is to appear in public. Sir Harold Nicolson has pointed out that the influence which any British king or queen is able to exercise is derived not only from the personal qualities of an individual sovereign but also from the respect and affection with which the monarchy as an institution is today regarded. Such is the strength of feeling towards the monarchy itself, however, that whatever the personal qualities of the individual sovereign they will grow in the esteem and affection of the public, who require with any certainty only two things – that the king or queen shall be a respectable, God-fearing character, and that he or she shall be seen. Thus at any particular moment the sentiment of the public for the monarchy as an institution and for the personal qualities of the sovereign or for his heir will be inextricably mixed. The warmth and affection which is felt for the Royal Family always has a strongly personal element in it which must also be felt in a personal way by those who are the object of it, and, since they are human, presumably welcomed and in some sense returned.

When King George V visited the Commonwealth as Duke of Cornwall it was a turning point in his life. He worked so hard and put so much of himself into each and every occasion and almost for the first time tasted the pleasures of public success. Far more important, nevertheless, were the impressions he received in every Colony he visited of the strength and depth of loyalty to the Crown. As John Gore says:

> It was forced in upon him that nothing had contributed so much to produce those unmistakable manifestations of loyalty and love of England as the life and example of Queen Victoria.... He was thenceforth in no doubt about the importance of the Monarchy and the heavy responsibilities of a democratic sovereign and the purpose and policy of his life were founded from these days on that knowledge.... He saw then the extent to which the whole Empire might stand or fall by the personal example set from the Throne, and to assure the integrity of that example he was to sacrifice much that men hold dear, much that makes life sweet.

George V was the first member of the Royal Family to pay an extended visit to the Commonwealth and Empire. It was not surprising, then, that he regarded himself as an authority upon them. Now he sent his eldest son forth to represent him.

It was a foregone conclusion that throughout his tour the Prince of Wales would be met by cheering, enthusiastic crowds, that, bowing, smiling and waving his hand, he would drive through lanes of loyal subjects, and that he would come back to England impressed by the strength of the feeling for the Crown. Was there, in addition, anything special about this visit?

This famous photograph of Edward
signing a visitors' book was taken in
Canada in 1919, on the first of
Edward's highly successful foreign
tours. The broad grin was provoked
by a wag in the crowd, who shouted
to him, 'Look out, Prince, you're
signing the pledge!'

This famous photograph of Edward signing a visitors' book was taken in Canada in 1919, on the first of Edward's highly successful foreign tours. The broad grin was provoked by a wag in the crowd, who shouted to him, 'Look out, Prince, you're signing the pledge!'

Did he by his own qualities arouse some particular enthusiasm or particularly genuine emotion? The answer to these questions, which must in each case be 'yes', can be given with some confidence. There are many witnesses to its truth.

One of the most convincing is a few reels of film that have been incorporated into the film made from the Duke of Windsor's book *A King's Story*. When he arrived in Canada the Prince immediately inaugurated a function which he put into practice as far as possible on all his tours and which became famous. Everywhere he went, in the large cities or at stations where there was little more than a platform and a grain elevator, although a crowd was always waiting for him, he held an open, public reception at which all and sundry could come and shake him by the hand. In the film of *A King's Story* he can be seen at one of these functions, standing at the end of a kind of wooden platform. People file by him in a never-ending stream and, as each passes him, he extends his hand to shake theirs (at one point on his tour his right hand became so bruised and sore that he had to use his left) and for each individual he has a separate smile. Suddenly, as man after man passes by him, one of them halts and speaks a few words. Instantly the Prince's face, which has never lost attention or recognition of the uniqueness of each meeting, lights up with a more particular response and he answers the man immediately with some words that cannot be heard. The man who spoke to him nailed for all time the Prince's awareness of those others passing him and the intensity of his desire to please.

Compton Mackenzie once wrote: 'If one may so put it, King George had all the talents but none of the genius of royalty. If his son may have lacked some of the talents he had the genius of it beyond any except a dozen princes in the history of man.' At the time Mackenzie was in a mood for chivalrous hyperbole. If one paraphrased him to say that King George had the character for royalty and the Prince all the talents 'beyond any except a dozen princes

in the history of man', a great many people would feel that it was not an exaggerated statement.

On the first of his tours the Prince landed in Canada at the port of St John and, travelling through Halifax, Charlottetown and Quebec, boarded a train just outside Quebec which carried him across Canada to Vancouver, stopping not merely at the major cities but also at dozens of small stations, at every one of which people were gathered, often having come a long way to meet him. The train was a kind of hotel *de luxe* on wheels, in which the Prince had a dining-room, drawing-room, bedroom and bath as well as room for all his staff.

At all the big cities he attended functions, luncheons and dinner parties, made speeches, shook hands, smiled and bowed, untiringly willing, physically strong. At Nipigon he spent a few days roughing it in a camp with some Indian guides, eating Indian food and fishing for trout. At Saskatoon he watched a demonstration of bronco-busting and achieved everlasting fame by mounting one of the broncos and staying on it until the end of the course. In Alberta he bought a ranch for himself. Most striking of all, he received as great a welcome from the French-speaking population as from the English. Everywhere he met companies of men who had fought in the war, and one of his chief functions was to review men who regarded him as an old comrade.

Hundreds of thousands of words were written about him. Newspapers all over the world were in those days prepared to devote columns to a description of such ceremonies. The accounts of journalists covering a tour of this kind seldom survive the event they are written about and nothing is so stale as the cheers of yesterday. Here and there, however, some writer was so struck by what he witnessed that he recorded the event in words sufficiently fresh to convey the spirit of it. Here are two excerpts from the account of

Edward's Canadian tour even included a brief taste of the Indian way of life, at a camp in Nipigon where he spent a few days fishing and eating Indian food.

the special correspondent of *The Times*:

> Some of his speeches he reads; sometimes he speaks from notes which he hardly
> looks at; sometimes he just talks as a friend to friends. When he is on his feet
> he loses all self-consciousness. You hear without effort every word he says. He
> has a happy knack of saying the right thing in the right way, and his clear boyish
> voice has a quality of sympathy and sincerity which makes the speaker one with
> his audience.

And on 4 September 1919 at Winnipeg, in an account of a ceremony at which
the Prince bestowed decorations on returned soldiers or on their nearest
relation, this correspondent wrote:

> For each old mother or father, all of whom seemed to look into his face as if
> he himself was their son, for each pathetic widow, for each wounded soldier he
> had an especial word of sympathy and praise and understanding ready, and not
> a short one either, so that before he gave them his left hand to shake after pinning
> on the medal won in the great struggle, he never stopped talking for a moment....
> For him and for the Empire this gift of human sympathy and kindliness is a very
> great and valuable possession.

*The wistful Prince, sitting on the
steps of a ranch he bought in
Alberta.*

At the end of his Canadian tour, at the invitation of President Wilson
the Prince crossed the border into the USA. In Washington he met the President and in New York huge crowds turned out to welcome him. As he passed
beneath the offices of the stockbroking community, streams of ticker tape
floated down from the windows, and in response he rose from his sitting
position in the car and stood up bowing and smiling. The next day the *New
York World*, reporting his arrival, said: 'It was not crowd psychology that
swept him into instant popularity but the subtle something that is called
personality. Three months ago the *World* correspondent wired from St John,
N.B., "New York will fall in love with this lad." New York did.'

In the USA, as much as in the British Dominions and Colonies, the Prince
of Wales, by his personality and behaviour, lifted his hosts off the horns
of their dilemma. They longed, like humanity everywhere in the world, to
be allowed to idolize royalty; yet to do so was against their whole culture
and philosophy, against the idea they wished to preserve of themselves as
citizens of the New World. In the aftermath of the war the revulsion against
the forms and ceremonial of European society, a society which had so conspicuously broken down, was particularly strong. Democracy was thought
of not so much as a political method, but as a romantic ideal. If a kingly
figure had come among the peoples of the West, dressed in ceremonial costume, holding himself aloof and silent, bowing and waving, they would no
doubt have been moved to much the same emotion, but there would have
been a sense of unease and shame in showing it so openly. When they saw
this smiling, friendly, handshaking boy with his obvious desire to please
and his intense awareness of each and every one, they were able to adore
in him qualities they believed in and which they felt it respectable to praise.
In all the countries he visited, the same words and phrases could be heard:
'A real democrat', 'a good sport', a 'Prince with no pretence', 'Sailor Prince',
and 'Our Prince'.

All courtiers and most royal personages have believed that if the 'mystery
and the magic' are to be preserved, royalty must remain on a pedestal,
although there has never been much evidence for this view. It is clear, however, that it is safer to remain on a pedestal. To come off it, to behave in
a natural and human way, to let the mystery and magic take care of themselves, requires an unusually unaffected nature, a lack of a narrow kind of
vanity, a real interest in other people. The odds against these qualities being

part of the equipment of a member of the Royal Family must be very high indeed.

The Prince of Wales had them. He also had another quality which reinforced them and which was to prove less fortunate in the long run. Like his father, he was exceptionally opinionated. He believed that he understood his own generation, the generation that had been through the war, as none of his family or their advisers could. As he sailed home from New York, he was able to reflect that it was exactly by ignoring the views of his father and his courtiers and by going his own way that he had made a success of his tour beyond anything that had ever been seen before.

Within four months of arriving home from Canada and America the Prince set out to tour New Zealand and Australia. He landed at Auckland on the eve of Anzac Day and it was said that he seemed embarrassed by the depth of the welcome he received. His first act was to attend the service at St Mary's Cathedral in commemoration of the men who had died five years before, and throughout his tour of New Zealand and Australia, as in Canada, he was continually met by small groups of ex-soldiers and sailors, with some of whom he had served at the front. During the summer he visited over 200 different places and travelled by sea and land a total of nearly 46,000 miles.

Everywhere he went his popularity increased and everyone found him irresistible. His talent for the easy exchange, the touch of personal interest, raised the natural enthusiasm of the crowds to a pitch of adoration. And above all they were moved by his capacity to be moved himself. One man told the reporter from *The Times* that he had been near the Prince and seen his eyes fill with tears again and again as working women and children filed past him in an interminable stream. 'He could not have spoken then however much a Prince he was.'

Although, as it turned out, no opportunity could have been more propitious, probably no one in our history has ever had so marked a power as this young Prince to rivet the ties of emotion and sympathy between the mother country and the millions of men, women and children in the outlying Commonwealth of nations. The emotions felt for England could never be explained merely by political or economic advantage, and there is no doubt that the monarchy was the greatest single influence in welding the disparate nations together and in creating the feeling of integration and patriotism which was so remarkable and so spontaneous in both of the World Wars. After the First World War, when the monarchical principle proved in Europe too weak or too unpopular to hold the allegiance of the people, it would have been easy to predict that the young countries of the western world would soon outgrow its influence. The effect of the Prince of Wales' tours can never be exactly measured, but he aroused emotions then which attached the people to the Crown, survived the restlessness of the post-war years, the abdication crisis, and the transfer of loyalty to the new King and Queen, and brought the Dominions in to stand unquestioningly by Britain's side on the declaration of the Second World War. The populations of the countries he travelled through would no doubt have found much to love in any royal personage who visited them, but the manners and the personality of this young Prince were in tune with a philosophy they cherished deeply, and were marvellously reassuring to the sense of uncertainty and insecurity inevitably felt by the citizens of these aggressively young countries.

His physical energy was as usual extraordinary, and in addition to his public functions he joined enthusiastically in any sport provided for his entertainment. Violent physical exercise seemed necessary to him all his life, but this fact should not be allowed to minimize the physical and mental strain of these tours, the real slogging hard work he undertook. He was never for long at one place, while he had to speak, lunch, dine, receive addresses, shake hands, smile, wave, for day after day, week after week at a time. In Melbourne, for instance, he replied to twenty-six addresses. The enthusiasm of the people was sometimes expressed in ways that must have become difficult to bear. Writing many years later, he said that in Australia even a car was often no protection against his welcoming hosts, who would snatch him out of it and pass him from hand to hand in the streets. Worst of all was the touching mania which caused crowds to close round him and, pushing and shoving and treading on his feet, to aim the end of a folded newspaper at him if they could not reach him with their hands. On all public occasions he drove himself to do all that was required of him and showed an almost obsessive desire to give to each individual and every occasion. By the time he left Australia he was physically and mentally exhausted.

From the autumn of 1920 until the autumn of 1921 the Prince stayed at home. His own recollections of that year are chiefly concerned with the splendours of the London season. This was the year of the coal strike and the first post-war slump, but it was also the year in which a full return to peace-time conditions was attempted. The wealth and splendour of the 1920s would never approach that of the years before 1914, particularly in relation to the numbers of servants kept and the plurality of houses in full commission, but servants in livery once more served food on gold and silver plate in the great houses of London and a whole society gave itself up to entertaining. The Prince of Wales belonged to a generation of *jeunnesse dorée* who danced with a feverish determination to shut out the memories of the terrible past.

In the winter of 1920–1 he started hunting fairly regularly. Hunting was regarded then with uncritical affection as a national sport, and the Prince's courage as he hurled himself across country did as much to please the population here as riding the bronco had done to please the crowds in Canada. He never acquired a strong seat on a horse and, without this, but with an absolute determination to surmount every obstacle that came in his way, he earned a reputation for the ease with which he parted company with his horse as well as for the courage with which he continued to invite this fate. But he rode very good horses and was very light, and when in the spring he started to ride in point-to-point races, he did so with some success, winning two races and being placed in a third.

In spite of all this, what is most notable in the record for the year is still the rigour with which he performed his public duties. Once more he drove himself beyond what even the strongest physique could endure, and, in addition to the endless round of speeches, dinners, luncheons, horse shows, ex-servicemen's associations and so on, he undertook a series of special visits to the provinces. He visited Glasgow, South Wales, the West Country and the Scilly Isles. In July he went to south and west Lancashire and in five days he visited Ormskirk, Southport, Formby, Great Crosby, Waterloo, Litherland, Bootle, Liverpool, Ashton-under-Lyne, St Helen's, Manchester, Salford, Eccles, Orlam, Prescot, Fleetwood, Clevelys, Blackpool, St Anne's, Lytham, Kirkham, Mowbreck, Hale, Preston, Leyland, Chorley and Wigan. Enormous and wildly enthusiastic crowds attended him

(Opposite) A keen sportsman, one of Edward's earliest hobbies was point-to-point racing. However, his propensity to fall off, as on this occasion, led his parents to forbid the sport as too dangerous for the heir to the throne.

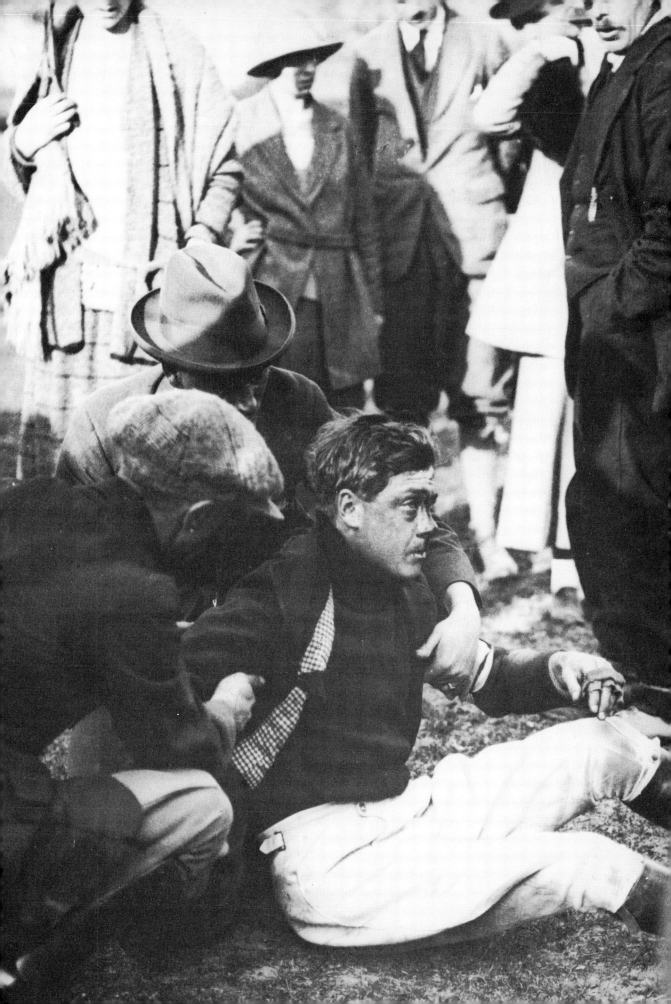

When not abroad, the Prince was kept busy touring Great Britain, and particularly the poorer, depressed areas. Here he has a 'Lucky Dip' at an ex-service men's exhibition in 1921.

throughout the tour.

Writing about the plans for the Prince's forthcoming tour of India to the Viceroy, Lord Reading, Lord Stamfordham said:

For the moment the Prince's health is suffering from the bodily and mental strain of the life which he almost insists upon following, and I am certain that when he comes to India he will have to take things much easier than he has done hitherto, either at home or in the Dominions.... I would strongly urge that his programme allows ample time for rest and recreation.

The tour of India had originally been planned for the previous year, immediately after the Prince's return from Australia. The Prince had objected strongly and ultimately the King yielded and the tour was postponed for a year. It seems, however, that the Prince was still not happy about it. Frances Stevenson, later Lady Lloyd George, wrote in her diary on 18 June 1921:

Went to Cuckoo Belville's party on Thursday night – lots of celebrities, including the King of Spain and the Prince of Wales. ... He must have had one of his gloomy fits, for he came up to me and remarked: 'There's more trouble about India – have you heard?' For the moment I thought he meant a rebellion, but then it occurred to me that he must mean his visit there, & I said: 'But I thought it was all settled. Don't you want to go?' 'Of course I don't want to go,' he replied petulantly – 'I know,' I replied, 'but I thought you had become more or less reconciled to the idea.' 'Oh! I suppose I can become reconciled to anything,' he replied. 'Does the P.M. think I ought to go?' I could not understand why he brought the subject up again, as I knew it had all been settled ages ago, but I suppose he must have been feeling particularly depressed about it. Apparently he had been having an argument with his father about it, for I heard that the Prince said he would ask the P.M. whether he really wanted him to go. Whereupon the King said: 'I don't care whether the P.M. wants you to go or not. *I* wish you to go & you are going.'

This evidence opens up a whole field for speculation. Were the King and Queen without feeling for their gifted if wilful son, who had worked so hard and known so little of the pleasures of youth? And, if they were ready to sacrifice him personally to the monarchy, were they unheedful of the need to nurture its heir? Probably not entirely. The Prince's visit to India had after all been put off for a year. Nevertheless, there is plenty of evidence that the schedules for his tours were exhausting and that the King agreed to programmes that were nearly impossible to undertake.

And what of the Prince himself? Were his remarks as recorded by Lady Lloyd George simply the result of a 'gloomy fit', or is it possible that he was cast in so private a mould that he had no public ambition, that he found no enjoyment in the excitement of his tours, the exercise of his natural talents, his popularity and the feelings he aroused in other people? Given hindsight, one may believe that his enjoyment was less, his demands on life more complex than his public appearances, standing smiling in uniform to receive the cheers of the crowds, would suggest. For the rest he was young, and loved above everything the pleasures of youth – dancing and night life, hunting and polo. It does not require much explanation if he sometimes longed to have time to himself. Above all, he was in love. At this time in his life he was forced, sometimes for years at a time, to put his public life before his strongest desires.

All through the summer the plans progressed for the Prince's visit to India, in spite of some uncertainty caused by the political disturbances there. The anxieties of the authorities as well as the importance attached to the Prince of Wales' tour were because it took place in the aftermath of the massacre at Amritsar. This is not the appropriate place to go into the details of that horrifying episode, one of the most tragic and shameful in British Indian history, and it is enough to say that it is chastening to read about it today. Only less terrible than the massacre itself were some of the cruelties and humiliations to which Indians were subjected during the period of martial law which followed, and it is impossible to overestimate the effect of Amritsar in India.

In 1920 Gandhi and the Congress organization struck a temporary alliance with the Moslem community and launched a movement of non-cooperation with the Government, which included abstention from the official celebration for the Prince of Wales' visit. Nevertheless, plans for the tour went ahead. Lord Reading, the Viceroy, pointed out that to postpone the tour because of the disturbances 'would be a confession of the impotence of the King–Emperor's Government in the face of the Gandhi opposition'.

The *Renown*, carrying the Prince of Wales, dropped anchor in Bombay very early in the morning on 17 November, to the salute of guns of the ships of the East India Squadron. For two weeks before, advertisements had been appearing in the Bombay newspapers urging the public to refrain from welcoming the Prince, to abstain from attending public functions and to stay in their houses as a sign of national mourning. The streets were placarded with notices calling for a boycott. Yet at dawn on the day of the Prince's arrival dense crowds were to be seen making their way to every part of the route the procession would take, until, in spite of the long wait that must follow under the dangerous Indian sun, every inch of standing room was occupied. As the Prince drove through the streets, Indians rushed to kiss the dust over which his car had passed. And, if there was any uneasiness as he passed through the cheering multitudes, it was noticeable that he did not share it. He stood up in his car and called to the guards not to press the people back.

In the meantime in the back streets of Bombay there was some fighting. But these disturbances were regarded rather as a sign of the general unrest in India than of any lack of warmth in the welcome to the Prince, and they only served to underline the element of risk that attended the whole of the Prince's tour in British India. However, if the success of his visit was ever in doubt, this was dispelled during his visit to Poona. The principal event here was the laying of two foundation stones, the first of the Maratha War Memorial and the second of a memorial to Shivaji, the hero of the Marathas. When he performed the second of these acts the Prince said in his clear voice:

A few minutes ago I laid the foundation stone of a memorial to the Maratha soldiers who laid down their lives in the Great War, men who proved that the spirit which animated the armies of Shivaji still burns bright and clear. And what could be more fitting than that the glory of the past and of today should be inaugurated in the presence not only of the representative of the house of Shivaji but also of those princes and chiefs who are descended from the soldiers and statesmen of the Empire which he founded.

When this speech was translated so that everyone present could understand it, it provoked shouts of victory, Maratha battle cries, blessings on the Prince's head, invocations of victory to his sword, in such a volume of sound as to be absolutely deafening. And as he left the enclosure those who were not near enough to touch him threw gold and silver coins in his path so that the royal feet might tread on them.

News of this personal triumph at Poona, following so quickly on that at Bombay, made a great impression throughout India and did much to ensure the success of the rest of the tour. Back in Bombay it soon became noticeable that, wherever HRH was due to pass, crowds began to collect at street corners

(Above) To the joy of his hosts and the Indian public, Edward took part in several polo matches during his tour.

(Opposite) Her Majesty the Begum of Bhopal entertains the formally dressed heir to the British Empire.

to welcome him. Most significant of all was the fact that these crowds, usually not much inclined to be vocal, began now to cheer him as he passed with the heartiness of an English crowd.

While the Prince was in Bombay an incident occurred that was to add unexpectedly to the success of the tour, and in addition to introduce to him someone who was to become a lifelong friend. He was disturbed one afternoon during a siesta by a young Indian Cavalry officer who entered without ceremony and stood by his bed. This was Captain Edward Dudley Metcalfe, popularly known as 'Fruity'. He made his mark without difficulty on this hot afternoon by telling the Prince that a number of maharajas were anxious to lend him some polo ponies, and asking him whether he would like to play. As a result of this conversation twenty-five polo ponies were added to the Prince's retinue and for the rest of the tour wherever possible the Prince and his staff played polo. These games became a very important part of the tour. The Indians are good judges of horses and riding and it is in accordance with their traditions for ruling princes to exhibit their prowess before the eyes of their subjects. The games attracted large crowds, and even at Allahabad, where the orders for non-cooperation were successfully imposed, the Indians, having satisfied their sense of duty by staying off the streets in the morning, rushed wreathed in smiles to cheer the Prince on the polo ground in the afternoon.

The Prince spent a total of four months in the sub-continent, during which he fulfilled his usual heavy programme, replying to addresses of welcome, driving through gaily decorated streets, reviewing troops, visiting colleges, attending banquets, garden parties and so on. Afterwards he travelled on to Ceylon, Japan, the Philippines and British North Borneo before returning home. On 20 June, after being away for eight months, he reached England.

So much for the public side of the tour. There is no doubt that it was brilliantly successful. Nevertheless, by this time the Prince had already begun to exhibit in private a duality in personality and behaviour. Genuine hardship seems to have been caused him, here as elsewhere, by the determination of private people to entertain him, and it is impossible not to sympathize with the young man who, at the end of a long day, was expected to appear, fresh and convivial, at private parties. But he responded to the pressures put upon him by a selectiveness which, as the years went on, involved the disappointment of very many people and which, in the circumstances, was not acceptable. Criticisms of this kind of behaviour were first heard after his Australian tour. They gathered strength in India and were soon heard all round the world. The letter which follows has been chosen because it is well authenticated and because it is typical of many letters which are part of a postbag following the newspaper serialization of the history of his early life, and described similar events all over the world:

My in-laws in Queensland organized a large dance when he was out there in 1920 and invited him to stay for it, & in fact had built on to the house! But he never came having said that he would – making out that the rains had made the roads impassable when in fact he had found the Bell girls in Boonah more to his liking and didn't want to leave them. Various people motored over the road to prove that it was passable – but he never came, and hurt a great many feelings in consequence.

It would not be easy – and indeed would be presumptuous – to suggest how the Prince might best have dealt with the pressures created by a combination of his own personality and conduct and the heavy schedules agreed

'I am having a great time, but it is very difficult to keep David cheerful. At times he gets so depressed and says he'd give anything to change places with me' – so wrote one of Edward's closest friends, Lord Louis Mountbatten (left in picture). On this occasion at least he seems to have succeeded.

to by the all-powerful, insatiable and unimaginative King, but it is clear how he did deal with them. He developed a callous irresponsibility to those parts of the programme he found unrewarding, and a stony disregard for the feeling of people whose hospitality or welcome proved inconvenient. He began to be ruthlessly unpunctual and his staff were often in real difficulty to explain his absence or delayed appearance at public functions. He had become very spoilt – how should he not? – and as Robert Sencourt so aptly puts it, he had been, 'subjected to a tension too unique, too subtle, too varied and too continuous for his character to ripen and strengthen'. Melancholy by nature, and easily bored when he was forced to appear at public functions which did not interest him, by his unresponsiveness and air of discontent he gave colour to the kind of rumour that he was 'still suffering from a hang-over from the night before' or 'was drunk at the time', while his passing flirtations were given more importance by offended civil servants and their wives than possibly, at least while he was young, they deserved. Neverthe-less, it is beyond doubt that from the time of his Indian tour he troubled less and less if he gave offence on dull or very formal occasions, although he never lost his ability to magnetize crowds.

His cousin, Lord Louis Mountbatten, who accompanied the Prince on his tours of New Zealand, Australia and India, and who was as close to him as anyone living at this time, bears witness to his melancholy nature. Writing many years later, he said: 'I soon realized that under that delightful smile which charmed people everywhere, and despite all the fun we managed to have, he was a lonely and sad person, always liable to deep depressions.' On one occasion during the tours Lord Mountbatten wrote to his mother: 'I am having a great time, but it is very difficult to keep David cheerful. At times he gets so depressed, and says he'd give anything to change places with me.'

In his autobiography, *A King's Story*, the Duke of Windsor reflected on the nature of his official duties during these years of travel:

Lonely drives through tumultuous crowds, the almost daily inspection of serried ranks of veterans, the inexhaustible supply of cornerstones to be laid, the com-memorative trees to be planted ... sad visits to hospital wards, every step bringing me face to face with some inconsolable tragedy ... always more hands to shake than a dozen Princes could have coped with....

These words were written many years after the event, but if they really represent – and there is some reason to believe they do – the thoughts of the young Prince of Wales, it suggests that, whereas the cheering populace can easily dispense with, or compensate for, the 'mystery and the magic' of monarchy, some elemental faith in it is necessary to the man himself. When one contrasts the Prince's perfectly reasonable and understandable words, his all-too-realistic visions of cornerstones and commemorative trees, with the awe experienced by his father in similar circumstances, the almost sacrificial sense of dedication, one cannot feel moved to the award of praise or blame; but one must pity the young Prince, born in many ways so suited to his inexorable fate, but with a clarity, a *practicality* of vision which, in some spheres most valuable, was here such a desolating gift.

5

The Prince at Home

In a television interview with Kenneth Harris in 1970 the Duke of Windsor betrayed an interest in the word 'establishment'. Asked what he thought it meant, he replied:

> Well, the establishment was a new word to me until about fifteen years ago when I heard it and I asked people to explain it to me. It's not easy to explain, it's rather an obscure word, but it must always have existed. I think it means authority, authority of the law, of the Church, of the, well, I suppose, the monarch to a certain extent. And universities and maybe the top brass of the army and navy.

The Duke's definition misses a little of the subtlety in the use of the word today, but there is no doubt that he welcomed it, with its slightly but unmistakably disrespectful air, as a delightful generic term for a great many things he disliked.

This is typical of an immaturity of outlook which he never outgrew. All his life he tended to view his fellows as might a schoolboy, setting a demarcation line between himself and kindred spirits on the one hand, and authority and the friends of authority on the other. His failure to develop in depth may be partly attributable to heredity. According to John Gore, his father's immaturity in his youth caused concern, while according to many authorities, his three younger brothers developed fully only with marriage. What is beyond doubt, however, is that the most important influences of his childhood and youth – his relationship with his parents, his restricted education, the arid discipline of the naval colleges, the lack of close contact with civilized minds, as well as the freak of birth which placed him in a unique position of isolation and pre-eminence – all contributed to it. As a young man such stability as he might have achieved in this unparalleled position came under a continual barrage from the hectoring and complaints, the bombardment of instructions to which his father subjected him, as well as the insurmountable fact that he could never please the King.

While the Prince was a child there were many signs of the fondness that existed between his father and himself, but they were incompatible in taste. The King loved everything old, the Prince loved everything new (possibly in reaction), and they were separated by a generation gap that had been unnaturally widened by the war. In a different sphere they would have gone their separate ways. As it was, the King's authority was absolute and he wished to live the life of a family man with his wife and children around him. His dictatorial attitude spoiled to some extent his relations with all his sons, and the happy family existed only in his imagination. 'The King is in a very good form,' Lord Hardinge wrote once to his wife, 'which I hope will survive the arrival of his sons.' It is constantly said that his attitude to his children changed completely with their marriage, but there seems also to have been a well-defined difference in his feelings for his first and second sons beforehand. 'You have always been so sensible & easy to work with,' he wrote to the Duke of York at the time of his marriage in 1923, '& you have always been ready to listen to any advice & to agree with my opinions about people & things, that I feel we have always got on well together (very different to dear David).'

In return there was some ambivalence in the Prince's feeling for his father. We are told that he talked almost excessively about him, telling stories which reflected admiration and respect. Nevertheless, he can often be seen attempting the forlorn task of cutting the King, indeed all the Royal Family, down to size. When he was shown Lytton Strachey's recently published *Queen Victoria*, the Prince remarked: 'That must be the book the King was talking about this morning. He was very angry and got quite vehement over it.' 'P of W had not seen the book,' Lady Lloyd George records, 'so we showed it to him & presently he was discovered in roars of laughter over the description of the Queen and John Brown.'

Much damage was done to the relationship between the King and his heir by the fact that the King managed to keep himself so well informed of the Prince's movements and behaviour. The Prince came to regard with

King George rides with three of his sons (Albert, Edward and George) in Windsor Great Park – the kind of Royal Family image that the King struggled to present, in the face of Edward's increasingly unconventional behaviour.

dislike and distrust people who might have his father's ear. But it was almost certainly as much from taste as because of their access to his father that the Prince avoided the big guns of the establishment.

It is impossible to understand the Prince of Wales' tastes and pursuits without reference to the time in which he lived. From the beginning of the war there had been a tendency to react to the unbearable strain by escaping into triviality in everyday life. Such records as Lady Cynthia Asquith's diaries give an astonishing picture of the superficiality of the civilian upper classes. Then, in the aftermath of the war, there occurred a transitional period between the old rich civilization and the poorer and more democratic world of the future. Large sections of society were bereaved, uprooted and emotionally exhausted and at the same time had an entirely new freedom from convention. Against a background of booms and slumps, of the homeless and the jobless, the first Labour Government in 1924, the General Strike, the betrayal of agriculture, and later under the shadow of the great army of unemployed, they spent their time in the pursuit of pleasure with a single-mindedness which marks them off from almost every other generation in history. In spite of his position and his essentially unreal relationship with his fellows, the Prince was a genuine product of his period. Indeed it is impossible to refrain from speculation as to whether he could have progressed so inexorably to his fate if he had been born at any other time – one of the very few fields for speculation in a progress which was soon to take on the predestined air of a Greek tragedy.

The most extraordinary phenomenon of the post-war years was the mania for dancing: all over London, hotels were forced to hire bands and clear part of the restaurant floor. At the same time dozens of new establishments called night clubs opened their doors. The most famous of these and the one which the Prince attended night after night, was the Embassy Club in Bond Street. He has described it as 'that Buckingham Palace of night clubs', an inapt description for what was simply a long underground basement, however luxuriously furnished.

To this room, night after night for years, came dukes and earls and princes and their wives and the women they loved, writers, actors, press lords, politicians, all the self-made men from the war who were trying to break into society, all the riff-raff and the hangers-on. At home in many of the houses in which these people lived there were cooks and kitchen-maids waiting to cook a dinner, butlers waiting to serve it. But their masters and mistresses at the Embassy Club sat at their tables only until the waiters served the soup, and then, as though mechanically activated, they all got up and began to dance. In this restaurant one could eat as well as anywhere in the world, but the food was always crammed down between dances, drowned with gin and tonic, blown over by cigarette-smoke.

Here the acute observer could watch the rules of an older society gradually being broken down. For the first time in history the British upper classes were opening their ranks and allowing wholesale ingress to rich or famous men and women, notorieties, anyone who could add a scrap to their entertainment. At the Embassy most of the clientele knew each other, and met there as in their own drawing-rooms. The nodding and waving and calling out and transferring to one another's tables that went on gave unequalled opportunities for social climbing from outside this group.

The question of money had great relevance. These young people had been brought up in the Edwardian age to an aristocratic role. They had an absolute

if discreet belief in their own superiority and their natural right to certain
material things, yet their role, their lands and their incomes were all
diminished. They adjusted themselves as best they could. They lived in
small houses in Westminster, they sold the gold plate and they managed
without a footman, sometimes without a kitchen-maid. They dined out, they
said, because they could not afford to dine in – by which they meant they
could not entertain on the scale of their parents. They seemed to themselves
to be making endless economies, constant adjustments, and they could not
go further or faster in one generation. This, as much as their desire for entertainment, caused them to open their doors so easily to many people they still
regarded as their inferiors – the ability to pay being less rare and even more
necessary than wit.

Yet this society, like all others, was composed of individuals. Some were
very rich, some hard-working. Some would become conventionally and un-
compromisingly staid when they inherited from their parents, while a few
had a great future to fulfil. Collectively they had a slightly raffish air.

If the Prince was seldom to be seen in the company of members of those
great political families who for generations had played their part in the
government of the country, or of the lesser nobility who undertook the
serious work of the counties, they, in return, began quite early to adopt a
somewhat scornful attitude towards him. It would be too crude to say that
he regarded them as 'stuffy' while they regarded him as 'rather vulgar', but
these words do represent the spirit of the thing.

In this matter the Prince played unwittingly if unconcernedly into the
hands of his critics. One of the oddest things about him – until one remembers the isolation of his youth – is that he was singularly uninformed about
all those shibboleths which go to make up what has been so conveniently
and compactly labelled by the single letter 'U'. The Prince was in some ways
surprisingly 'non-U', most noticeably in the clothes he wore. It was not
merely that the upper classes agreed with his father in disliking the loudness
of his tweeds and the cut of his clothes: the Prince wore his top hat on the
side of his head out hunting, suede shoes or brown and white brogues, things
even schoolboys at Eton or Harrow knew were done only by cads. Such
matters were taken with the utmost seriousness then, not for themselves
but for what they told people about one another in a class society which
was deeply divisive and made possible by the complete acceptance of the
superiority of one class over another.

Yet we can be sure that all of this was forgiven him whenever he chose
to exert himself, partly because no one in England of any class can resist
overtures from a member of the Royal Family, but also for qualities of his
own. Before we can decide what these were, we must follow him into the
society of the people he trusted and loved.

In contrast to his attitude of rebelliousness and mistrust of any kind of
masculine authority, in his relationship with first one and then the other
of the two women for whom he cared deeply the Prince seemed, on the contrary, to be actively seeking a dominating, quasi-maternal partner. There
was a slavish quality in his devotion that prevented it being fully returned
by any woman who sought a lover rather than a son. Mrs Dudley Ward
was extremely fond of him and she exercised enormous influence over him,
but he must always have been aware that the intensity of his love was not
returned. If she had loved him more than she did, or if she had been in-
sensately ambitious, history might have been, not completely different, but

*The Prince's choice of clothes was
an increasing source of annoyance
to his father: (opposite, left) a
definitely 'non-U' outfit, with loud
stripes, turn-ups and brown and
white brogues; (opposite, right) a
more 'acceptable' Edward
(although his father might regret he
could no longer order his son's
trouser pockets to be sewn up).*

altered, because it seems possible that from the earliest time the Prince regarded his predestined role as not inescapable, and viewed the Duke of York much as one brother might another in the case of a family firm.

People speaking of these years almost invariably remark of Mrs Dudley Ward that 'she was very good for him', and, asked for a more specific account, explain that, although in public her attitude towards him was extremely correct, in private she 'teased' him (counteracted a tendency to become rather spoilt) and took a strict view of his obligations.

She had two little daughters, whom the Prince of Wales adored. His favourite, Angie, attended a day school but also took several special classes in languages, dancing and so on. Discovering that it was impossible for the mistresses of the school to be quite sure when these extra classes took place, she would sometimes play truant. When this happened she would wait on a seat outside the school until a car drew up, and the chauffeur got out to tell her that 'His Royal Highness' would like her to go to tea at St James's Palace, or to play golf, as the case might be.

Mrs Dudley Ward's maid, McCann, has said that the servants both in their household and in the Prince's were devoted to him and that his popularity with them was at least as great as with the public. People whom he trusted or loved almost invariably speak of his essential simplicity, and they use a word about him that is also used about his father. 'We liked him', Mrs Colin Buist said, 'because he was so straightforward.' And she added: 'You know, I have known him all his life and I have never seen him angry. If he hears something he doesn't like or doesn't understand, he never speaks strongly. He just says: "Oh! well, I suppose he thinks...."' His preferences were always for a private life. He liked to dine two or four – alone with the woman he loved, or with one other couple. One reason for his addiction to night clubs was that there people dined in small parties.

Instances are given of his generosity. Lady Hardinge speaks of his generosity both to charities and individuals, and she says: 'He used, long ago, to be lavish with tips. A shockingly bad but brave rider, he was reputed to give a five-pound note to anybody who opened a gate for him out hunting. A story circulating at the time said that his route across country was marked by attentive members of a famous banking family, each one holding open a gate.'

But the qualities for which above all he was famous were his exceptional ability to handle a crowd and a quite irresistible personal charm. He had the gift of command combined with a special quickness and adroitness in extemporization and a flair for saying and doing exactly the right things without prompting. His extraordinary charm is well attested, not merely by immense numbers of simple people, but again and again in the memoirs of courtiers and others with a wide experience of meeting people. 'He had an absolutely magnetic charm,' Lord Mountbatten has said, while a typical comment is this one taken from the autobiography of the Duchess of Atholl: 'We also saw a little of the Prince of Wales lately returned from his trip to India. I think it was the first time I had met His Royal Highness and I began to realize something of his great charm.'

While it is true to say that the qualities of any member of the Royal Family cannot be separated from their royalty, there may, nevertheless, be some that are particularly suited to set this off. From most accounts of Edward VIII as Prince of Wales, it seems he had qualities which, attractive in anyone, become irresistible in a member of the Royal Family. In attempting to analyse them one cannot disregard his looks. His fair face under his thatch of yellow hair was both exceptionally beautiful and ineffably sad in repose. 'He is sad', Lord Esher had said, 'with the sadness of the world's burdens.' And we know from Lord Mountbatten that this air of having been blighted by some vision too immense for him to bear did represent a genuinely melancholy temperament. This suggested vulnerability, attractive in almost anyone, and in a royal personage enough by itself to account for the sympathy he aroused. Then, on occasion, the sad, royal face would light up with an intensity of desire to please which transformed the expression to one of youthful, almost conspiratorial gaiety. And, although there were other things – the natural manner, the mild sense of humour, the infallible memory for faces and names – it was this desire to please that was found irresistible by the population of whole continents and also by individuals quite accustomed to displays of exceptional charm.

However, one cannot spend the whole of one's life in an effort to please, and, as the Prince grew older and more confident of his powers, he began to lose the desire to please everyone he met. When he was uneasy or bored, he either sat melancholy and aloof (as time went on he chose this alternative more and more often), or he 'switched on' an imitation of feeling and behaviour which experience had taught him was effective. If almost the whole of one's duty is publicly to please people, it cannot be considered a crime to counterfeit emotions which never could be at command. What was sad, and unusual in his family, was that as he grew older these emotions became less and less spontaneous; almost as though he had worn out the whole stock in the exceptional ardour of his youth.

There is really no doubt that the Prince had a genuine simplicity and naturalness of manner. From the time when he was a child playing football with the village children at Sandringham, he seems always to have suffered from a genuine uneasiness about his enforced elevation, and from a desire, no less honourable for coming sometimes into conflict with other desires, to enter on equal terms the world from which he felt shut out. It was this sense of being shut out that accounted for much of the duality of his nature. His books are full of sentences expressing his dislike of ceremony, his consciousness of the loneliness of his lot, and a wistful envy of the ordinary man.

The difficulty arose not so much because this natural simplicity, so admirable in itself, was in some ways inconvenient in the heir to the throne, as that because of his immaturity of mind he was unable to reconcile it with the exceptional demands life made upon him, or even with other aspects of his own character. Thus he was sometimes accused of suddenly turning 'royal'. Probably every member of the Royal Family who attempts to break the rules of isolation from the rest of the world will be compelled to administer the 'royal snub', and this would be true irrespective of any natural tendency to arrogance. If the rules are kept on one side they will be kept on the other, but, if they are waived, too much is left to the judgment of any and every man. The Prince may not have been arrogant by nature but he was extraordinarily spoilt and self-indulgent, and he was clearly very haughty when his ideas for fulfilling his public duties were interfered with.

Many rumours and anecdotes, some of doubtful truth, have grown up around the person of this Prince. One of these, widely believed by many people who should know better, is that the Prince customarily drank too much. It is completely untrue. The Prince had an obsession with physical fitness; he ate very little, often nothing at luncheon, and drank nothing until after seven o'clock in the evening except tea, a beverage for which he had

an enduring passion the whole of his life. A story is told of how on one
occasion both his pilots were with him in his aeroplane when they had to
make a forced landing. Sick with apprehension themselves, they found their
anxiety relieved by the obvious enjoyment of their passenger in the back,
and later by the fact that, to keep him happy while arrangements were made
for their rescue, it was necessary only to introduce him to the cottage of
a woman who made him a cup of tea.

Nor can one close this account of the impression made by the Prince in
his youth without one more quotation from Lady Hardinge, a truthful witness but one by no means biased in his favour. 'Never think,' she said, 'never
think there wasn't quality there.' And she waved her hand in the air. 'He
had only to arrive at Windsor....'

It is often argued that the King arrested the development of his eldest son
by his unwillingness to allow him adequate opportunities to acquaint himself
with the affairs of the realm. Indeed, he was unwilling for his son to see
anything except a very limited selection of Foreign Office and Dominions
Office telegrams, and discouraged his association with political leaders.

It is nevertheless doubtful whether, unless temporarily thwarted in something he seriously wished to do, the Prince of Wales expected or even desired
to anticipate the responsibilities of the King. Brought face to face with the
appalling poverty of the late 1920s and early 1930s, to his infinite credit
his distress was genuine and spontaneous. Under this influence he was inclined to make apolitical statements and to believe that something could and
should be done to alleviate the desperation he found. As a result, it has sometimes been thought that he had a genuine interest in politics, even one of
a progressive, almost radical kind. Nothing could be further from the truth.
He was concerned, as almost everyone is, with certain political questions,
and by the nature of his work his attention was drawn to them again and
again, but, if allowance is made for this, it can be seen that his serious interest
in the government of the country was hardly greater than that of any other
easy-going, under-educated, unintellectual young man. The King was responsible for discouraging his association with professional politicians but
he could hardly have prevented, and indeed would not have wanted to
prevent, his gravitating towards those noble families, such as the Stanleys
and the Cecils, to whom politics was the stuff of life. This, as has been said,
the Prince notably failed to do.

Again, it is perfectly clear that, as far as he was a political animal, he was
as unthinkingly conservative in outlook as ninety out of every hundred
young men born outside the working class. His books are restrainedly but
quite definitely full of nostalgia for 'the good old days', while his accounts
of political occasions are couched in the language of a faded reactionism
which, although it expresses sentiments still held by many people of his class
and age, falls oddly on the modern ear. Here is what he has to say about
the General Strike of 1926:

What was unique about the strike of 1926 was the reaction of the upper and
middle classes. They regarded it as a blow aimed at the constitutional foundations
of English life. In response to the Government's appeal thousands left their business desks and their suburban homes or emerged from their landed estates, their
clubs, and their leisure, determined to restore the essential services of the nation.
The people I knew felt they were putting down something that was terribly
wrong, something contrary to British traditions. And they put on a first-class show.

He goes on to say that his father, who clearly had difficulty in deciding

(*Above*) *The Prince of Wales* (*near
the wall on the left*), *visiting a
depressed area in Wales.*
(*Opposite*) *At a Toc H ceremony in
the Royal Albert Hall.*

whether the strike fell within the ordinary meaning of party politics or was of a more revolutionary nature, was anxious that his sons should keep out of it. This the Prince found impossible to do, and he adds that he hopes he will not at this late date be accused of party politics when he says he lent his car and chauffeur to transport the *British Gazette*, the government newspaper edited by Winston Churchill, to Wales.

What he does not say, but which is greatly to his credit, is that he also contributed to the miners' relief fund. The Prince took an absolutely genuine, deep and imaginative interest in the welfare of the working man and in particular of ex-servicemen, towards whom he felt a very real comradeship. Whenever he was in England he supported Toc H, the religious movement based on the complete equality of its members, and the British Legion, never failing to attend their functions, to take part in their ceremonial occasions and to give them a warmth of interest and patronage which clearly exceeded mere attention to duty. 'I feel more at home with the Legion than anywhere else,' he said once, and whether or not this was completely true, he succeeded in making the people of Britain feel it was. In those days the Prince could not captivate the whole nation by one or two television appearances, but, by his continual visits to the branches and headquarters of the working men's associations, he earned the love of large sections of the population.

Yet even in this sphere, where his son was so obviously successful, the King's attitude was invariably churlish and discouraging. He seems never to have made any attempt to understand the younger man's point of view or to sympathize with his aspirations. The Prince received the equivalent of a summons to the library as a result of a press photograph showing him dressed in the uniform blazer of Toc H. And while the King often gave him formal praise for some obviously successful public appearances, he could never put much warmth into his speech because he felt nothing but irritation at and disapproval of the Prince's methods. 'The King argues', Lord Stamfordham once wrote to Sir Godfrey Thomas, 'that he never made jokes in any of his public speeches.'

6

No Doubt of the Young Man's Capacity for Goodness

The Prince of Wales was nothing if not an original personality; no faceless royalty he, and, if it is not always possible to catch the exact mixture of talent, charm, obstinacy, flair for public relations and callow lack of judgment which combined to make him unique, it is not because of any attempt at disguise on his part.

In 1924 he broke his journey to his ranch in Canada to stay with Mr and Mrs James Burden of Syosset, Long Island, in order to see the international polo matches between Great Britain and America. After his long and strenuous years he was in holiday mood and his affinity with what almost overnight had become the richest and the most undemanding society in the world was immediately apparent. In the early days of their supremacy the

The Prince of Wales and two of his personal staff, Captain Allen Lascelles (centre) and David Boyle, on arrival in America in 1924.

American nation required of a visitor only that he should be a 'good fellow', and that he fully deserved this name the Prince had demonstrated all over the world. He now set about his holiday-making with an assiduousness and a carefree lack of particularity that startled his staff and his father even though it delighted his hosts. The Prince's own account of the King's re-action to this visit is among the most disingenuous passages in his book. He quotes a headline PRINCE GETS IN WITH THE MILKMAN and then blames the American press for the fact that his father refused after this to let any of his sons visit America again. The King did not openly ban a return to America but, whenever this was suggested by either the Prince of Wales or his brothers, he managed by some means to prevent it.

The American press did indeed take an avid interest in his visit, and even such serious organs as the *New York Times*, *New York Herald Tribune* and *Chicago Tribune* devoted every day a front-page column to his movements as well as a further column on the inside pages, sometimes two or three. Thus the *New York Times* on 1 September, after calling him 'the indefatig-able vacationist', told its readers that the morning before, in very hot

The Prince chats to ladies at the Belmont Park races. His suede shoes, sign of a 'cad' in his father's opinion, carried the different but equally unfortunate connotation in America of homosexuality, a fact eventually pointed out to Edward who then ceased to wear them there.

weather, the Prince had practised polo for more than two hours, running three ponies into a lather and exhausting two companions, and went on to say that for hours in the afternoon no one had known where he was, 'no one that is except the Prince and a few boon companions who knew that he was streaking it up Long Island in one of the fastest motor boats extant'. On the following day the Prince went to a luncheon party where 200 guests were assembled to meet him and where dancing had been arranged. From there, against the advice of his staff and his hosts who warned him of the heat and the holiday crowd, he went to the races at Belmont Park. On 3 September he is reported as having gone to a dance and stayed out until six o'clock in the morning, and on 4 September as having disappointed many people by failing to turn up for a drag hunt arranged for five o'clock in the morning, for the good reason that he had only just gone to bed. That evening he attended another dance, left at 2.30 in the morning and went once more to some destination unknown until about 5 a.m. when he returned to bed.

The Prince's staff were anxious to counter the air of frivolity which between them the press and the Prince had contrived to create. It was announced that reports of the Prince's late rising were mistaken: the truth was that he was out of bed by ten o'clock every morning, and began his day with a swim in the pool. Again, it was a mistake to think that the Prince was a pleasure-lover and a sportsman only, an idea based on his diversions while on an American holiday, and to counter this suggestion it was made known that in spite of his many social and sporting engagements the Prince had been reading *The Life and Letters* of Walter Hines Page during his stay in America.

The following year the Prince visited West Africa, South Africa and South America and arrived back in England in October at the end of his last official overseas tour, having visited forty-five countries and travelled a distance of 150,000 miles.

On 17 October *The Spectator* devoted an article to the Prince of Wales' return in which, after saying that everywhere he went he left behind most pleasant memories of his charm, modesty and friendliness, the writer referred to certain criticisms that had been made of him in the Argentine newspapers. This article is remarkable in two ways: for the astonishing servility of its language, and because it marked one of the few occasions on which criticisms quite often heard abroad were openly referred to in the British press.

The writer speaks of a day when the Prince was due to visit a school at eleven in the morning. The building had been specially decorated and the children taught to sing in English 'God Bless the Prince of Wales'. Two ministers were at the school to receive the guests. The assembled company waited for some time and then one of the two ministers went to the Prince's house where he was merely told without explanation that the engagement had been cancelled. The writer goes on to say that, in his opinion and the opinion of the correspondent he quotes, it was inconceivable that the Prince himself was responsible for this blunder, but that, in spite of this, it was impossible to prevent people from talking and drawing comparisons between his apparent willingness to attend supper parties into the small hours of the morning and his failure to keep an engagement a few hours later. Then, in slavishly apologetic tones, he suggests that, whatever the difficulties, the Prince should avoid giving people the excuse to say that he was either unduly restless or exhausted by giving to amusements too many of the hours which might have been spent in preparation for work that was necessarily exacting and tiring. And he went on to say that the Prince would do well to attach himself seriously to some public cause entirely beyond and above faction.

Following this article A.G. Gardiner drew attention to it and, having first catalogued with perfect sincerity the Prince's many good qualities, continued as follows:

There is a feeling that there is a lack of seriousness which, excusable and even natural to healthy youth, is disquieting in the mature man. This implies no disapproval of the Prince's love of sport, of fun and of innocent amusement. Nor does it imply a demand that the heir to the throne should have intellectual tastes that nature has not endowed him with. Least of all does it imply that the qualities of a snob would be a desirable exchange for the Prince's high spirits and companionable temper. But it does mean that the public would be relieved to read a little less in the encomiums of the Press about the jazz drum and the banjo side of the Prince's life....

The Prince's future is not a personal affair only, but an affair of the nation and of the world. His apprenticeship to life is over. His career is henceforth in his own hands. He commands an affection and goodwill on the part of the nation that cannot be overstated and that a man of his genuine kindliness of heart must wish to repay. He can repay it by emulating the admirable example which is offered by his parents of how a modern democratic throne should be filled. It is the general wish, now that his travels are over, that he should take up some task which will reflect his interest in the weightier matters of the national life and that will prepare him for the heavy responsibilities which will one day fall upon him. And finally, it is proper to say that the nation would be gratified and relieved to find that the heir to the throne, like Dame Marjorie in the song, was 'settled in life'.

The British press were presently to show that they were capable of imposing upon themselves a quite extraordinary degree of reticence in relation to the affairs of this royal young man. The fact that these articles were published reflects the growing understanding of the defects in his character which, alongside his popularity, continually increased.

The trouble was that as the Prince neared middle age the polarity between his response to people and occasions that awoke his interest and imagination, and those which failed to do so, became increasingly obvious. More and more often he gave demonstrations of an immature callousness and indifference to other people's feelings, and he troubled less and less to control the weariness and sadness with which he went about so much of his work. Yet, in that part which he undertook from choice, he still had a marvellous capacity to please and he made a genuine contribution to the evolution of the role of modern royalty.

As the great depression of the late twenties and thirties hit first one industry and then another, and the vast armies of unemployed men and of under-nourished children stood on the streets, a living condemnation of modern civilization and government, the Prince no more than any other man could offer a political solution to the problems that beset his country. But it would be wrong for this reason to underestimate the very real contribution he made to the relief of human unhappiness. Whether calling in at branch meetings of the British Legion, or leading thousands of ex-servicemen from the Albert Hall to the Cenotaph in a torchlight parade, he succeeded in giving sincerity and genuine enthusiasm to the performance of what might have been a purely dutiful role. He spoke to the men on his travels in tones of equality as well as concern, and in return they openly adored him. It was not uncommon for scenes of spontaneous enthusiasm to be evoked by the mere mention of his name.

In 1928 he became patron of the National Council of Social Service, an event which according to its official historian was to lead to some diversion from its original broad aims and purposes through concentration on one specific type of activity. From now on the work the NCSS undertook on behalf of the unemployed was to take precedence over everything else. It is not a polite exaggeration to say that the Prince inspired a great deal of this work, that other people were fired by his enthusiasm or that he constantly suggested new spheres where he might be of use to the institutions working in this field.

Nor did he ever spare himself physically. He travelled continually all over the worst areas of Wales, Tyneside, Lancashire, the Midlands and Scotland, and to quote the historian of the NCSS:

The Prince knew more than some of his Ministers about the problems of the derelict valleys and the silent mills. Nor were the endless ceremonies, openings and presentations accomplished without personal cost in nervous strain and sheer fatigue. On one occasion, worn out with day-long travelling in Wales and the pain of helpless sympathy, the Prince slept exhausted on the shoulder of Sir Percy Watkins, chief NCSS officer for Wales, waking dutifully each time Sir Percy warned him that the car was approaching groups of children waiting to see their Prince.

The sphere which the Prince made his own was that of voluntary service. He helped to raise funds where necessary, but his heart was in the effort to raise volunteers. It says much for the achievements of the Welfare State that to a later generation his appeals seem rather naïve against the background of the depression and the appalling numbers of unemployed. At that time, however, even the hospitals were dependent to a very large extent on voluntary effort and, if any help was to be given to individuals other than that of a purely economic kind, it had to be done by voluntary workers. These were unable to touch the basic problems but they made an enormous contribution to the welfare of thousands of people. Because of his immense personal prestige the Prince was able to coordinate the work of the various institutions with far more ease than is usually possible, and he launched an appeal for volunteers to which the response was immediate and temporarily overwhelming.

Those who then worked with the Prince in the fields where his enthusiasm combined with his natural flair for casual communication to make him one of the best-loved figures in modern history would have felt bewildered if they had known that elsewhere so much anxiety was felt. In 1927, when the Prince was thirty-three, a member of his own household expressed this anxiety in a letter to Baldwin in which he asked the Prime Minister to use his influence with the Prince. For 'there is no doubt', this writer said, 'of the young man's capacity for goodness.' The Prime Minister's response to this letter, according to some accounts, took an unexpected and rather exaggerated form. In 1927 the Prince, accompanied by his brother, Prince George, visited Canada for the Diamond Jubilee of the Confederation and Baldwin travelled with them. He was quickly given an example of the kind of behaviour that had upset so many people. The Prime Minister and his wife were invited to dine at Government House where the Prince of Wales and Prince George were staying. Arriving punctually for dinner, they passed on their way into the house the two brothers dressed in shorts and shirts going out to play a game of squash. The whole party was then kept waiting until, the game being over, the princes had had time to dress for dinner.

The irresponsible, almost hostile attitude to obligations which bored the Prince, and the immaturity exhibited by his choice of leisure pursuits, were well guarded from the British public; and his popularity with the public

was equalled by the strength of his hold on the imagination of individuals – many of them people of experience and knowledge of the world. Nothing illustrates this better than Baldwin's own account of an incident which occurred on the Prince's return from a shooting expedition in East Africa in 1928.

The Prince had been summoned home urgently because the King had been taken seriously ill, and when he arrived at Folkestone he was met by Baldwin who travelled to London with him.

When we had to call him from Africa at the time of the old King's first serious illness, I had gone down ... to meet him with the delicate task of explaining to him exactly how the land lay. We had dined together as we travelled up by train to London and during the meal we had talked more or less indifferently of this

In 1927 the Prince of Wales, accompanied by his brother Prince George (left) and Mr and Mrs Baldwin, travelled to Canada. Baldwin, later to be so deeply involved in the Abdication crisis, had a genuine affection for Edward.

and that. At last he said to me:

'You know, Prime Minister, I should like you to remember that you can always speak of anything to me.'

I seized on this and I answered: 'Sir, I shall remind you of that!'

And as I said it a most curious impression came over me, a feeling of certainty that one day I almost certainly *should* have to 'say something to him' – and that it would be about a woman. And then, as suddenly as it had come, it was gone....

When he arrived at ... Buckingham Palace he was told that he might not on any account go *near* his father, who was, we all thought, near death, for at least 48 hours. He simply took no notice, damned everybody and marched in. The old King, who had for nearly a week been practically unconscious, just opened half an eye, looked up at him and said: 'Damn you, what the devil are you doing here?' And from that moment he turned the corner and began rapidly to get better. It was exactly like the scene in *Henry IV* when Prince Henry tries on the crown....

It will not be found possible to reconcile Baldwin's version of the Prince's arrival at Buckingham Palace with that given by the Duke of Windsor himself. Yet even if Mr Baldwin is in error, as people speaking from memory so often are, the passage shows how romantic was the feeling he still had for the Prince a year after the Abdication.

(Opposite) When strong pressure led Edward to give up his beloved steeplechasing, he turned to the safer sport of golf. Here he drives off at the opening of Richmond Golf Course, Surrey.

An aerial shot of Fort Belvedere.

King George had continually criticized his son in his choice of leisure pursuits, but his illness in 1928 had a particularly significant effect on the Prince in this respect. The Prince most enjoyed two things: the life in the night clubs of London, and hunting. He found nothing as exhilarating as riding a good horse and taking a line of his own across country, and his success in point-to-point races was immensely important to him because it was his only opportunity to compete with the rest of the world in circumstances that could by no conceivable means be weighted in his favour. However, from the autumn of 1924 when he had a rather bad fall, he was under constant pressure from his family, from the press and even from politicians to give up the hazards of steeplechasing. Then, at the time of his father's illness, his mother made it a personal point that with his father so ill he should give up race riding and be content with hunting. And he told her that he would of course do as she asked.

He may well have felt that without the climax of the spring point-to-points, the few days' hunting he could fit in between public duties were not worth the trouble and expense. In any case in the winter he sold all his horses and gave up the house he had taken in Melton Mowbray. The anxiety of his parents and the continual pressure brought upon him is perhaps understandable. Nevertheless, one of its effects was to narrow his vision to the golf courses round London, and Fort Belvedere.

Fort Belvedere is a 'grace and favour' house situated on land bordering Windsor Great Park near Sunningdale. A strange, castellated house begun in the eighteenth century and twice enlarged, it had been neglected for many years when the Prince first saw it in 1930. He says that it was a 'pseudo-Gothic hodge-podge' and that the garden was untended and the surrounding woods wild and untidy. With the help of Mrs Dudley Ward, he turned the Fort into a comfortable home 'where he could rest from his labours at the week's end'. He was happy in this house and entertained there frequently at weekends. Friends like the Metcalfes stayed regularly and it was here that he brought Mrs Simpson.

7

Mrs Simpson

'"You'd think", said Aunt Bessie with some heat, "that we'd all come right out of *Tobacco Road*."'

Mrs Merryman was speaking at the time of the Abdication of King Edward VIII, and she referred to what her niece, the Duchess of Windsor, has called 'the wild *canards* being circulated that my family had come from the wrong side of the tracks in Baltimore'. And it is true that large sections of the British people were, and have remained, convinced that, in addition to the obvious disadvantages as a prospective wife for the King of England of having been twice married, Mrs Simpson had also that of being of lowly, even disreputable birth. This conviction seems to have been arrived at without much knowledge of the facts but through a kind of complacency which caused the English of that day to be easily persuaded that a twice-married American woman might also be of low birth. Yet this was particularly irritating to Mrs Simpson, as well as to Mrs Merryman, because, although in childhood and youth she had known poverty and insecurity, no one had ever before questioned her breeding. In fact she belonged to one of the first families of Baltimore.

The populations of the eastern seaboard towns of America are largely descended from the first English settlers. As a result they have often maintained a tightly cohesive society, with a well-defined class system, which considers itself to have a superior culture and higher moral principles than the rest of the nation. Moreover, families who can trace their descent for more than 200 years in one place customarily place greater weight on birth and breeding than, as in the rest of the United States, on money. This has made for a development which is essentially different from that of the populations of the cities of the north and west and the cultivation of the virtues, if also the vices, of a genuinely aristocratic society.

The future Duchess of Windsor was born on 19 June 1896, almost exactly two years after the Duchess of York gave birth to her eldest son in England. She was named Bessiewallis, in accordance with the Baltimore habit of giving children two names and running them together – Wallis after her father and Bessie after her mother's sister. She disliked the name Bessie, however, which she associated with cows, and as she grew up this was dropped in favour of the more simple Wallis. When her father, Teackle Wallis Warfield, died a few months after she was born, she and her mother were left dependent on their relations.

Bessiewallis Warfield was surrounded by solidly wealthy relations. Uncle

Mrs Simpson was born Bessiewallis Warfield, in June 1896. Her mother, Mrs Alys Montague Warfield (seen here holding her daughter), brought up young Wallis in circumstances of genteel poverty.

Solomon, Uncle Henry and Uncle Emory Warfield all had farms in the country where the little girl was sent for the long summer holidays, and the two latter had sons and daughters who grew up in houses with spacious verandahs, rambling rooms, and Negro servants, with horses in the stables behind and cattle that grazed the land. On the other side, her mother's family, the Montagues, had a country house in Virginia.

It was Uncle Sol who took it upon himself to see that his niece was educated as befitted a Warfield child, sending her, if not to the best, to the second best school in Baltimore. Thus, among her own relations and also among the girls she met at school, she alone knew the pinch of poverty and deprivation. For although Uncle Sol placed a sum of money each month in Mrs Warfield's bank account, every month the amount was different, sometimes barely covering the rent. Their fortunes improved considerably, however, after her mother's second marriage, for Wallis's stepfather, John Freeman Rasin, was a member of a rich and politically prominent Baltimore family.

Among the few memories her schoolfellows have of her is that, apart from working hard and doing well in examinations, she was always very well and neatly dressed. Her mother sewed everything herself or gave the patterns to a dressmaker, but both mother and daughter had such a natural sense of clothes, both how to fit and how to wear them, that Wallis did not suffer on this account. She is remembered as being reserved in her dealings with other people, although, if this concealed ambition and a certain ruthlessness, it held no malice. Wallis was a 'good fellow' and out for a good time, attractive to the other sex and, according to most accounts, 'rather fast'.

At the age of sixteen she was sent to a boarding school named Oldfields, which seems to have been the equivalent of what in England was known as a 'finishing school'. Speaking of her time there in her autobiography, the Duchess of Windsor has told us that the thought of going to college never occurred to her. 'It just didn't exist for girls of my age.' And in reply to her own question, 'What, then, was life supposed to hold for us?', she answers, 'Marriage'. When she left, she made her début in Baltimore society, and at her first ball she found herself in an element where she would be happy and successful for the rest of her life.

In 1916 she married Earl Winfield Spencer Jr, an officer in the air arm of the United States Navy – a not very ambitious choice. There seems to have been no very far-reaching strategy in her mind when she made her first marriage and to do it she broke her own candidly declared intention to marry money. Earl Winfield Spencer – 'Win' to his wife – had neither very much money nor any great career in front of him. But Wallis found him physically attractive, she had been brought up to get married, and she wanted to get away from Baltimore.

Her first husband soon turned out to be a neurotic alcoholic and obsessively jealous. 'I am naturally gay and flirtatious,' the Duchess writes in her autobiography, 'and I was brought up to believe that one should be as entertaining as one can at a party. ... My gaiety, and even more the response of others to it, made Win jealous.' Win had a propensity for practical jokes and this now took a sadistic turn. He used to lock his wife up in a room for hours on end, and one afternoon he locked his wife into the bathroom and left her there into the night. Next morning Wallis went to see her mother and told her that she felt the only honest course left to her was divorce.

It is a matter of astonishment to the English reader at this point to be told by someone who two divorces later aspired to marry the King of England that on both sides of her family the consternation was extreme. The

English when discussing the Abdication invariably put down the King's and Mrs Simpson's fatal preference for marriage, over the time-honoured arrangement usual in such cases, very largely to the fact that she was an American. Americans, they argue, have to get married and do not mind divorce; the English, on the other hand, are not always marrying but they do mind about divorce. In this the English show a total ignorance of the difference between Hollywood and Baltimore. Wallis's mother and her Aunt Bessie Merryman both believed that marriage was indissoluble – or if not indissoluble, indissoluble by a Montague. Aunt Bessie said that Wallis must go away for a while, or, as a last resort, agree to a temporary separation, but on no account get a divorce. 'The Montague women', was her unanswerable dictum, 'do not get divorced.' Uncle Sol's reaction was predictably stronger. 'I won't let you bring this disgrace upon us!' he said. 'The Warfields in all their known connections since 1662 have never had a divorce. What will the people of Baltimore think?'

At the time of her decision to leave Spencer, he had a staff appointment at Washington and, when he was ordered to the Far East, she merely remained behind – a lone young woman in an apartment in Washington. In her autobiography she tells us that the 1920s were a particularly hazardous era for a lonely woman, 'especially on sofas and in rumble seats'. 'I had ... a code,' she says, 'which was never to allow myself to drift into light affairs of the moment. But one must pay the price – many evenings alone.' Having delivered herself of these excellent sentiments she goes on to give a description of her experiences of Washington society which seems to leave very little time for evenings alone. The surplus of attractive, cultured, unattached men made the diplomatic service a paradise for women on their own. In this sophisticated circle brilliant conversation was carried on at luncheon and dinner parties, at Sunday night suppers, impromptu excursions to little country restaurants and picnics in the Virginia countryside.

At this time in her life Wallis Spencer fell deeply but rather unsatisfactorily in love. She writes: 'I was conscious of drifting dangerously, and yet I was reluctant to free myself from so beguiling a current. I knew that I could not continue to have it both ways. I must go through with my divorce or return to Win.'

In the event she did neither. Her young diplomat married someone else and she cajoled five hundred dollars out of Uncle Sol and sailed for Paris with a Montague cousin. In Paris the diplomatic service once more provided escorts for the two young women and soon, the Duchess explains, 'our evenings were taken up with exploring the city while our weekends were solidly booked for trips through the French countryside'.

Something nevertheless seems to have been missing. All this time Win had been writing to his wife pleading with her to forget the past and return to him. When an American woman friend invited her to accompany her home on the *France*, Wallis agreed with an eagerness that surprised herself, and in July 1924 she travelled to China to join her husband.

When, as was inevitable, she left him for a second time, she went to Shanghai to try to get her divorce from the US Court for China. Soon after her arrival she encountered a young Englishman from the embassy. 'We had a drink together, very pleasant. Then he suggested dinner, and it proved to be even more pleasant. This was the simple beginning of a delightful friendship. Robbie knew everyone in Shanghai....' She was once more drawn into the world of garden parties, race meetings, dancing by moonlight and so on...

When eventually Wallis arrived back in Washington a friend advised her that at a cost of about three hundred dollars and after one year's residence she could obtain a divorce in Virginia on the grounds of desertion after three years' separation from her husband. Wallis therefore took up residence in a small hotel in a little town called Warrenton. Before long she ran into an old Baltimore acquaintance who worked in the local bank, and who, as the Duchess records, 'took me in tow and launched me in the social whirl of the local horsey set'.

At this time there also occurred a more important meeting. Wallis used to go to New York occasionally to shop for clothes and on these occasions she stayed with a friend from her Oldfield days, Mary Kirk, now married to Jacques Raffray. With the Raffrays she met Mr and Mrs Ernest Simpson. Simpson's first marriage was already in difficulties and he and Wallis were immediately attracted to each other.

In December 1927 Wallis Spencer's petition for divorce from Winfield Spencer was granted and in July 1928, having spent some of the intervening time with friends in the South of France in order to consider her future, she married Ernest Simpson.

Ernest Simpson, Wallis's second husband, photographed after his secret wedding in 1937 to the former Mrs Jacques Raffray, Mary Kirk, at whose house Wallis had met Simpson in the early 1920s.

Simpson was the son of an English father and an American mother. He was born in New York and went to Harvard. While still an undergraduate he crossed to England, joined the Grenadier Guards as a second lieutenant and later became a British subject. He and Wallis were comfortably off and they seem to have been happy together. The Duchess of Windsor describes

Ernest Simpson as a man with quiet, rather scholarly tastes who loved reading, the theatre, opera and ballet. They shared an interest in antique furniture and, when they moved to a flat in Bryanston Court in London, Mrs Simpson was able for the first time to indulge the taste for fine things which was to be a source of happiness to her for the rest of her life.

When Mrs Simpson first arrived in London she knew almost nobody, but Ernest Simpson's sister (Mrs Kerr-Smiley, at whose house in Belgrave Square the Prince of Wales first met Mrs Dudley Ward) took her under her wing. One gets the impression, nowhere stated, that Mrs Simpson found neither her sister-in-law nor her sister-in-law's friends entirely sympathetic and soon she began to make friends of her own, among them American expatriates and Americans from the embassy. These included Benjamin Thaw and his wife, the former Consuelo Morgan, the sister of Thelma, Lady Furness. Some time in the autumn of 1930 Lady Furness introduced her to the Prince of Wales.

There are several accounts of this meeting and the memories of the protagonists vary a little. Lady Furness gives the following account:

I went over to Wallis, took her to the Prince, and introduced her. This meeting has been the subject of an enormous amount of fiction. It has been written, for example, that the Prince, on being introduced to Wallis, asked her if, in England, she did not miss the comforts of central heating, and that she had answered, 'I'm sorry, sir, but you have disappointed me. Every American woman who comes to your country is always asked the same question. I had hoped for something more original from the Prince of Wales.'

Had this been true, it would have been not only bad taste but bad manners. At that moment Wallis Simpson was as nervous and as impressed as any woman would have been on first meeting the Prince of Wales. Another apocryphal story is that when the Prince first met Wallis an electric tension was set up between them, and he then and there decided he could not live without her. This is utter nonsense. Wallis and I became great friends; actually I came to regard her as one of my best friends in England, and the Prince and I often would include Wallis and her husband in our parties. The Prince, consequently, saw her at least once a week for the next three and a half years. It was only after this that he discovered she was more important to him than the throne.

According to the Duchess of Windsor's account, it was six months before she saw the Prince again and then six months more. It is sometimes said that when he first met her he did not like her very much, although there does not seem to be much evidence for this. He was invariably pleasant to her, and out of the blue in January 1932 he sent her an invitation to Fort Belvedere.

This was the first of many visits to the Fort. At first Lady Furness, with whom the Prince had a brief and not very serious love affair, was always present and acting as hostess, and Prince George was often a fellow guest. In June 1933 the Prince gave a party at Quaglino's for Mrs Simpson's birthday and in July he dined for the first time with the Simpsons at their flat.

Lady Furness went to America from January to March 1934 and she asked Mrs Simpson to look after the Prince of Wales while she was away. In America she behaved sufficiently indiscreetly for the attentions paid her by Prince Aly Khan to reach the Prince's ears. He had begun to dine informally with the Simpsons, often choosing, apparently by chance, the very evenings on which Ernest Simpson had brought papers home to work on. When this had happened several times, Simpson adopted the habit of leaving his wife

alone to entertain their royal visitor. Finally the Prince asked the Simpsons whether they would like to bring some of their friends with them to the Fort.

When Lady Furness returned from America, she found the Prince formally cordial but personally distant in his manner to her. Unable to understand what had come between them, she visited her friend Wallis Simpson to ask her advice. The Duchess has given an account of the meeting:

It was an unhappy call. She told me that the Prince was obviously avoiding her – she couldn't understand why. He would not speak to her himself on the telephone. No more invitations to the Fort were forthcoming. Finally she asked me point-blank if the Prince was interested in me – 'keen' was the word she used.

This was a question I had expected, and I was glad to be able to give her a straight answer. 'Thelma,' I said, 'I think he likes me. He may be fond of me. But, if you mean by keen that he is in love with me, the answer is definitely no.'

In May Mrs Dudley Ward's elder daughter was taken seriously ill and for weeks her mother thought of little else and spent most of her time at the nursing home. Only when her daughter was out of danger and on the way to recovery did she begin to consider the fact that, for the first time in nearly seventeen years, although the Prince of Wales was in England, a period of weeks had gone by without his visiting her house or telephoning her. She put a call through to St James's Palace. For years she had spoken to the girl on the switchboard nearly every day. Now when the telephonist heard her voice she immediately replied in tones of the greatest distress. 'I have something so terrible to tell you', she said, 'that I don't know how to say it.' And when pressed to continue she said sorrowfully: 'I have orders not to put you through.'

(Opposite) Edward takes his dog for a walk in the grounds of Fort Belvedere (he owned a succession of Cairn terriers, 'Pookie' being the most famous).

A visit to Balmoral – (left to right) Edward, in Scottish costume, Louis Mountbatten, Mrs Herman Rogers, Mrs Colin Buist, Wallis and Edwina Mountbatten.

(*Opposite*) *Edward and Mrs*
Simpson at Ascot, 1935.

Within a matter of weeks the gist of these matters was widely known. When a new favourite arises it causes great excitement because people not previously in the inner circle recognize an opportunity, and speculation and gossip about Mrs Simpson had begun before this, soon after Lady Furness went to America.

We have several descriptions of Mrs Simpson at or about this time. One of these was written by her defeated rival Lady Furness:

She did not have the chic she has since cultivated. She was not beautiful; in fact she was not even pretty. But she had a distinct charm and a sharp sense of humour. Her dark hair was parted in the middle. Her eyes, alert and eloquent, were her best feature. She was not as thin as in her later years – not that she could be called fat even then; she was merely less angular. Her hands were large; they did not move gracefully, and I thought she used them too much when she attempted to emphasize a point.

Chips Channon describes her as 'a jolly, plain, intelligent, quiet, unpretentious and unprepossessing little woman', but he adds: 'She has already the air of a personage who walks into a room as though she almost expected to be curtsied to. At least she wouldn't be too surprised. She has complete power over the Prince of Wales, who is trying to launch her socially.' Before long he is telling us that she is 'a woman of charm, sense, balance and great wit, with dignity and taste'. It does not seem to have been quickly perceived that Mrs Simpson had a strong and also a magnetic personality, although this is positively asserted by people who know the Duchess of Windsor. Possibly she was not aware of her own potentiality at this time, but the ability to adjust personality to changing circumstances is a not uncommon female characteristic. It seems unlikely that the attractions she so quickly acquired were entirely in the eye of the beholder.

Harold Nicolson, who accompanied Mrs Simpson to the theatre, describes her as 'bejewelled, eyebrow-plucked, virtuous and wise'. He then goes on: 'I was impressed by the fact that she forbade the Prince to smoke during the *entr'acte* in the theatre itself. She is clearly out to help him.' Yet, to those not bewitched by the immediate presence of royalty, it is exactly these proprietary attentions which seem so inappropriate. One has only to visualize Mrs Keppel ordering King Edward about with the confidence which only intimacy can give, to realize how little Mrs Simpson was equipped to be Queen of England or even for the role of the king's mistress.

Within a matter of weeks more gossip and scandal had been created than in the whole of his previous forty years. Until now, although he had followed his inclinations in his private life and at times had stretched the resources of his Household in covering lapses due to his idiosyncrasies and unpunctuality, while he had obstinately refused to follow the conventions suggested to him by his father, there is no doubt that the Prince had added more to the brilliance of the Crown, to the magic of the monarchy, than he had taken away. From now on he was to behave with a senseless recklessness in minor matters, an imperviousness to other people's opinions and feelings, which, carelessly and publicly proclaimed, could not for long have been covered by his Household and must in the end have undermined even his extraordinary popularity.

Almost immediately they had London society by the ears. Initially this was because, if we are to believe Chips Channon, there was a rift between the Prince's old friends who had been given such short shrift, and all those struggling to get on the band wagon, but chiefly it was owing to the childish ostentation with which the Prince and Mrs Simpson conducted themselves.

Mrs Simpson's appearances in society were designed to invite gossip about the unprecedented splendour of her jewels. Diana Cooper described her as 'glittering', and said she 'dripped in new jewels and clothes', and Chips Channon speaks of her variously as 'dripping with emeralds', 'literally smothered in rubies', and 'wearing new jewels – the King must give her new ones every day'. Probably the most amusing account of her appearance – at a weekend dinner party in the country – is given by Marie Belloc Lowndes:

> She wore a very great deal of jewellery, which I thought must be what is called 'dressmaker's' jewels, so large were the emeralds in her bracelets and so striking and peculiar a necklace. ... Several of my fellow-guests asked me what I thought of her. I said what had struck me most were her perfect clothes and that I had been surprised, considering that she dressed so simply, to see that she wore such a mass of dressmakers' jewels. At that they all screamed with laughter, explaining that all the jewels were real, that the then Prince of Wales had given her fifty thousand pounds' worth at Christmas, following it up with sixty thousand pounds' worth of jewels a week later at the New Year.

Marie Belloc Lowndes nevertheless put firmly on record that she liked Mrs Simpson.

By the summer of 1934 Mr and Mrs Simpson had become an almost permanent part of the Prince of Wales' private life. They were constantly at the Fort, where by now, rather to the chagrin of the servants, Mrs Simpson had begun to take an interest in the arrangement of the furniture, the running of the household and the menus. When they were in London the Prince's chauffeur, Ladbroke, often waited for hours outside her flat. In August the Prince took a house in Biarritz and invited the Simpsons to accompany him and a party of other guests. Ernest Simpson had already arranged to go to the USA on business, and Aunt Bessie Merryman took his place and acted as chaperone. Soon the Prince and Mrs Simpson formed the habit of leaving the others once a week and dining alone in one of the little bistros in Biarritz; and, when presently the whole party took a short trip on Lord Moyne's yacht *Rosaura*, the Duchess tells us that, sitting alone together on deck in the evenings, she and the Prince crossed the boundary between friendship and love. When they reached Cannes, although the party had been meant to disband there, the Prince, unable to bring his happiness to an end, decided to continue to Genoa and from there to travel by train to Lake Como. In the ecstasy he felt, he showed a reckless disregard of the conventions which should have bound his behaviour and an insensate determination to break the barriers which stood between him and this woman who had succeeded in appeasing his everlasting need for fulfilment, not as a Prince, but as a human being. On the *Rosaura*, as later on the *Nahlin*, he showed that he lacked the maturity to accept easily the role of a lover and combine it with that of a man of affairs – his childish exhibitionism taking the form, as often as not, of stripping off his clothes; the clothes which, ever since his pockets had been sewn up to prevent him putting his hands in them, had been a bone of contention between himself and his father. Thus he appeared in shorts and sandals, not merely on the yacht and on the beaches, but when visiting the Borromeo Palace, where, instantly recognized though posing as a tourist, he was welcomed by Prince Borromeo in a morning coat and striped trousers.

The Duchess's reflections on this trip show her at her most honest and attractive, but they also underline the fact that in spite of his genuine simplicity and real dislike of ostentation, the Prince took it absolutely for granted that, while indulging in his every like and dislike, he might nevertheless continue to wield all the appurtenances of power – a belief that in the long run would cause him an infinity of pain. She could not, she tells us, find any reason why this most glamorous of men should have been so much attracted to her. She was not a beauty and she was no longer young. 'In my own country I would have been considered securely on the shelf.' On the other hand, and it is this paragraph that is so revealing, she found no difficulty in explaining why the Prince should be so overwhelmingly appealing to her:

Over and beyond the charm of his personality and the warmth of his manner, he was the open sesame to a new and glittering world that excited me as nothing in my life had ever done before. For all his natural simplicity, his genine abhorrence of ostentation, there was nevertheless about him – even in his most Robinson Crusoe clothes – an unmistakable aura of power and authority. His slightest wish seemed always to be translated instantly into the most impressive kind of reality. Trains were held; yachts materialized; the best suites in the finest hotels were flung open; aeroplanes stood waiting. What impressed me most of all was how all this could be brought to pass with no apparent effort: the calm assumption that this was the natural order of things, that nothing could ever possibly go awry.... It seemed unbelievable that I, Wallis Warfield of Baltimore, Maryland, could be part of this enchanted world. It seemed so incredible that it produced in me a happy and unheeding acceptance.

Those who cannot understand and sympathize with this passage should not judge the Duchess. Yet judged she must be, because the extent of her hold upon the Prince of Wales and the completeness of his subjection to her were soon to be remarked by every perceptive observer. After the Abdication Walter Monckton wrote:

No one will ever really understand the story of the King's life during the crisis who does not appreciate two factors: the first, which is superficially acknowledged

On holiday on the Rosaura in 1934. It was in the evenings on deck that, in Wallis's own words, she and Edward 'crossed the line that marks the indefinable boundary between friendship and love'.

by many of those who were closely concerned in the events of these days, was
the intensity and depth of the King's devotion to Mrs Simpson. To him she was
the perfect woman.

Because of Edward's obsessed absorption in his love for Mrs Simpson
and more especially because of the Abdication, it has become widely believed
that the bond between them was a purely physical one and that she was
the only woman to satisfy this side of his nature. It is clearly not very easy
to find evidence for or against this theory, but people who hold it must reconcile it with the fact that it comes as a surprise to those who travelled with
him on his tours as Prince of Wales and had so often to deal with situations
created by a healthy interest in the other sex. Indeed it might be true to
say that during the whole of his youth the Prince was criticized for over-
indulgence in the sexual act, while ever since he has been believed incapable
of it until he met his wife.

For some people the purely sexual explanation of a relationship which
inspired an act unique in history and also the slavish devotion of a lifetime
is in any case too simple. It is interesting, therefore, that, following the passage just quoted, Walter Monckton recorded the view that it was a great
mistake to assume that the Prince was merely in love in the physical
sense. 'There was an intellectual companionship, and there is no doubt
that his lonely nature found in her a spiritual comradeship.'

Some time during the Abdication crisis one of Mr Baldwin's entourage
amused himself by sending a specimen of Mrs Simpson's handwriting to
a graphologist, and it is not necessary to have any considerable belief in
graphology to be struck by this particular example of its analysis. 'A woman
with a strong male inclination in the sense of activity, vitality, initiative.
She *must* dominate, she *must* have authority, and without sufficient scope
for her powers can be disagreeable ... primarily all she does comes from
her wish to be important.' All his life the Prince of Wales had sought a
'woman with a strong male inclination' and one of the most enduring links
between these two was that, in the context of their relationship although
apparently in no other, he was made for domination, while she was made
to dominate. He and Wallis Simpson were quite unusually suited to each
other; they were two parts of a whole and it was her misfortune as well
as his that, when two complementary natures join, it is not merely the best
in each that finds completion. The time might come in the crisis that was
to follow – although even here the evidence is not strong – when she would
temporarily lose her power to influence his behaviour, like someone who,
having whipped up a sensitive horse, momentarily loses control of it; but
she must bear a large responsibility for everything that follows, because his
greatest happiness in life was by now to obey her slightest wish.

Yet there seems little doubt that he misled her. For different reasons, her
euphoria was as great as his, and nothing in her character, background or
experience enabled her to see beyond hotel suites and yachts to the realities
of power, or to recognize that the choice was not between being Queen of
England or the King's mistress, but between mistress of the King and exile.
Even if it is an intellectual absurdity to attribute to the whole American
nation an inability to understand that divorce constitutes a total prohibition
on becoming Queen of England, all the evidence suggests that Mrs Simpson
did not understand it. She did not understand it in her bones, as every
English woman would have done, and this, more than anything else, may
have accounted for his obsession. So many people were deceived about his
true nature, because in all his life he had seriously loved only married

women. Yet he was exceptionally domestic and was later to show that for true satisfaction he needed not merely the durability and dependability of marriage but also the delight of shared household goods and household chores which only the long habit of married life affords. When he asked Mrs Simpson to marry him, he almost certainly made her believe that what he offered was in his power to give. Whether he believed it himself no one will ever know. For almost as long as he could remember he had defied tradition and the views of the King's Household, and, in the phrase which he is said to have favoured himself, 'had got away with it', and he certainly saw himself as standing for the principles of the young against the old and well established. At this period of his life, it is possible that in a dangerously superficial way – which was to leave him at a loss when he came up against reality – he believed that he could get away with even this.

It is not intended to suggest that there and then on the yacht *Rosaura* thoughts of becoming Queen occurred to Mrs Simpson, but the narrative which follows will be more readily understood if one believes that ideas of the sort began gradually to have a stronger and stronger hold on her, while at the same time she continued to abandon her will to what she called a 'happy and unheeding acceptance' of the strange fate that was hers.

In the autumn of that year, at a reception given at Buckingham Palace a day or two before the wedding of the Duke of Kent, she was presented to the King and Queen for the first and last time. This wedding marked the end of the particularly close relationship between the Prince of Wales and his younger brother which, outside those with women, must be regarded as the only important relationship of the elder man's life. After this only one member of the Prince's family remained a fairly constant visitor at the Fort – Lord Louis Mountbatten.

In February of the following year – 1935 – the Prince asked Mr and Mrs Simpson to accompany him to Kitzbühel for the winter sports, and again Mr Simpson refused on the grounds of business in New York. Once more,

Kitzbühel, February 1935. It was after this holiday that Wallis Simpson first experienced the 'dark loom of doubts and questions unexpressed' that marked the end of her relationship with her husband.

at the end of the prearranged fortnight's skiing, the Prince could not bear
to return home; he and his party were transported to Vienna and, after a
brief interlude there, continued to Budapest. It is not surprising that when
Mrs Simpson returned to her flat in Bryanston Court she found that her
relationship with her husband had undergone a change. Here again we owe
to her own revelations our knowledge of what passed in her mind:

I was troubled, but my concern was no more than a tiny cloud in the growing
radiance that the Prince's favour cast over my life. I became aware of a rising
curiosity concerning me, of new doors opening, and a heightened interest even
in my casual remarks. I was stimulated; I was excited; I felt as if I were borne
upon a rising wave that seemed to be carrying me ever more rapidly and even
higher. Now I began to savour the true brilliance and sophistication of the life
of London.

One might expect that she would follow this by telling us something of what
passed in her mind about the work and the unique public position of the
man who opened the doors of all these hotel suites and society houses, but
curiously enough there is not one word on these matters. From what she
tells us, and we must accept that it may be all she chooses to tell us, her
life with the Prince of Wales was merely one long, glorious, extended holiday.

In the summer of 1935 the Prince of Wales and Mrs Simpson repeated their
holiday of the previous year – cruising in the Mediterranean and later revisit-
ing Vienna and Budapest. It was October before they were back in London.

In his autobiography the Duke of Windsor tells us that he was by now
conscious of the overwhelming love and surpassing need he had for Mrs
Simpson, and he tells us that his dream of being able to bring her permanently into his life was, although quite vague, extremely vivid. He dis-
cusses the attitude that in court circles is likely to be taken on the question
of the divorce, and tells us that he wished to discuss the whole thing with
his father. Then he says quite openly that he did not discount the possibility
that he might have to give up the Crown and took comfort in the fact that
his brother, Bertie, was temperamentally so much more like his father. He
says that he did not talk to his father because a concatenation of events prevented him doing so, and he lists such objections as the Silver Jubilee
celebrations, the holiday season, the Duke of Gloucester's wedding, a
general election and the death of his father's sister Princess Victoria. At
Christmas at Sandringham the King seemed too old and too ill to be worried.
Only the last two of these objections seem entirely valid. All the rest are
in the category of the kind of event which might be expected to occur at
any time. It is very hard to believe that the Prince could ever have found
the courage to face the father whom he had been so conditioned to fear with
the news that he intended to marry a married woman, already once-divorced,
and that in order to do this he would if necessary renounce the throne.

What is more curious is that King George did not speak to him. News
of the Prince's latest love had quickly reached the Palace and the anxiety
that it caused the King spoiled the last year of his life – some believe hastened
his death. We know that he discussed this matter with the Archbishop of
Canterbury, Cosmo Lang, to whom he said that he was much concerned
about the Prince of Wales' 'latest friendship'. The Archbishop said that the
Prince had had previous friendships, like most young men, and especially
those who had grown up during the war. But the King replied that he
believed this affair was more serious than any of the others. We know too

that he appealed to the Duke of Connaught to intervene and that he asked
the advice of the Prime Minister, Stanley Baldwin, to whom he made the
dramatic statement: 'After I am dead the boy will ruin himself in twelve
months.' And finally we have been told that only a few weeks before his
death he exclaimed passionately: 'I pray to God that my eldest son will never
marry and have children and that nothing will come between Bertie and
Lilibet and the throne.' In the aftermath of the Abdication, criticisms were
levelled at certain people – Stanley Baldwin and Lord Hardinge of Penshurst
in particular – because they had not spoken sooner to the King (Edward VIII)
on the matter of Mrs Simpson. Very little attention has been paid to the
fact that neither his father nor his mother ever spoke to him at all. George V
had never ceased to hector his son about such things as his clothes and
his deportment, but on this matter, which he was well aware sapped the
life of the monarchy itself, he could not bring himself to intervene. This
is surely a commentary not merely on the relationships within this family
but on any tendency to criticize others in contact with Edward who intervened, if at all, very late. The truth is that the Prince of Wales, whose
obstinacy in any case 'constituted power of a kind', was in this matter so
early armed by certainty of purpose as to check advice or warning on the
lips of those who tried to utter them. When he chose, he was a formidable
personality.

On Thursday 16 January 1926 the Prince of Wales was shooting in
Windsor Great Park when a letter was brought to him from his mother asking him to propose himself for the weekend at Sandringham because,
although there seemed to be no immediate danger, the King's doctors were
not too pleased with his health. The Prince flew to Sandringham in his own
aeroplane the next morning, and on the Sunday he motored to London to
inform the Prime Minister that the King was not expected to live more than
a few days. On the Monday night the famous bulletin was issued – 'The
King's life is moving peacefully to its close' – and George V died in the presence of his wife and children. Hardly was the King dead than Queen Mary,
taking the hand of her eldest son, kissed it. 'The King is dead, long live
the King.'

Queen Mary and George V, on their way to church in Scotland, shortly before George V's death.

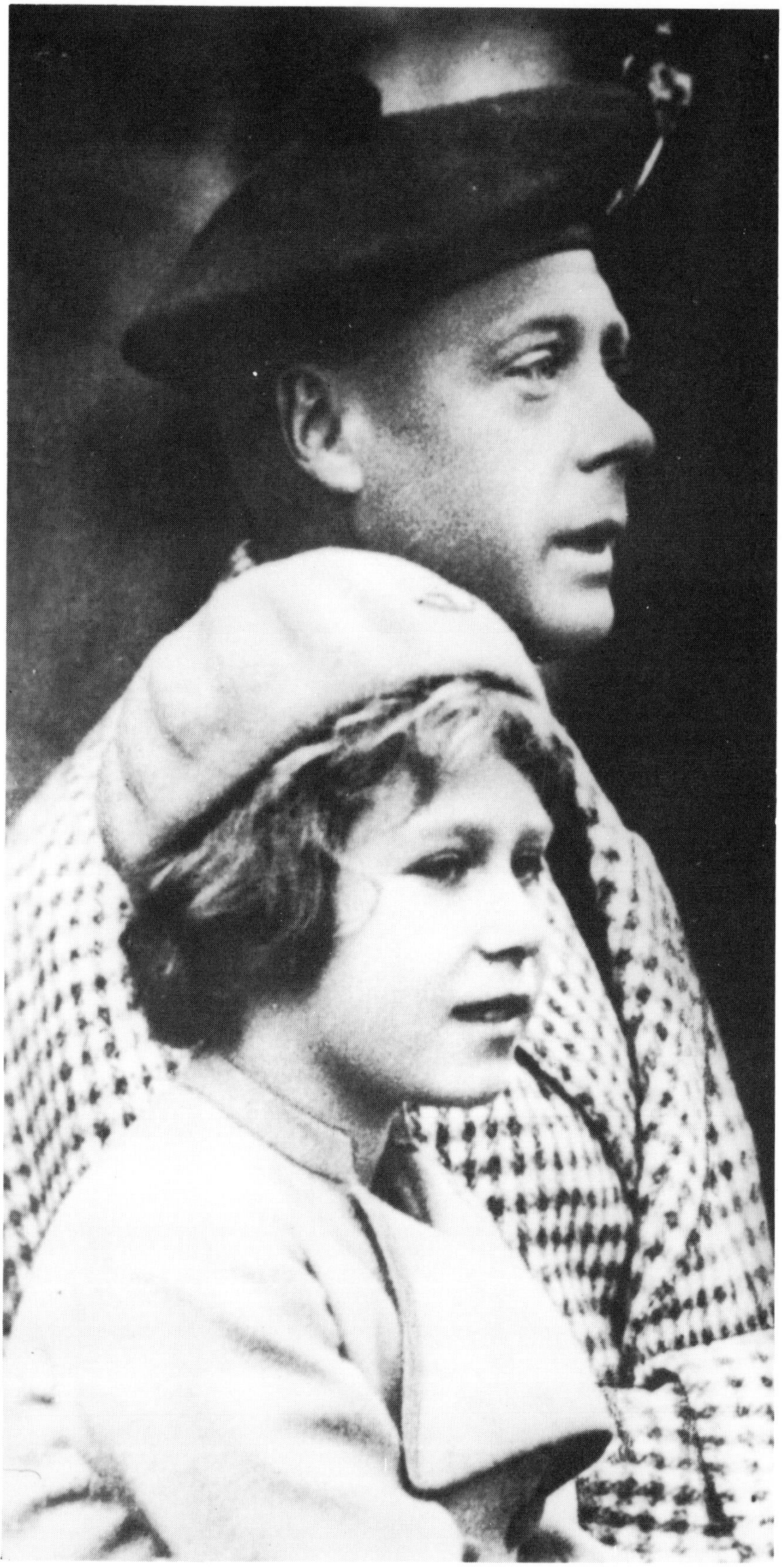

Edward and his niece, now Queen Elizabeth II.

PART II

8

King Edward

According to many accounts of Edward VIII's reign it began with an act almost as difficult to explain as the one with which it closed, and which to a small circle and on a small scale was as unpredictable and shocking. At Sandringham, where George V died, the clocks had always been kept half an hour fast ever since the days when Edward VII assembled his guests in the morning for shooting. It was done to ensure their punctuality but must also have acted as a forerunner of daylight saving. On the night the old King died, Edward VIII is said to have left his bedside and gone immediately downstairs to give orders that the clocks should be altered to normal time. More attention has been given to the lack of feeling in this extraordinary gesture than to the lack of reason. Yet there is a senselessness about this early exertion of an unquestioned power that surely needs explanation.

We owe to a member of the Prince of Wales' staff the most probable one. During the long hours while the King's death was awaited some small mistake occurred because of the discrepancy between Sandringham time and real time. 'I'll fix those bloody clocks,' the Prince cried angrily, and without further consideration gave an order which in the event was not carried out until immediately after the King's death. The effect was horribly offensive and can be explained only by the idea that the Prince was so closely imprisoned in his own personal crisis that he had no thoughts for anyone else. And it was a presage of all that was to follow that this man, who for so many years had seemed to have an unerring flair for doing and saying the right thing, should in the first minutes of his reign have disturbed and distressed everyone about him and alienated the sympathies of servants who had been with his family for years.

This strange and callous act was accompanied in private by excessive emotion. Lady Hardinge has described his grief as 'frantic and unreasonable' and says 'it far exceeded that of his mother and three brothers'. The intensity of his suffering suggests a subjective involvement different from grief or even from the guilt which might be normal to a son whose relationship with his father had steadily deteriorated. The King had made up his mind to marry Mrs Simpson but he had allowed himself to drift into a situation in which, since he resolutely refused to face facts, the pressures must have been intolerable. During the whole course of his reign this inner tension remained and his public as well as his private behaviour must be related to it.

His public appearances were cushioned by his enormous popularity which it is impossible to overstate. The strength of the monarchy which had

steadily grown from the reign of Queen Victoria had reached a climax with
the jubilee of King George v. As Prince of Wales, the new King had become
known all over the world, largely through his own efforts, the beauty of his
appearance, and his ability to please, but also with the help of modern transport and communications not previously available. His personal popularity
was something that had never been seen before, and, in the numbers of
those who loved and looked up to him, has not been seen since. Nor was
it as yet understood how suddenly and completely popularity, which had
taken years to build up, could be dissipated.

Edward VIII broadcasts to the nation on his succession to the British throne.

The King began his public duties with his accustomed flair and with
words that gave hope, even to his critics, that he might be capable of rising
to the new demands to be made of him. The first public act of the new
King was to present himself before an Accession Privy Council. More than
a hundred Councillors assembled in the Banqueting Hall of St James's, and,
after referring to the irreparable loss of his father, Edward addressed them
as follows:

> When my father stood here twenty-six years ago he declared that one of the
> objects of his life would be to uphold constitutional government. In this I am deter-
> mined to follow in my father's footsteps and to work as he did throughout his
> life for the happiness and welfare of my subjects.
>
> I place my reliance upon the loyalty and affection of my peoples throughout
> the Empire, and upon the wisdom of their Parliaments, to support me in this heavy
> task, and I pray God will guide me to perform it.

The following day the Accession was proclaimed at four different points
in London – first at St James's Palace, then at Charing Cross, Temple Bar
and the Royal Exchange. And immediately the new King made a characteristic departure from precedent. He had arranged that certain friends of his,
including Mrs Simpson, should watch the Accession ceremony from a room

in St James's Palace. The thought came to him, he was later to say, that he would like to see himself proclaimed King, a thought almost certainly made urgent by the fact that he would inevitably be parted from Wallis Simpson for the next few days and one that he immediately obeyed. As he stood talking to her by the window, a photographer caught them, so that the next day she appeared in the newspapers, a strange and nameless woman for the first time by his side. And, as he escorted her down at the end of the ceremony and she thanked him for arranging for her to see it and said she realized how different his life would now be, he told her that nothing could ever change his feeling for her.

After this he returned to Sandringham where his father's body rested in the little church, watched over by gamekeepers and other servants, who paid their last tribute to him. Next morning the coffin was taken to London. On foot, the King and his brothers followed the gun-carriage bearing the coffin through the streets of the city of Westminster. Here is a description given by Tom Jones in his *Diary with Letters*:

From the window of my second-hand bookseller, I saw the mournful little procession pass on its way from King's Cross to Westminster Hall – perhaps 40 men in all counting mounted and on foot. The King plodded heavily along weighed down by a thick long overcoat, looking utterly done. The only patch of colour was the Royal Standard on the coffin. The absence of the military and of music, the walking of the King and the Dukes, the fewness of those taking part, the intense quiet of a thronged street, made the sight a most moving one. I suppose it could happen in this simple way nowhere but in London.

The new reign had an inauspicious beginning when, during George V's funeral procession, the Maltese cross on top of the Crown, which was balanced on the coffin, fell off into the gutter.

The royal crown had been taken from its glass case in the Tower and secured to the lid of the coffin over the folds of the royal standard. The jolting of the heavy gun-carriage must have caused the Maltese cross on the top of the crown – set with a square sapphire, eight medium-sized diamonds and 192 smaller diamonds – to work loose. At the very moment when the

small procession turned into the gates of Palace Yard the cross rolled off and fell on the road. Two members of parliament – Walter Elliot and Robert Boothby – stood on the pavement watching the procession. As a company sergeant-major, bringing up the rear of the two files of Grenadier guardsmen flanking the carriage, bent down and in a swift movement picked up the cross and dropped it into his pocket, they heard the King's voice say: 'Christ! What will happen next?' 'A fitting motto', Walter Elliot remarked to his companion, 'for the coming reign.'

Edward and his three brothers, Prince George (far left), Prince Albert and Prince Henry, follow their father's cortège. According to one observer, the grief Edward showed on his father's death far exceeded that of his mother and three brothers.

There was no lack of people willing to see this incident as an omen. At the Accession Council, Baldwin had expressed his anxiety to Attlee, and his doubts as to whether the new King would 'stay the course'. But probably J.H. Thomas lamenting to Harold Nicolson about the death of the old King put with the greatest precision the sense of uneasiness felt by so many people. 'And now,' he said, '' 'ere we 'ave this obstinate little man with 'is Mrs Simpson. Hit won't do, 'arold. I tell you that straight.'

However, the King began by giving proof of his talent for public gestures. As long as his father's coffin lay in Westminster Hall, officers of the Household Troops, together with the Gentlemen-at-Arms and the Yeoman of the Guard, maintained a continuous vigil, while members of the public in enormous numbers filed by to pay their last respects. At midnight on the evening before the King's body was taken on its last journey to Windsor, people still moved past the coffin in spite of the lateness of the hour. A few minutes later four figures in full-dress uniform descended the staircase and took their places around the catafalque between the officers on vigil and, bent over their swords, stood there motionless for twenty minutes – the new King and his three brothers. It was a fine romantic action which caught the imagination of the public and gave great pleasure to Queen Mary.

In the early part of his reign the King did not wish to disturb Queen Mary, who, before moving to Marlborough House, had to pack or dispose of the accumulation of a lifetime. The offices of his secretariat therefore remained at Buckingham Palace but he continued to occupy York House and to spend much of his time at Fort Belvedere.

In retrospect it is apparent that only the small, enclosed world of Fort Belvedere really mattered to him, and his self-engrossment was such that he felt the presence of those who were outside it no more than an actor feels the presence of his audience, who, although living, sentient creatures, are bystanders to the theme which stirs the emotions and stops the breath. His situation was unique in that nothing checked his growing exaltation or his increasing divorce from reality, because whichever way he turned he was confirmed in the validity of his fantasies. He continued at times to respond to crowd scenes which sustained him in the central role, and when this happened he had lost none of his power to bewitch. But to a dangerous extent he reacted to the outside world only with anger and impatience because it kept him from the woman on to whom he had transferred his emotional needs. Alexander Hardinge, the King's Private Secretary, was later to write:

It was scarcely realized at this early stage how overwhelming and inexorable was the influence exerted on the King by the lady of the moment. As time went on it became clearer that every decision, big or small, was subordinate to her will.... It was she who filled his thoughts at all times, she alone who mattered, before her the affairs of state sank into insignificance.

It would be some time too before it was understood that 'the lady of the moment' was not an adequate description of Mrs Simpson. The estrangement of the Prince of Wales not merely from his father but from all those who surrounded him meant that almost none of those who had to deal with him really knew him. They believed Mrs Simpson to be merely the last of a succession of passing affairs, and since they had not witnessed the extent of his dependence on Mrs Dudley Ward, nor understood the importance of his relationship with her, they were completely unaware both of his need to submerge himself in a domestic situation and of his fidelity.

Proofs of Mrs Simpson's power were soon forthcoming. In the first place the King surrounded himself only with people who were friends of hers, and cut out of his life even those who had been closest to him unless they were part of this company. Even Fruity Metcalfe, his closest man friend from whom for years he had been inseparable and who for long had been promised a place in the King's Household, was hurt and disappointed to be overlooked. Members of the Household were not expected to go to the Fort unless sent for, and those who had been accustomed to go there as guests were no longer invited. At the time of the Abdication crisis this greatly increased the King's isolation and the lack of communication between him and those who might have been expected to advise and warn him, while at the beginning of the reign it added considerably to the difficulties under which they worked.

His staff complained of his unpunctuality, inconsequence and conceit, and most of all his lack of consideration. He worked at odd hours and thought nothing of calling his secretaries from their dinner, their baths or their beds. Worst of all was a lack of method with state papers. All his life Edward had been accustomed to watch his father 'doing his boxes', and when he first came to the throne he made a great show of carrying out this part of his duty, working assiduously through the papers and initialling everything he read. His first enthusiasm was soon his undoing, however, and a shortage of initials betrayed him. This acquired a serious aspect because the red boxes

were invariably taken to Fort Belvedere, where there was no responsible
person in charge of them, and it was often days, as time went on sometimes
weeks, before they were returned. Given the negligence of the King there
could be no absolute certainty that no one besides himself had access to
them.

This was a circumstance which would in any case have given cause for
great alarm, and fears were much increased by the King's quite open German sympathies. Neither now nor at any other time was his patriotism in
doubt but, as Prince of Wales, he had been rebuked by his father for unwise
public statements, and, although the extent of his indiscretions in conversation with German diplomats was not known until the German Foreign
Office Papers were captured after the war, he made no secret of his opposition to much of the foreign policy of his government. In addition it was
feared, without (the evidence shows) good reason, that Mrs Simpson was
on friendly terms with Ribbentrop. She was constantly under surveillance
by security officers and, for the first and last time in history, Foreign Office
papers were screened before they were sent to the sovereign.

He was full of ideas and he liked change for change's sake, but there were
only a few things in which his interest was sustained. He showed a continuing
and almost pathological preoccupation with finance. At the end of any régime
which has lasted a long time many abuses will usually be found to have crept
in on the one side and a certain indulgence on the other. There was plenty
of room for reforms in the palaces and at Sandringham and Balmoral, but
in his desire for retrenchment the King betrayed a small, compulsive stingi-
ness and a lack of regard for men who had rendered long and faithful service,
which contrasted oddly with the splendour of his almost daily gifts to Mrs
Simpson, and lost him a great deal of sympathy. Thus there was understanding for the servants of Buckingham Palace, who resented having their beer
money cut down at a time when they were often employed loading cases
of champagne or furniture and plate destined for Mrs Simpson's flat.

The strangest demonstration of an obsessive concern with even quite
small sums of money took place not at one of the royal palaces but at Fort
Belvedere. One day King Edward sent for his head housemaid and asked
her what happened to the guests' soap after they had left the house. She
replied that it was taken to the servants' quarters and finished there. The
King instructed her in future to bring it to his rooms for his own use.

The lack of consideration shown to members of his Household, and the
near-hysterical impatience of the incident of the clocks at Sandringham, was
from time to time displayed to a wider audience. Because of the period of
court mourning, the four annual courts, at which women of position and
debutantes were presented to the King, had been postponed, creating a back-
log of some 600 ladies waiting for presentation. It was therefore decided
that presentations should take place at two garden parties at Buckingham
Palace in July. For some reason which is not now clear, no adequate arrangement seems to have been made in case of rain. At the first of these functions,
while the debutantes passed the King one after another, a storm broke out.
He immediately gave orders that the presentations were to be taken as made
and disappeared into Buckingham Palace. The shower soon passed over but
the King did not reappear. This incident affected very few people directly,
but it made history because, as the curtseying girls passed the King, a photographer caught the look of thunderous boredom on his face and the press
next morning revealed to the world the picture of a monarch clearly failing
in one of the most elementary of his duties. By such behaviour he gave

needless offence which must sooner or later have undermined his popularity. The childishness which is apparent in that photograph was sometimes more endearingly revealed, however, and even the most censorious of his staff were amused when the King, wishing to avoid a meeting with Lord Wigram, climbed out of one of the windows of Buckingham Palace and went off to see Mrs Simpson. Probably his most serious omission, however, was that, in spite of the exhortations of his staff, he went to church only two or three times throughout the whole summer.

Yet when he was good he was still very very good. If he felt in the mood he still performed what he called his 'field work' with the energy and enthusiasm and the happy knack for which he had become famous. An incident

Trooping the Colour: it was during this ceremony that an apparent attempt was made on Edward's life.

which increased his enormous popularity occurred when he was returning
from presenting the colours to three Guards regiments. He noticed at the
top of Constitution Hill a slight commotion in the crowd, and a moment
later a man pushed through the police line and what later turned out to
be a loaded revolver struck the pavement beside him and skidded under
his horse's hooves. The police had actually been watching the man and when
he raised his arm one of them had fallen upon him and caused the gun to
jump out of his hand. The King believed that an attempt had been made
on his life, but with the courage that was a part of his nature and one of
the most striking attributes of his family he rode on without flinching.

And in his private life, at Fort Belvedere, where fantasy merged with
reality, and in London where he was always accompanied by Mrs Simpson,
most people found him delightful. Because of his royalty his extraordinary
immaturity passed as naturalness, an endearing lack of 'side'. Chips Channon, for instance, wrote: 'Afterwards we played a game, introduced by the
King. He gave us each ten matches and we sat huddled in a circle on the
floor, and an empty bottle was sent for and the idea was to pile matches
on the top, in turn, without letting the pile collapse. It seems silly and it
was, but it was most innocent and enjoyable.'

Lady Diana Cooper was to say later that 'What would King George think
of that?' was a favourite question of the King's and also that his desire to
be free of fuss was sometimes embarrassing. 'Diana, will you have a glass
of champagne?' 'Well, Sir, I'd much rather have white wine if there is any.'
'Yes, of course,' and off he would go and fumble about for too long looking
for it himself. One of the odd things about Fort Belvedere was that it seems
to have been accepted ever since the days of Lady Furness that one of the
women of the party should act as hostess. This was a convention not often
observed in bachelor households in England except in a slightly embarrassed
and half-hearted way by whoever knew the host best, and even then only
in relation to such matters as the whereabouts of the lavatory, and her obser-
vance of it led Mrs Simpson to give a certain amount of offence. When she
apologized to members of the King's Household, or other people who had
been his friends for years, for not being present to welcome them, and then
warmly pressed them to a drink, what was intended as a courtesy was often
resented as an insolent show of power. The division between Mrs Simpson
and her friends – nowadays the King's friends – and everyone else grew
more and more complete.

9

The *Nahlin*

In the early days of the King's reign it did not occur to anyone that he intended to marry Mrs Simpson. In the first place, she was married to Mr Simpson, and this by itself made the idea so unlikely that it only gradually began to take hold of men's minds. Even Walter Monckton who, long before the Abdication crisis when he represented the King, was on terms of close friendship with him, recorded that he always underestimated the strength of the King's devotion and 'of their united will'. And he says in words which are the nearest to criticism he ever comes: 'I thought, throughout, long before as well as after there was talk of marriage, that if and when the stark choice faced them between their love and his obligations as King-Emperor, they would in the end each make the sacrifice, devastating though it would be.'

Yet there were signs which, if they had been believed, would have made the King's intentions perfectly plain. One, so odd that it was barely understood by those concerned, was that in the long discussions about the new Civil List, the King laid much emphasis on the provisions to be made for a queen, concentrating on this aspect more than any other. A second, which was also disregarded, was a strange story told by Sir Maurice Jenks, a former Lord Mayor of London, to Baldwin. He said that, some time before, Ernest Simpson had applied for admission to a Masonic Lodge over which he, Jenks, presided, his candidature being supported by the Prince of Wales. Simpson was refused entry and the Prince of Wales, who naturally demanded an explanation, was told that it was against the Masonic law for the husband of his mistress to be admitted. The Prince gave his word that this was not the situation and Simpson's candidature was accepted. Now Simpson had come to see Jenks – 'the *mari complaisant* is now the sorrowing and devoted spouse' – and told him that the King wished to marry his wife. Simpson had said that he would like to leave England but that would make divorce easier, and Jenks suggested that Baldwin should see him. Baldwin refused flatly, saying that he was the King's adviser, not the Simpsons', but he saw Lord Wigram and told him all he had heard. Walter Monckton was also told.

I did not know Mr Simpson, nor indeed have I ever spoken to him, but I confess that I was afraid (and so, I think, were my informants) of the possibility of blackmail upon an extravagant basis; and I did not believe that the King had said what was attributed to him at third hand: nor was I at liberty to pass the rumour on to him.

However, years later, after the war had begun, Monckton met an old friend of the Simpsons, Bernard Rickatson-Hatt. He told Monckton that he had been at York House with the King and Ernest Simpson. When he had risen to go, Simpson had asked him to remain, and turning to the King had made a dramatic statement. Wallis, he said, would have to choose between them; and he asked the King what he intended to do about it. Did he intend to marry her? The King then rose from his seat and said: 'Do you really think that I would be crowned without Wallis by my side?'

Rickatson-Hatt also gave Monckton the following analysis of Mrs Simpson's character which Monckton wrote down because 'he clearly has a considerable knowledge of the parties':

I asked him about her attitude towards Simpson. He said that Simpson was extremely fond of her but that she was incapable of being in love with any man. She was extremely attractive to men, amusing and kind on most occasions but capable of hardness. She often used the same technique which I think she has used with the Duke, namely making him supremely unhappy and then overwhelming him with kindness and affection in making up the difference. He remained and I think still remains extremely fond of her. Rickatson-Hatt says she is not the sort of woman who could be relied upon to stand by a man in poverty or misfortune. She likes the good things of the earth and is fundamentally selfish. He thinks her intention was to have her cake and eat it. She was flattered by the advances of the Prince of Wales and the King and enjoyed his generous gifts to her to the full. She thought that she could have them and at the same time keep her home with Simpson....

Rickatson-Hatt himself thinks that but for the King's obstinacy and jealousy the affair would have run its course without breaking up the Simpson marriage.

Whether or not the King spoke the words to Simpson attributed to him by Rickatson-Hatt, he began now with the utmost coolness to thwart conventional ideas of discretion in his relationship with Mrs Simpson, and to make it plain that she was to occupy a position never before accorded to the King's favourite. On 27 May he gave a dinner at St James's Palace to which were invited Lord and Lady Mountbatten, Lord and Lady Wigram, Mr Duff and Lady Diana Cooper, Lord and Lady Chatfield, Mr and Mrs Baldwin, Colonel and Mrs Lindbergh, Lady Cunard and Mr and Mrs Simpson, and he placed Lady Cunard and Mrs Simpson one at each end of the table. This admixture of the two worlds he was usually so anxious to keep separate seemed designed to cause comment. The following morning the King made quite sure of it by publishing the list of his guests in the Court Circular, an official and wholly unusual method of announcing his friendship with the Simpsons.

Before the first of these dinner parties, at the end of May, the King had said to Mrs Simpson: 'Sooner or later my Prime Minister must meet my future wife.' This, according to her account, was the first time he mentioned marriage to her, although later in the year he told Walter Monckton that he had intended to marry her ever since 1934. At about the same time Mrs Simpson discovered that her marriage to Ernest Simpson was dead, that he had found a new emotional centre, in short another woman. She therefore decided on divorce, a decision which she imparted to the King.

It would be wrong, the Duchess of Windsor tells us, dropping into the sententious, women's-paper style which, although so open about much of her early life, she invariably uses when speaking of the King or the Abdication, it would be wrong, he told her, for him to try to influence her in any way. 'You can only do what you think is right for you.' But he arranged for her to have legal advice. Walter Monckton says that the King and Mrs Simpson visited him several times at his chambers during the summer to discuss the divorce, and the King said that he was not going to allow her friendship with him to prevent her from obtaining release from her husband. Monckton says that by the end of June he became seriously disturbed 'not by the prospect of the King marrying Mrs Simpson if and when she got her freedom, but about the damage which would be done to the King if he continued to make his friendship with her even more conspicuous'. But the King said that 'he was not ashamed of his friendship, and he was not going to hide it or try to deceive people.'

None of these things was known at Buckingham Palace until several months later, but the King's Household had other things to worry about. Edward showed a total disregard, even a lack of comprehension, of the lines he was expected to draw between his public and official position and his private life. For the sake of economy he arranged that the Air Ministry should take over the upkeep of his aeroplane and the salaries of his pilots and mechanics. Yet he continued to use the aeroplane for the benefit of his friends and even for the importation of goods on which duty should have been paid. This almost innocent assumption of his inalienable right to do as he pleased was paralleled by the use he made of the two detectives provided by Scotland Yard for his protection, one of whom as often as not was detailed to look after Mrs Simpson. His staff were nervous that a question might be asked on these matters in the House of Commons, which they were afraid would produce an awkward situation, but nevertheless they still believed that they were dealing with different manifestations of the new King's irresponsibility and lack of understanding of his constitutional position, and did not understand that these were deliberately flown signals of his intention to raise Mrs Simpson to a position where the attention he bestowed on her would become appropriate. No one could control the King, indeed no one seems to have been able to speak to him, and the only hope therefore lay in the idea, which seems to have occurred to almost everyone concerned with the events of this time, that sooner or later he would tire of 'the lady of the moment' as he had of others; and that, once freed from his obsession, all the capacity for good, the genuine devotion to duty, the straightforward nature, the extraordinary charm and flair for public life, would reassert themselves and balance the immaturity and lack of discipline, the instinctive and genuine dislike of so much of his job and the life he had to lead, and enable him with the aid of a well-trained staff to make a good King. Since no one could solve the problem, there was a strong temptation to hope that, if one refrained from looking at it for a while, it might go away.

However, this hope reckoned without the King, who now went on holiday. He chartered a large yacht, the *Nahlin*, and invited a party to accompany him on a cruise along the Dalmatian coast. The King had originally intended merely to take a holiday and he ventured forth, under the romantic rules of an earlier century, as the Duke of Lancaster. This fiction soon had to be dropped because he was given a vociferous welcome wherever he went, and because, in addition, his journey acquired a semi-official aspect owing to the necessity for him to fall in with the wishes of the Foreign Office and undertake some diplomatic duties. However, it is not for its diplomatic results that the King's holiday will be remembered. For this journey was the beginning of what would so shortly be the end.

The King and his party travelled by train to Yugoslavia and reached the port of Sibenik on 10 August. Here there awaited them not merely the yacht

Nahlin and the two destroyers which were to accompany the yacht, but in addition a crowd of about 20,000 peasants who had assembled to welcome them. And it was immediately remarked that this laughing, shouting mob was as much interested in Mrs Simpson as it was in the King, a curious circumstance considering that no English crowd would have recognized her, and a tribute to the efforts of American pressmen, who now proceeded to follow the yacht wherever she went. This exuberant welcome was to be repeated at every port of call, on one occasion the whole of the King's party being nearly pushed into the sea as they returned to the yacht; while in Dubrovnik they were greeted with a cry of '*Zivila Ljubav!*', the Yugoslav equivalent of '*Vive l'amour!*'.

The couple who were the cause of this enthusiasm were elated by a sense that all the world loves a lover and, whereas they might have been expected to feel some anxiety, even some guilt, at this extraordinary public recognition of their relationship, they felt only happiness. 'It delighted both of us that strangers of uncomplicated hearts should wish us well.'

In retrospect there may appear something almost purposeful about the conduct of the King on the *Nahlin*. Everywhere they went he and Mrs Simpson were photographed together, passing through Salzburg, driving in Athens, bathing in the sea and on one occasion in a small boat, her hand on his arm and he looking down at her. Every line of his face and body told, and still tell, of his unutterable devotion.

After Athens the *Nahlin* continued in a leisurely manner in stages to Istanbul. But now, so different is life from how we imagine it, no one any longer enjoyed the holiday. The King had relapsed into a mood which subdued and disheartened his guests. Anxiously they searched their memories. What could have happened? What had been said? At meals they tried desperately to amuse or interest him, even to keep up some show of the amity which had gone from their association. No lip service to courtesy disturbed his melancholy, no concern for his guests diminished an unrelenting fit of the sulks.

'What are the plans for the day, Sir?'

'Wallis, what are the plans for the day?'

It will never be known what passed in his mind. Two possibilities suggest themselves. The first, that he simply considered his position. Perhaps at this moment, in spite of the deliberate exhibitionism, the determined indiscretions, he reflected on his future: on the sacrifice that must be made in one direction or the other, of the dereliction of duty which had become inevitable, either to the woman whose name he had so completely and publicly associated with his own, or to the Crown.

There is another possibility, however. When the yacht rested in Greek waters the conversation turned one night to the relationship between King George of Greece and a woman who was his constant companion. 'Why doesn't he marry her?' the American, Mrs Simpson, asked, upon which one of the guests replied in astonished tones with a simple statement of fact: it was impossible for the King to marry a woman who was both a commoner and already married. No one ever related this innocent answer to the King's mood, because no one had any idea what passed in his mind, no smallest inkling of his intentions. Yet he had already given several demonstrations that those who were not with him were against him, as well as of an absolute disregard for old ties and outworn affections. Did he in his disturbed state feel the irrational anger which can be provoked in an undisciplined mind by a messenger with bad news? It might have been so, or it might have

(*Above*) *In a café.*

(*Opposite*) *With Mrs Herman Rogers, one of their guests on the cruise.*

been a mixture of the two, one being a starting point for the other. As long ago as his tour of Australia with his cousin Louis Mountbatten, the King had had fits of melancholy. In any case the party broke up without regrets.

When the King arrived back in England he went to dine with Queen Mary at Buckingham Palace. He told her that he meant to spend the last two weeks of September at Balmoral, which he says was a source of pleasure to her, signifying as she thought a return to traditional ways. If this was so, her pleasure was short-lived. It was customary for the list of guests at Balmoral to record the names of Cabinet ministers, bishops, admirals, generals and so on. In 1936 the King, who felt he gave sufficient of his time to such dignitaries when in London, asked whom he pleased. Among his guests there were many people who had been at Balmoral through the years – the Duke and Duchess of Marlborough, the Duke and Duchess of Buccleuch, the Duke and Duchess of Sutherland, the Mountbattens and the Roseberys. The Duke and Duchess of York were at Birkhall, and the Duke and Duchess of Gloucester at Abergeldie, nearby. The King had nevertheless decided in the words of his future wife 'that this grouping would be improved by a leaven of less exalted but nonetheless stimulating people', and her name and those of her friends, Mr and Mrs Herman Rogers, were recorded in the Court Circular. So also was that of Mr Esmond Harmsworth.

Nor was this all. If one had to choose one example to illustrate the extent of the King's alienation and oblivion to everything except the emotion which dominated his life, one could hardly choose better than the action with which he began his holiday. Months before he had been asked to open some new hospital buildings in Aberdeen on a day in September, and with ineffable negligence had refused on the grounds that he would still be in mourning for his father (there had been no mourning at Ascot in June and it was part of his whole philosophy to reduce the traditional mourning), deputing

his brother the Duke of York to take his place (although one would suppose that what applied to one brother applied also to the other). On the day that the Duke undertook this task the King himself was seen openly arriving at Ballater station to meet Mrs Simpson, whom he put into the front of his car beside him, while Herman Rogers got into the back. This became extremely widely known, indeed exaggerated, and not merely in Scotland. Chips Cannon recorded a month or so later: 'The Mediterranean cruise was a Press disaster, the visit to Balmoral was a calamity, after the King chucked opening the Aberdeen Infirmary, and then openly appeared at Ballater station on the same day, to welcome Wallis to the Highlands. Aberdeen will never forgive him.'

The rest is mainly surmise. According to one authority, 'the Duchess of York openly showed her resentment at being received by Mrs Simpson', and certainly, if the latter carried as far as Balmoral her belief that one of the women in a bachelor household should act as hostess, one can understand that it might be regarded as very insolent indeed.

However, by now it did not need personal or private antipathy for the King's family to regard Mrs Simpson with anxiety and horror, because the American papers were in full cry. Almost daily, articles and photographs appeared showing the two together, while rumour became more and more scurrilous. On 23 September the *New York Woman* pointed out that if Ernest Simpson should wish to divorce his wife the King could not be sued for adultery in England.

Meanwhile at Balmoral the King took the opportunity to devise economies, and Mrs Simpson to introduce the three-decker toasted sandwich to the kitchens.

By 1 October the King was back in London and this time he returned to Buckingham Palace. He hated this Palace and never lost the feeling of not belonging there, and says that he made few changes because of a presentiment that he would not live in it for long. Walter Monckton wrote: 'He could not bear to feel that he would be cooped up in Buckingham Palace all the time within the iron bars.' And he added, 'He never spoke to me of any doubt or hesitation about accepting his position as King. It was only later on in the year, when the controversy was upon him, that he would sometimes say that they must have him for what he was or not at all, and that, if they were wanting someone exactly reproducing his father, there was the Duke of York.'

10

The Divorce

When the King returned from his holiday it seemed to his staff that his nervous condition was greatly improved and he began to talk of visiting the provinces during the coming winter. Plans were discussed for visits to the Black Country and to South Wales. Nevertheless anxiety about him continually grew because, although the national newspapers still refrained from any gossip, American newspapers now began to find their way into England as well as into the Dominions, and, even more, because letters of a most critical kind began to reach Buckingham Palace, Queen Mary, the Prime Minister and Cabinet ministers, the Archbishop of Canterbury and many other leading men. During the whole course of the Abdication crisis a selection of those reaching Buckingham Palace was sent to the King at Fort Belvedere, so that it is not true, as is so often stated, that he was later taken completely unaware by the attitude of the government and his subjects.

All through the summer Major Hardinge had found it impossible to get Baldwin to address himself to the serious situation which he believed to be developing. 'The Prime Minister's natural reluctance to interfere in the private life of the Sovereign,' Hardinge wrote later, 'in spite of the pressure that was already considerable, was reinforced by the fact that no constitutional issue could arise as long as Mrs Simpson remained married to Mr Simpson.' Yet on 14 October, while waiting to see the King in connection with his forthcoming visit to the Fleet, the Prime Minister volunteered to Hardinge that he was increasingly anxious about the King.

Baldwin too had been on holiday and on his return he had had a great shock. At the beginning of the parliamentary recess he had been in a dangerous state of nervous exhaustion. In a year which included the Hoare-Laval Pact, the occupation of the Rhineland and the outbreak of the Spanish Civil War, as well as such small but pregnant signs of the times as the public exhibition of a gas mask, Tom Jones listed among the causes of the Prime Minister's condition both the death of the old King and anxiety about the new. All through the summer letters of protest about the King and Mrs Simpson had been sent by British citizens abroad and members of nations of the Commonwealth to the Prime Minister, but they had been largely kept from him by his staff because of his nervous exhaustion. On his return there awaited him on his desk the accumulation of several months' letters as well as all the American press cuttings and the photographs of the King and Mrs Simpson among cheering crowds, walking, or driving, or alone on the beaches, and he had learned during two or three hours' concentrated reading

'King Presents Gems to Wally': although the British press kept their promise with the government and were silent about Edward's affair with Mrs Simpson, American newspapers were under no such limitations, and their gossip features inevitably filtered through into Britain, and to the attention of Stanley Baldwin and his Cabinet.

of the world-wide scandal surrounding the British Crown.

When the Foreign Secretary, Anthony Eden, called on the Prime Minister at this time, he found Baldwin's attention wandering. Presently the Prime Minister asked him whether he had received any letters about the King. 'I expect you have some,' he said. 'I fear we have difficulties there.' And then he made the astonishing statement: 'I hope that you will try not to trouble me too much with foreign affairs just now.' Eden – suspecting, he has said, that this was merely 'another example of Baldwin's reluctance to face the unpleasant realities which were our daily fare at the Foreign Office' – returned to his office where he found the conversation explained by the number of letters he had received in a similarly critical strain.

Baldwin proceeded slowly and when, in his conversation with Hardinge at Buckingham Palace, the Private Secretary warned him that the day would come when he would be forced to intervene, he replied that he agreed but was hoping to stave it off until after the Coronation, an astounding remark considering the Coronation was still six months off. However, his conversation with Eden had been in the opposite sense, and it seems likely that he was merely warding off pressure to act before he was ready to. His hand would soon be forced.

Once Mrs Simpson had decided to divorce her husband, she had taken a house in Cumberland Terrace, Regent's Park, and another at the small seaside town of Felixstowe in Suffolk. The reason for the Suffolk house was that her divorce suit had been put down for hearing at Ipswich and it was necessary for her to comply with a residential qualification. It has always been assumed that the divorce suit was heard at Ipswich because of a desire to avoid publicity, although it has never been sufficiently explained how it could have been achieved in that way. The truth seems to be that the London

courts were full for more than a year. Nevertheless, Theodore Goddard, Mrs
Simpson's solicitor, saw a great deal of difference between normal publicity
of the actual proceedings and press comment beforehand, and when he received a telephone call from Lord Beaverbrook, who as it happened was
an old friend of his, and who told him that he proposed to publish a statement
in the *Evening Standard*, he went to see him to dissuade him.

Lord Beaverbrook had learned of the impending divorce 'in the ordinary
way of news gathering', that is to say before knowledge of it reached the
public, or, in this case, the Prime Minister, and, since by now Mrs Simpson's
name was beginning to be known to a great many people, her divorce was
undoubtedly news. Beaverbrook was not much impressed with Goddard's
representations and the solicitor left him without having received any
assurance that publication would be withheld. In consequence he went on
the following morning, in company with Walter Monckton and Mr Allen,
the King's solicitor, to see the King at Buckingham Palace where he told
him exactly what had happened. He suggested that the King should telephone Lord Beaverbrook himself and 'make it clear that there was no desire
whatever to stop any report of the proceedings but merely to stop press
announcements beforehand'. With this suggestion he ensured Lord Beaverbrook a place in the history of the Abdication.

On Tuesday 13 October, the day before Baldwin's visit to Buckingham
Palace, the King telephoned Lord Beaverbrook and asked him to go to see
him and to name his own time. Lord Beaverbrook seems to have been in no
hurry to reply to his request, and, suffering rather mysteriously from tooth-
ache, he became so 'heavily engaged with his dentist' for the next two days
that the interview did not take place until Friday 16 October. (According to
an editorial footnote to Lord Beaverbrook's account, there is no record in his
diary of an appointment with his dentist on either of the intervening dates, although at 5.30 on 15 October there occurs the name Mr Ernest Simpson.)

The King knew Lord Beaverbrook only slightly, yet he now went much
further in his request than Goddard had suggested, asking for help not
merely in suppressing all comment in advance of the Simpson case but also
'in limiting publicity after the event'. He stated his case calmly, Lord Beaverbrook says, and with considerable cogency and force. 'The reasons he gave
for this wish were that Mrs Simpson was ill, unhappy and distressed by
the thought of notoriety. Notoriety would attach to her only because she
had been his guest on the *Nahlin* and at Balmoral. As the publicity would
be due to her association with himself, he felt it his duty to protect her.'

Lord Beaverbrook found these reasons satisfactory and he undertook to
do what the King wanted. In company with Walter Monckton he called
on Mr Esmond Harmsworth (son of Lord Rothermere, the owner of the
Daily Mail, who was chairman of the Newspaper Proprietors' Association)
who, it will be remembered, had stayed with the King at Balmoral. They
then approached the other British newspapers who consented without much
difficulty to a policy of discretion. Lord Beaverbrook writes:

> While I was engaged in these activities directed to regulating publicity I had
> no knowledge that marriage was in the mind of the King. He himself had given
> me no hint of the matter, and, at the same time, I had been told by Mrs Simpson's
> solicitor, Mr Theodore Goddard, that His Majesty had no such intention. I
> repeated that assurance to other newspaper proprietors. And I believed it.
>
> Even if I had known that he did propose marriage, I would still have done what
> I did. But the fact remains that I did not know, although I was having conversa-
> tions with the King almost every day.

*Anthony Eden, then Foreign
Secretary, in Downing Street*

*Lord Beaverbrook, whose influence
in Fleet Street on Edward VIII's
behalf made the British press's pact
of silence possible.*

On Friday 16 October, the day that Lord Beaverbrook called on the King, Baldwin went in company with his wife to Cumberland Lodge, a house in Windsor Park, to stay the weekend with Lord FitzAlan, a former Conservative Chief Whip and Viceroy of Ireland. He found staying there the Duke of Norfolk, Lord Salisbury and Lord Kemsley, another press lord. The main topic of conversation was naturally the Simpson divorce (although facts do not support the suggestion sometimes made that this house-party had been gathered together to discuss worries about the King). There had by now been sufficient evidence that the King might be intending to marry Mrs Simpson for it to be immediately obvious that the latest event brought the prospect of a constitutional crisis uncomfortably near. It was calculated that, if Mrs Simpson received a decree nisi on 27 October, this would be made absolute on 27 April, just in time for the King to marry her before the Coronation in May.

On the following morning Major Hardinge arrived to beg Baldwin to see the King and urge him to prevent the divorce going through and to avoid flaunting his friendship with Mrs Simpson in public. He believed that Baldwin was the only person who could do this, and he thought it of vital importance that the King should be given a warning.

If the King desired to marry a woman who was twice divorced there would be two people primarily concerned – Stanley Baldwin, as Prime Minister, and Cosmo Gordon Lang, the Archbishop of Canterbury and Head of the Church. The Sovereign is not, as is sometimes thought, Head of the Church, but is bound by an Act of Settlement of 1701 to be a member of the Church of England, and is officially designated 'Defender of the Faith'. The Church regards marriage as indissoluable and does not accept divorce and remarriage. After the Abdication an idea gained ground that these two men, the Prime Minister and the Head of the Church (the names of Geoffrey Dawson, the Editor of *The Times*, and Alexander Hardinge, the Private Secretary, are sometimes joined to theirs), plotted together to rid themselves of the King for unworthy political motives not connected with his wish to marry a twice-divorced woman. There is no real evidence for this theory, in fact the reverse, but, vaguely held by a great many people, it has led to the equally false idea that the King was too 'radical' for the leader of the Conservative party and the leader of the Church. The King was accustomed to make unconstitutional interventions on domestic as well as on foreign affairs, and internally the most important question of the day was the vast army of the unemployed, for whom his genuine sympathy cannot be called in question. He was accustomed to speak of his ministers loudly and critically at semi-public functions such as dinner parties. None of this made him a 'radical' however, and it is unbelievable that any politician who had any real acquaintance with him ever mistook him for one.

It would be pleasant to cast Lord Beaverbrook as inventor of the plot and villain of the piece, and indeed he made a bid for the role in his account of the Abdication. But in fact it grew up years before this account was published. What makes it worthy of discussion is that it seems to have had a natural attraction for all those who, being unable to believe that the King gave up the Crown merely for the sake of a woman, needed some more complicated explanation.

The history of the Abdication entirely absolves the Prime Minister. The very qualities which made him a dangerous leader for England in the peril that menaced her became the rarest of virtues in his dealings with the King. He was an experienced and cunning politician but he was a kindly man who was fond of the King. By temperament slow, some said lazy, he was never precipitate and he relied very much on his instincts, which were for the most part good. He remained completely and marvellously free from the indignation so many people felt, and the consequent wish to chasten the King. Again and again he can be seen warding off the attempts of others to speed events or administer rebukes.

In his account of the Abdication the Duke of Windsor gives the impression that from the first he saw Baldwin as an enemy. These are the broodings of exile, however, and none of the accounts written at the time suggest that the dealings between him and the Prime Minister were anything but frank and friendly. On the other hand it is probably an exaggeration to say that he had a real affection for Baldwin.

If Baldwin was not plotting, there could be no plot. Nevertheless, since other names are sometimes mentioned in this connection, it must also be said that they are almost invariably those of men who were exceptionally devoted to the monarchy, taking for granted its power for good and the damage to the Commonwealth that would follow any damage to the Crown. In hindsight it can be seen that the loyalty of the British people was so much to the institution that one king could be removed and another take his place without a tremor of hesitation in the transfer of feeling. But that could not be known beforehand, and no one has ever attempted to explain how it was intended to remove the monarch without risk to the monarchy.

Cosmo Gordon Lang, the Archbishop of Canterbury, who with Baldwin had most cause for concern, was perhaps not so strong in Christian charity and patience as the Prime Minister. He had for many years been a friend of King George and Edward had known him – even felt affection for him – as a child. But he was too close both to the old King and to his staff to retain the young man's friendship when he grew up. All through the summer

Cosmo Gordon Lang, Archbishop of Canterbury, leaves 10 Downing Street. He took a grave view of Edward's behaviour, which he felt 'vulgarized and degraded' the monarchy, and doubted whether he would be able, in all conscience, to consecrate Edward as 'Defender of the Faith' when that faith did not accept divorce or remarriage.

the Archbishop received press cuttings and photographs and letters from overseas expressing dislike and dread of the King's behaviour, and he felt that 'the monarchy was being vulgarized and degraded'. The Archbishop had the appalling personal difficulty that he would have had to crown the King if Edward had succeeded in his purpose of marrying Mrs Simpson and retaining the crown. 'As the months passed . . . the thoughts of my having to consecrate *him* as King weighed on me as a heavy burden. Indeed, I considered whether I could bring myself to do so.' He would undoubtedly have liked to intervene. In fact he could do nothing; the King 'would listen to nobody but Mr Baldwin'. Baldwin kept him informed but otherwise the Archbishop could only watch and wait.

To return to the day in October when Baldwin stayed at Cumberland Lodge, he had previously received a letter from Major Hardinge telling him of the impending divorce and begging him 'to see the King and ask if these proceedings could not be stopped, for the danger in which they place him [HM] was becoming every day greater'. Baldwin had therefore arranged with his host, Lord FitzAlan, to invite Hardinge and his wife to luncheon, and afterwards he retired with Hardinge to discuss the matter. The Private Secretary confined his request to two things: that the Prime Minister should ask the King (1) that the divorce proceedings be dropped and (2) that he should cease to flaunt his association with Mrs Simpson publicly. The Prime Minister did not immediately agree but he suggested to his host that the Hardinges should return again for dinner, and after dinner he told him that he had in the end decided to ask for an audience. Three days later he went to see the King at Fort Belvedere.

Thousands of words have been written about the Abdication and every event, every detail of what happened is known. The only thing about which there will always be room for surmise is what was in the King's mind. Fifteen years later he purported to tell us, but by then fifteen years of exile and the persuasions of other people had intervened and he no longer remembered himself. Only one thing can be said with absolute certainty. The King was in every way more sympathetic, more considerate of the feelings of others, more honourable and more likeable than the picture he painted of himself. Throughout the crisis he behaved with a sincerity and straightforwardness which forced the respect and earned the affection of those who worked for him.

When Baldwin first arrived, the King was in the garden and the Prime Minister complimented him on the beauty of the grounds and their arrangement. Soon they repaired to the octagonal room and Baldwin, who was clearly nervous, became very restless and finally asked for a drink.

The conversation that followed has been reconstructed again and again. Baldwin began by reminding the King that, when they met at Downing Street on the eve of the King's death, he had said that he was glad Baldwin was Prime Minister and he recalled an earlier conversation when they travelled up from Folkestone together and the King (as Prince of Wales) had said that he was to remember he could always speak freely to him about everything. Did that – he asked – hold good when there was a woman in the case?

The King made some gesture of assent, and Baldwin went on to speak of his regard for him as a man and his belief that he had the qualities which might make him an admirable monarch during the transition period the country was going through, and he said: 'You have all the advantages a man can have. You are young. You have before you the example of your father.

You are fond of your house and you like children. You have only one disadvantage. You are not married and you ought to be.' Then he told the
King he had two great anxieties. The first was the effect of a continuance
of the kind of criticism that appeared every day in the American press and
the effect this would have in the Dominions, together with the effect it would
be bound to have in Britain. Recollecting the substance of this interview
for the benefit of the House of Commons, Baldwin said:

And then I reminded him of what I had told him and his brother in years past.
The British monarchy is an unique institution. The Crown in this country through
the centuries has been deprived of many of its prerogatives, but today, while that
is true, it stands for far more than it ever has done in its history. The importance
of its integrity is, beyond all question, far greater than it has ever been, being
as it is not only the last link of Empire that is left, but the guarantee in this country
so long as it exists in that integrity, against many evils that have affected and
afflicted other countries. There is no man in this country to whatever party he
may belong, who would not subscribe to that. But while this feeling largely depends on the respect that has grown up in the last three generations for the
monarchy, it might not take so long, in face of the kind of criticisms to which
it was being exposed, to lose that power far more rapidly than it was built up,
and once lost I doubt if anything could restore it. . . .

You may think me Victorian, Sir. You may think my views out of date, but
I believe I know how to interpret the minds of my own people; and I say that
although it is true that standards are lower since the war it only leads people to
expect a higher standard from their King. People expect more from their King
than they did a hundred years ago.

Baldwin told the King of the large correspondence he had received on
the subject of his friendship with Mrs Simpson. He produced, and later
left with the King, a folder containing many samples of this correspondence.
He also said: 'The American newspapers are full of it and . . . the effect
of such comment in the American press would be to sap the position of
the throne unless it were stopped.'

Then he said: 'I don't believe you can get away with it', a phrase he was
very proud to have thought of, and repeated to everyone he afterwards told
of this conversation, because it was one the King often used himself. And
when the King asked him what he meant he said: 'I think you know our
people. They'll tolerate a lot in private life but they will not stand for this
kind of thing in the life of a public personage and when they read in the
Court Circular of Mrs Simpson's visit to Balmoral they resented it.'

To this the King replied: 'The lady is my friend and I do not wish to
let her in by the back door, but quite openly. . . .'

And then, as it was now Baldwin's turn to be silent, the King said, 'I
hope you will agree that I have carried out my duties with dignity.'

To which Baldwin, understandably, if rather weakly, replied: 'I do agree
and all the more as I know that the duties of royalty are not much to your
liking.'

The King then said, 'I know there is nothing kingly about me but I have
tried to mix with the people and make them think I was one of them.'

Baldwin came to the point. 'Cannot you have this coming divorce put
off?'

'Mr Baldwin,' the King replied, 'that is the lady's private business. I have
no right to interfere with the affairs of an individual. It would be wrong
were I to attempt to influence Mrs Simpson just because she happens to
be a friend of the King.'

Baldwin was later to say that this was the only lie the King ever told

him, and Beaverbrook that, although it was a perfectly proper reply provided
the King had no feelings except those of friendship, 'if he had deeper feelings, and an intention to marry, it was no reply at all'. The King seems
always to have been quite satisfied with it, however, and as Duke of Windsor
he repeated it in his account of the interview with an effect of pride.

Before he left, Baldwin pointed out the danger of the divorce proceedings.
If a verdict was given that left the matter in suspense (by which he seems
to have meant a decree nisi, after which it would be six months before the
decree was made absolute), everyone would then be talking, and when the
press began, as it must begin some time, a most difficult situation would
arise. 'There might be sides taken and factions grow up in this country in
a matter where no factions ought to exist.' And he urged that Mrs Simpson
should be asked to leave the country for six months, hoping, as he later told
Tom Jones, that in the meantime the King's passion might cool and that
other influences might be brought to play on him. (Almost everyone who
spoke to the King during these weeks invariably urged delay in one form
or another for the same reason.)

When Baldwin left the King he was aware of his exaltation, and he told
his wife that the King had said that Mrs Simpson was 'the only woman
in the world and I cannot live without her'. It is curious that, presented
with this opportunity, he did not ask him exactly what he meant, but perhaps
at this stage he did not want to be told. He was satisfied to have got through
the interview and 'broken the ice'. He had made sure that the King knew
the extent of the press comment and the tone of the letters he was receiving,
and he had done this without personally antagonizing him. When he left,
the King had said to him (as he was to say many times in the days that
followed): 'You and I must settle this matter together. I will not have anyone
interfering.'

Major Hardinge was less satisfied. He felt that Baldwin had failed in not
mentioning the subject of marriage and emphasizing the dangers of any idea
of the sort. In the following week he discussed this with some of the heads
of the Civil Service and it was decided that Mrs Simpson should herself
be warned. Theodore Goddard (who it will be remembered had given his
word that marriage was not contemplated) was persuaded to undertake the
task and he travelled to Ipswich for the purpose. On his return he reported
that Mrs Simpson had derided any question of marriage to the King and
that the divorce would go on.

On 26 October *The New York Journal* – a newspaper belonging to William
Randolph Hearst – printed an article under the headline KING WILL WED
WALLY. This stated unequivocally that eight months after her divorce
Edward would marry Mrs Simpson and that after the Coronation she would
become his consort. Two things added to the impact of the article. The first
was that until now the Hearst papers had been singularly quiet on this topic,
and the second was that Hearst had recently been in England, where he
was believed to have visited Fort Belvedere. It was immediately assumed
that this was something in the nature of an inspired leak. (In fact, as Brian
Inglis has pointed out in his book on the Abdication, there was little in the
story that could not have been formulated by putting two and two together.)
In any case the idea that Edward might intend marriage had now appeared
for the first time in print and the sensation this made was by no means confined to America. (American newspapers were entering England, and the
story spread quickly by word of mouth.) One effect of it all was greatly to
increase the difficulties and doubts of the editors of English newspapers,

who were confined by Beaverbrook's 'gentleman's agreement', but only as
to comment on Mrs Simpson's divorce. Brian Inglis has analysed the
motives which were to keep them silent on all aspects of the greatest newspaper story in history for many days to come. Since not all the newspapers
and magazines came under the control or influence of Beaverbrook or Rothermere, he asks, why was the story not broken by some editor craving a
scoop to put his paper on the map?

The temptation must have been considerable, particularly for papers that
needed a circulation boost. But for once their managerial sides were not keen on
the idea. They were afflicted by fear of the unknown. What would the reaction
be, should a paper take a chance and spring the story? Obviously its sales for
that issue, and probably for the next few issues, would be prodigious, but what
thereafter? Suppose the public, though avid for the story when it appeared,
thought badly of the paper for having printed it. . . . And what of advertisers? The
weight of official and unofficial disapproval at such an act of lèse-majesté might
well lead to the withdrawal of promised advertisements. What too, of the legal
position? A single false step, a mis-statement, an unguarded innuendo, and
swingeing damages could be expected against the transgressor. No, on the whole
it was safer to wait.

The position of the 'quality' papers, London and provincial, he goes on
to argue, was rather different. He quotes Tom Jones as saying that their
silence 'is not enforced by government, but by a sense of shame', and goes
on: 'No quality newspaper cared to be the first to break the story. And their
reluctance to take the risk can only be attributed to the prevailing belief
that on this issue, the lead should be given by the government – or by *The
Times*, as it could be assumed that *The Times* would not pronounce without
government sanction.' The position of the editor of *The Times* was therefore
a particular one, and Geoffrey Dawson had told Tom Jones on 21 October
that *The Times* would have 'to do something about the King and Mrs Simpson but that the PM must tell him what he wanted done'. The reply to this
was that Baldwin would like him to continue to do nothing.

On 27 October, Mrs Simpson's divorce suit was heard at Ipswich and
evidence was brought of Ernest Simpson's having stayed at the Café de Paris
at Bray with a lady named Buttercup Kennedy. A decree nisi was awarded
with costs against Simpson. Too much can be made of the fact that the
divorce suit smacked of collusion because the actual mechanics of many
divorces were contrived at that date (the real co-respondent being guarded
from unpleasant publicity by an artificial arrangement with another woman),
but there were, nevertheless, circumstances which were unusual. Two press
photographers had their cameras smashed by the police, who also forcibly
prevented reporters from following Mrs Simpson; while Ladbroke, the
King's chauffeur, had to execute a skilful manœuvre to get her away from
the court.

The following morning the British press kept the gentleman's agreement
and reported the divorce only in the most formal way. Not so in America,
however, where the press had a field-day even by their own standard, the
palm being awarded to the oft-quoted headline KING'S MOLL RENO'D IN
WOLSEY'S HOME TOWN.

The first phase on the road to abdication was over.

11

The Letter

On 3 November the King opened parliament, giving short shrift to the first part of this ceremony and a display of his natural talent in the second.

Traditionally the monarch drives from Buckingham Palace to Westminster, in a gilt state coach drawn by eight grey horses and escorted by the Household Cavalry, through streets lined by loyal subjects come to assuage their desire for ceremony, for mystery and magic. And, although this drive is strictly a sideline, a by-product of the main occasion, it is, nevertheless, of the essence of modern majesty.

On the day when Edward VIII opened his only parliament it poured with rain. Edward underlined the fact that the 'Queen's' weather, so marked a seal of Heaven's approval of previous sovereigns from Queen Victoria onwards, had deserted this one by cancelling the state procession and driving to Westminster in a closed Daimler. Pageantry, he would write later, requires sunshine, and there are few sadder sights than a dripping cortège splashing down a half-empty street – a remark which shows him careless of the fact that those who half-filled the streets stood in the soaking rain merely for a glimpse of him.

Arrived at the Houses of Parliament, however, he was anxious to do well before his sophisticated and critical audience and above all one which knew of the reports in American newspapers and even of Mr Baldwin's interview with him. *The Times* leader said next day: 'A young King has made his first speech from the Throne. Not alone the fact that his was a Throne by itself, but his whole Royal demeanour bade one feel that in himself was all his state.' Sir Harold Nicolson recorded in his diary, 'The King looked like a boy of eighteen and did it well.'

Nine days later the King turned the rain which still splashed down on him to better account. On his visit to the Fleet at Southampton he won the hearts of the Navy because, unlike Sir Samuel Hoare, the First Lord of the Admiralty, he would not wear a waterproof while inspecting men in the rain – 'A small thing, but sailors take note of small things, and in this they saw the real difference between the Politician and the Monarch.'

And in Sir Samuel Hoare's account of the same occasion we find Edward, almost for the last time in his life, exhibiting those qualities which, in spite of everything, will ensure him a small place in history and make him of ever-lasting interest to the psychologist and the biographer:

On one of the evenings there was a smoking concert in the aircraft carrier *Coura-geous*.... The vast underdeck was packed with thousands of seamen. In my long

experience of mass meetings I never saw one so completely dominated by a single personality. At one point he turned to me and said: 'I am going to see what is happening at the other end.' Elbowing his way through the crowd, he walked to the end of the hall and started community singing to the accompaniment of a seaman's mouth-organ. When he came back to the platform, he made an impromptu speech that brought the house down. Then, a seaman in the crowd proposed three cheers for him, and there followed an unforgettable scene of the wildest and most spontaneous enthusiasm. Here, indeed, was the Prince Charming, who could win the hearts of all sorts and conditions of men and women and send a thrill through great crowds.

Edward arrives to open the Houses of Parliament, November 1936. Owing to bad weather, he decided to make the journey in a Daimler rather than the traditional gilt state coach, in spite of the crowds who had lined the wet streets to watch the procession. However, his conduct in the actual ceremony, which included his first speech as king, was exemplary.

Lord Templewood adds that the whole visit had been one long series of personal triumphs for the King and says that he was amazed by his liveliness as they travelled back after two days of continuous inspections in the worst possible weather.

The King had every cause to be pleased with himself as, weary and cold, he entered the doors of Fort Belvedere. He was met by his butler who told him that there was a letter from Major Hardinge who was anxious that he should read it without delay. And there on top of the usual red boxes was the document marked 'Urgent and Confidential'. Putting aside for the moment the thoughts of a bath he had looked forward to, the King opened it slowly and read it.

Buckingham Palace,
13th November, 1936

Sir,
    With my humble duty.
    As Your Majesty's Private Secretary, I feel it my duty to bring to your notice the following facts which have come to my knowledge, and which I *know* to be accurate:

(1) The silence of the British Press on the subject of Your Majesty's friendship with Mrs Simpson is *not* going to be maintained. It is probably only a matter of days before the outburst begins. Judging by the letters from British subjects living in foreign countries where the Press has been outspoken, the effect will be calamitous.

(2) The Prime Minister and senior members of the Government are meeting today to discuss what action should be taken to deal with the serious situation which is developing. As Your Majesty no doubt knows, the resignation of the Government – an eventuality which can by no means be excluded – would result in Your Majesty having to find someone else capable of forming a government which would receive the support of the present House of Commons. I have reason to know that, in view of the feeling prevalent among members of the House of Commons of all parties, this is hardly within the bounds of possibility. The only alternative remaining is a dissolution and a General Election, in which Your Majesty's personal affairs would be the chief issue – and I cannot help feeling that even those who would sympathize with Your Majesty as an individual would deeply resent the damage which would inevitably be done to the Crown, the corner-stone on which the whole Empire rests.

If Your Majesty will permit me to say so, there is only one step which holds out any prospect of avoiding this dangerous situation, and that is for Mrs Simpson to go abroad *without further delay*, and I would *beg* Your Majesty to give this proposal your earnest consideration before the position has become irretrievable. Owing to the changing attitude of the Press, the matter has become one of great urgency.

I have the honour, etc., etc.,

Alexander Hardinge

PS I am by the way of going after dinner to-night to High Wycombe to shoot there to-morrow, but the Post Office will have my telephone number, and I am of course entirely at Your Majesty's disposal if there is anything at all that you want.

Writing about his reactions to this letter fourteen or fifteen years later, the Duke of Windsor says that he began by being shocked and angry, shocked by its suddenness, and angry because it suggested that he should send 'from my land, my realm ... the woman I intended to marry'. And he says that the longer he read the letter the more puzzled he became by the motives that had prompted his Private Secretary to write it. The Duke did not question his right to address such a communication to his sovereign; indeed if a Cabinet crisis impended over any issue, it was his duty to warn his master. But, having said that what hurt was the cold formality of the letter, the Duke goes on, in language absurdly inappropriate to the nature of the issues involved, to ask himself what this could mean. Was it a warning or an ultimatum? Who but the Prime Minister could have suggested all this to his Private Secretary, and, if the Prime Minister, what was his purpose? The Duke speaks of himself as a man in love, and says if their intention was to make him give up Mrs Simpson they had misjudged him. 'They had struck at the very roots of my pride. Only the most faint-hearted would have remained unaroused by such a challenge.' And he says he decided to come to grips with Mr Baldwin and the 'nebulous figures' involved.

Yet the King, unless his mind was completely unhinged, could not possibly have been surprised or shocked. From the time of his return from the *Nahlin*, Major Hardinge had done everything possible in fulfilment of his duty to keep him informed of the trends of public opinion. Day after day, cuttings from the American press and letters from his subjects abroad had been selected and sent to him. The Prime Minister had been persuaded to see him; and, although at this interview he had failed to bring up the question

(*Opposite*) *The opening of Parliament was a formal success for Edward ; his visit to the Fleet at Southampton proved that he continued to possess the 'common touch'.*

of marriage, he had made absolutely plain the damage which in his opinion
was being done to the Crown and the dangers which threatened it unless
the King prevented the divorce and ceased to flaunt the friendship; moreover, before leaving he had given him a folder of cuttings and letters, the
general effect of which had been to frighten Baldwin himself into believing
that in the year 1936 it was his duty to leave foreign affairs to his Foreign
Secretary, while he dealt with this more pressing matter. Whatever the feelings of the King, he cannot surely have been unprepared for his Private
Secretary's letter.

It is necessary for the moment to digress from the King to examine the
events which had led Hardinge to write the letter at this particular moment.
Baldwin had spent the time since his interview with Edward 'in the steadily
diminishing hope that the King would listen to his warnings'. He had
employed himself in testing opinion in private conversations. Among the
most important people he saw at this time were Clement Attlee, the Leader
of the Opposition, and Sir Walter Citrine, the General Secretary of the
Trades Union Congress. Attlee's opinions are known to have coincided with
those of the Prime Minister, and Citrine, who had recently returned from
America, felt even more strongly. He had been humiliated by the fact that
'newspapers in other countries were carrying discreditable stories about the
King', and he agreed with Attlee that the Labour people in the country
would not countenance the idea of Mrs Simpson becoming Queen.

By the beginning of November many people began to be frightened of
Baldwin's policy of inaction, since it was clear that in view of the foreign
press the English newspapers were bound soon to break their self-imposed
silence. In what has been called 'a most striking exercise of back-stage
power', certain civil servants, including Warren Fisher and Horace Wilson,
'attempted to jump Baldwin into an ultimatum', by composing a draft for
him to submit to the King. The draft read as follows:

> Unless steps are taken promptly to allay the widespread and growing misgivings
> among the people, the feelings of respect, esteem and affection which Your Majesty
> has evoked among them will disappear in a revulsion of so grave and perilous
> a character as possibly to threaten the stability of the nation and the Empire. The
> dangers to the people of this country of such a shock, the disunity and loss of
> confidence which would ensue at a time when so much of the world is looking
> to the United Kingdom for guidance and leadership through a sea of troubles,
> cannot but be obvious to Your Majesty. In Mr Baldwin's opinion there is but
> one course which he can advise you to take, namely to put an end to Your Majesty's
> association with Mrs Simpson.

This draft was shown to Hardinge who regarded it as very drastic and
suggested some amendments. It was then passed to Neville Chamberlain,
the Chancellor of the Exchequer, who amended it as follows:

> I have before me an official communication in which the advice of Your
> Majesty's Government is formally tendered, to the effect that in view of the grave
> dangers to which, in their opinion, this country is being exposed, your association
> with Mrs Simpson should be terminated forthwith. It is hardly necessary for me
> to point out that should this advice be tendered and refused by Your Majesty,
> only one result could follow in accordance with the requirements of constitutional
> monarchy, that is, the resignation of myself and the National Government. If Mrs
> Simpson left the country forthwith, this distasteful matter could be settled in a
> less formal manner.

It is clear that, but for his Private Secretary in the first place, and the
Prime Minister (who when he saw the drafts suppressed them) in the second,

the King might well have had real cause for complaint.

On 11 November the Prime Minister received a warning from the editor of the *Morning Post* that the press could no longer stay silent unless the Government had the matter in hand, and Geoffrey Dawson, the editor of *The Times*, went to Downing Street to discuss the possibilities and dangers of publication. In the meantime Hardinge had learned that two affidavits had been filed, requiring the intervention of the King's Proctor in the Simpson divorce case on the grounds of collusion. (As the law stood at the time, the fact that two people both wished to divorce each other was an absolute bar to their being able to do so. Thus if it could be proved that the divorce was arranged 'collusively' between the two parties, the application would fail.)

Possibly more important than any of these things, Hardinge had written confidentially to the Governor-General of Canada, Lord Tweedsmuir, asking if there were any marked reactions in Canada to articles in the American press (which found its way freely over the border), and whether there was any evidence of damage to the prestige of the monarch. On 15 October he received a reply. Lord Tweedsmuir's impression was that the Canadians, whose reaction had at first been one of incredulity and indignation, had come to an unwilling belief in these stories. Canadian opinion intensely disliked the American element in the stories and the Canadian, although very friendly to the American, was quick to resent interference or patronage, and felt his dignity hurt in having his King so closely associated with gossip of an American flavour.

Tweedsmuir went on to make a special point in relation to the King's personality:

He is really idolized here. Canada feels that he is, in a special sense, her own possession. It is wonderful how strong the personal affection is in all classes.... Any smirching of their idol is felt as almost a personal loss.... Like all devotees, they are unwilling to believe that any clay can enter into the composition of their god. And if they are compelled to admit this there will be a most unfortunate reaction.

Tweedsmuir also wrote in the same strain to Baldwin, although it is doubtful whether the Prime Minister had yet received this letter when Hardinge wrote to the King on 13 November.

In any case both men came to the conclusion that the time had come to act. Baldwin called a meeting of some of his senior colleagues, MacDonald, Chamberlain, Halifax, Simon and Runciman, and began discussions with them; and Hardinge decided that it was his duty to warn the King.

On the morning of 13 November he had composed a draft of the letter he was eventually to send, when Dawson arrived to see him. Hardinge showed his letter to Dawson, who found no fault with it. Hardinge then called at Downing Street to ask the Prime Minister's authority to tell the King of his meeting with senior ministers and to ask whether the meeting could be postponed until they learned the King's reaction. Baldwin replied that he could postpone it no longer as the pressure was overwhelming.

One further event must have influenced Hardinge. On that day he lunched with Stanley Bruce, the High Commissioner for Australia. As a result of this luncheon Bruce sent a communication to the Prime Minister in which he indicated the views of Australia, which were that 'if there was any question of marriage with Mrs Simpson the King would have to go, as far as Australia was concerned'. Hardinge must have been completely informed of the High Commissioner's views by the end of the luncheon.

Considering this and the attitude of the Leader of the Opposition and Sir Walter Citrine, the restiveness of the press, the draft memoranda of back-benchers and civil servants, and of the meeting of senior members of the government, how better could he have performed his duty than by the letter he sent to the King?

The King thought less coldly, or so he would later write, with more sympathy for the fact that he was in love. Yet he had cut himself off completely from Hardinge and the rest of his staff, who could not approach him except in the line of duty, and he had made it plain that no man might address him on the subject of Mrs Simpson. The idea that he was hurt because Hardinge did not approach him in person or in a less formal way simply will not do.

The truth is that he found Hardinge personally unsympathetic. There was no approach the Private Secretary could have made which the King would not have found distasteful. But he did like Godfrey Thomas, the Assistant Private Secretary, who had been in his service for years. Nevertheless, when shortly after this Thomas felt that he must make an attempt to save his master from the future he so clearly intended for himself, he, too, could only write. It is often said that none of the King's servants ever attempted to dissuade him or to tell him the truth about where he was heading, but this is completely untrue. And, although Thomas wrote informally and with sympathy and love, speaking not merely of the King's duty to his country but in graphic and moving terms of the inevitable consequences to himself of abdication, his letter had no greater effect than Hardinge's. Neither man ever received an answer.

12

'Something Must Be Done'

The King was correct in believing that many people now knew that Baldwin had been to see him and also that increasing numbers had seen, or seen reports of, the gossip in the American press. By Friday 13 November, when he returned from his visit to the Fleet, Tom Jones was writing, 'There is only one topic in London – Mrs Simpson', and Chips Channon, 'We are faced with an impasse. The country, or much of it, would not accept Queen Wallis, with two live husbands scattered about', while on the following day he recorded that the House of Commons was openly talking of abdication.

Mrs Simpson, accompanied by Aunt Bessie, was awaiting the King at Fort Belvedere, but he did not immediately tell them of the letter he had received. During the night he decided that, although the Private Secretary was the normal channel between the Palace and 10 Downing Street, he could no longer work with Alexander Hardinge. He therefore asked Walter Monckton to meet him on Sunday afternoon at Windsor Castle. Monckton had been a friend of the King since their days at Oxford and had a considerable reputation as a barrister.

The King had already taken him into his confidence and one evening, about a week before he met him at Windsor Castle, he told Monckton that he meant to marry Mrs Simpson. On that occasion Monckton, like everyone else when first confronted with this intention, counselled delay in making any decision, particularly as there was no possibility of marriage before 27 April, still six months off. The King then explained to him that he could not go forward to the Coronation meaning in his heart to make the marriage whatever happened, and deceiving both the government and the people.

At the meeting at Windsor Castle he showed Monckton the letter he had received from his Private Secretary. The King, according to Monckton, regarded the letter as forcing the issue (which it undoubtedly was) and thought that it compelled him to take some action, either to dismiss Major Hardinge or in some other way to bring the matter to a head. Monckton advised him not to dismiss Hardinge – which would indicate a breach over Mrs Simpson – and 'to wait and be patient'. But he agreed to act as the King's adviser and liaise with Baldwin in this crisis, 'thus temporarily taking over Hardinge's principal duty as the constitutional link with the Prime Minister and the Cabinet'. And Edward then told him that he proposed to send for Mr Baldwin and tell him that if the government were against his marriage with Mrs Simpson he was prepared to go.

'He will not like to hear that,' Monckton said gravely.

'I shall not find it easy to say,' the King replied.

When he got back to the Fort the King showed Hardinge's letter to Mrs Simpson who, according to her own account, 'was stunned' and said she thought the only thing for her was to follow the Private Secretary's advice and leave the country. The King was adamant that she should not do that and he said that Hardinge's letter was 'an impertinence'. And he told her that he had discussed it with Monckton and was going to send for Baldwin on the next day. 'I'm going to tell him that if the country won't approve our marrying, I'm ready to go.' And on the next morning the King asked his secretaries to inform Mr Baldwin that he wished to see him at 6.30 that evening. In the meantime he telephoned Lord Beaverbrook, who was on the high seas on his way to the USA, and appealed to him to return immediately.

At some time, and the indications are that it was probably before this second interview, Baldwin sent for the Attorney-General, Sir Donald Somervell, and asked for his advice on three matters: marriage, abdication and the possibility of an intervention by the King's Proctor. On the question of marriage the Attorney-General gave the opinion that the King's marriage was outside the Royal Marriages Act but that it would be unconstitutional for him to marry contrary to the advice of his ministers. It is a difficult question, but the history of the Abdication seems to prove that the sovereign is free to choose his own consort providing his choice is approved by the Prime Minister and government of the day. If, on the other hand, he chooses someone generally regarded as unsuitable to be Queen, it becomes a constitutional matter.

On the question of the Abdication, Sir Donald Somervell said this could be done with the King's Assent by an Act of Parliament; and on the question of the King's Proctor he took the view that it would be contrary to the constitutional position of the King for the King's officer in the King's courts to investigate allegations against the King, but he added that this view was debatable.

Baldwin arrived at the Palace at 6.30 to be warned by Hardinge that he might expect something dramatic, and the King came straight to the point: 'I understand that you and several members of the Cabinet have some fear of a constitutional crisis developing over my friendship with Mrs Simpson.' Baldwin replied that this was true. According to Lucy Baldwin's account, the King then raised the question of marriage. Baldwin told him that he did not think this 'particular marriage was one that would receive the approbation of the country'.

I pointed out to him that the position of the King's wife was different from the position of any other citizen in the country; it was part of the price which the King has to pay. His wife becomes Queen; the Queen becomes the Queen of the country; and, therefore, in the choice of a Queen, the voice of the people must be heard.

When Baldwin had said this the King said to him: 'I want you to be the first to know that I have made up my mind and nothing will alter it – I have looked at it from all sides – and I mean to abdicate to marry Mrs Simpson.'

To this Baldwin replied 'Sir, this is a very grave decision and I am deeply grieved.'

Then Baldwin told him that Mackenzie King of Canada and Bruce of Australia both agreed that the throne was the one thing that held the Empire together, and that this might break it up. The King repeated that he intended

(Opposite) Walter Monckton, an old Oxford friend of Edward's and a lawyer, acted as go-between for the King and his Cabinet. He is seen here leaving 10 Downing Street.

to marry Mrs Simpson as soon as she was free. If he could marry her as King, well and good; he would be happy and in consequence perhaps a better King. But if on the other hand the government opposed the marriage, as the Prime Minister had given him reason to believe it would, then he would go. Baldwin replied that this was the most grievous news, on which he could not comment that day.

Then the King said that he meant to go and tell his mother of his decision that evening, and he gave Baldwin permission to tell two or three privy councillors whom he trusted. That evening Lucy Baldwin wrote: 'All the time the King was most charming but S. said the King simply could not understand and he couldn't make him. On leaving, the King held Stanley's hand for a long time and there were almost tears in his eyes when he said goodbye.' And at this interview Baldwin was more than ever conscious of the other man's exaltation. 'The King's face wore at times such a look of beauty', he told his family, 'as might have lighted the face of a young knight who caught a glimpse of the Holy Grail.'

That night the King went to dine with his mother, having asked that his sister Mary should be present. After dinner, Edward – David to his family – told them of his love for Wallis Simpson and his determination to marry her and of the opposition of the Prime Minister and other members of the government. Presently he made it clear that he intended to abdicate. This was not completely unexpected to Queen Mary, who had lived in an agony of shame and apprehension for months. Even before her husband died she had realized that there was a dangerous recklessness in her son's feeling for Mrs Simpson, and in the last months she, like everyone else, had learned from American newspapers of his total disregard for the dignity of the Crown. Because of the long silence of the British press it is hardly realized in England how much suffering the King inflicted on his family, not merely by leaving the throne but by the manner in which he went.

The Queen, who had so long and so painfully failed in communication with her children, now implored her son to reconsider his decision. In July 1938 she wrote him the following letter:

You ask me in your letter of the 23rd June to write to you frankly about my true feelings with regard to you and the present position and this I will do now. You will remember how miserable I was when you informed me of your intended marriage and abdication and how I implored you not to do so for your sake and for the sake of the country. You did not seem able to take in any point of view but your own. . . . I do not think you have ever realized the shock, which the attitude you took up caused your family and the whole Nation. It seemed inconceivable to those who had made such sacrifices during the war that you, as their King, refused a lesser sacrifice. . . . My feelings for you as your Mother remain the same, and our being parted and the cause of it, grieve me beyond words. After all, all my life I have put my Country before everything else, and I simply cannot change now.

Queen Mary refused her son's plea that he might bring Wallis Simpson to see her. She was both shocked and angry. In the following account, which Baldwin gave his niece, some of the shock is apparent:

Queen Mary is one of the shyest women I have ever met in my life. This shyness puts a kind of barrier between her and you which it is well nigh impossible to get across.

I had suffered rather from this, though she was always very nice to me. But I was always expected to keep the conversation going; and it sometimes flagged.

She had a way, too, of standing at the end of the room when one was shown

Armistice Day, November 1936: one of the last photographs of Edward and his mother, Queen Mary, before the Abdication. On the left are Edward's brother, Albert, and his wife, soon to become George VI and Queen Elizabeth.

in at Buckingham Palace; and she would remain there like a statue while you made your bow and walked over a sometimes very slippery floor to kiss her hand. But all that was one day changed quite suddenly and I will tell you how. . . .

The first time I was sent for to see her at the beginning of this Simpson story, I had a tremendous shock. For, instead of standing immobile in the middle distance, silent and majestic, she came trotting across the room *exactly like a puppy dog*: and before I had time to bow, she took hold of my hand in both of hers and held it tight. 'Well, Prime Minister,' she said, 'here's a pretty kettle of fish!'

After that, I can assure you, my dear, the barriers were down.

We know from her biographer that if Queen Mary was shocked she was also humiliated and very angry. 'It can be simply stated that Queen Mary greeted her son's decision . . . with consternation, with anger and with pain. . . . No single event in the whole of her life . . . had caused her so much real distress or left her with so deep a feeling of "humiliation".' Nevertheless, at the time, the Queen wrote these words to her son in a letter: 'As your mother, I must send you a line of true sympathy in the difficult position in which you are placed – I have been thinking of you all day, hoping you are making a wise decision for your future – I fear your visit to Wales will be trying in more ways than one, with this momentous action hanging over your head.' On the following day the King told each of his brothers of his decision. The Duke of York, he says, was so taken aback that he could not bring himself to say anything.

At his meeting with Baldwin the King had also asked whether he might, without a breach of constitutional practice, seek the independent counsel and advice of other members of the Cabinet. He still had some hope that, even though the senior members of the Cabinet were behind Baldwin, there might be among the younger ones, particularly those who were his personal friends, someone who could be persuaded to speak for him. When Baldwin agreed, he asked to see Sir Samuel Hoare and Mr Duff Cooper, and he saw

Duff Cooper, who had been one of Edward's guests on the 'Nahlin' cruise in the summer, was the only member of the Cabinet to plead for a delay on the question of Edward's relationship with Mrs Simpson until after the Coronation.

both of them on the following morning, 17 November.

Sir Samuel Hoare had been not an intimate but an acquaintance of his for some time, and the King failed to win him as an ally. Hoare told him that Baldwin was in command of the situation and the senior ministers solidly behind him. If the King were to press his marriage on the Cabinet he would meet a stone wall of opposition.

The Duke of Windsor said that Duff Cooper (with whom he was on far more intimate terms) was as encouraging as Hoare was discouraging, but this seems to be a misinterpretation of Duff Cooper's attitude. He began by asking whether it was any use trying to dissuade the King from his intention or whether his mind was made up.

He said that it would be quite useless, and I believed him. I then suggested postponement. . . . I thought that if they would agree not to meet for a year, during which he would be crowned and perhaps attend a Durbar, of which there seemed some possibility at the time, he would at the end of that period have grown more accustomed to his position and more loth to leave it. I also secretly thought that he might in the interval meet somebody whom he would love more. He never has.

In answer, the King made an explanation which is important because in the first place it exposes exactly what Duff Cooper's suggestion would have meant, and in the second it outlines an attitude from which he could never be persuaded to depart.

The Coronation, he said, is essentially a religious service. The King is anointed with oil; he takes the Sacrament; and as Defender of the Faith he swears an oath to uphold the doctrines of the Church of England which does not approve of divorce. 'For me to have gone through the Coronation ceremony harbouring in my heart the secret intention to marry contrary to the Church's tenets would have meant being crowned with a lie on my lips. . . . Whatever the cost to me personally I was determined, before I would think of being crowned, to settle once and for all the question of my right to marry.'

On the same day, 17 November, Miss Ellen Wilkinson asked a question in the House of Commons of the President of the Board of Trade. 'Can the Right Hon. Gentleman say why in the case of two American magazines of the highest repute imported into this country in the last few weeks, two and sometimes three pages have been torn out; and what is this thing the British public are not allowed to know?' To this Mr Runciman answered: 'My department has nothing to do with that.'

Since Miss Wilkinson knew, as by now did every member of the House of Commons, why these American magazines had been censored, the question must have seemed to the watching press a warning that, if they remained silent much longer, the news of the King's love for Mrs Simpson might break for the first time elsewhere. Nevertheless, the Prime Minister had sent for Geoffrey Dawson after his interview with the King the night before and 'made it clear for the first time that any Press comment at this moment might weaken his influence such as it was'.

And the press were in a further difficulty. 'If newspaper criticism were to begin before these engagements,' Geoffrey Dawson wrote, referring to the intended visit to Wales and also to the visit to the Fleet, 'it might be taken as an attempt to undermine H.M.'s popularity in advance; if immediately after them as an attempt to minimize his influence. It was a very difficult problem on which S.B. professed himself quite unable to give advice.'

The King began on 18 November the journey through South Wales which, more than anything else he ever undertook, has lingered in the minds of his fellow countrymen. In one of the blackest periods of British industrial history South Wales was the blackest part of the country. In the Rhondda and Monmouth valleys, against a background of slag heaps and shuttered and empty shops, hosts of men stood on the road or at abandoned works to meet the King. These men and their families were short of food and clothing and many of them had been out of work for years. As he moved among them the King spoke to dozens of men directly, showing the utmost concern for their plight. A hundred times an hour his obvious sympathy encouraged sad-faced, ill-clothed men to speak to him of their troubles. And he showed even in these unpropitious circumstances the old flair for public relations, the same instinct for maximum effect. He entered Merthyr Labour Exchange at a time when it was full of men waiting hopelessly for work, and, moving up to the grill, spoke to them individually, showing openly his sorrow for their plight; and he ended his already long day almost an hour late because he made a detour, not in the original schedule, to visit the Bessemer Steel Works at Dowlais. Here 9000 men had been employed a few years before, while now it was a vast derelict area. Hundreds of men awaited him, sitting on piles of twisted and rusting metal where demolition had taken place, and when he arrived they arose and sang an old Welsh hymn. The King stood bareheaded, his face grave and set, plainly intensely moved. Turning to an official, he said: 'These works brought all these people here. Something must be done to find them work.'

That night he dined with Malcolm Stewart, former Chief Commissioner for the Special Areas, and Sir George Gillett, his successor. Ernest Brown, Minister of Mines, and Sir Kingsley Wood, Minister of Health, who accompanied him throughout the tour, were also there. At this dinner he was told something of the plans for re-starting derelict pits and steelworks in South

Despite growing personal troubles, Edward still felt deep concern for the plight of the unemployed, as his famous tour of South Wales in November, during which this picture was taken, revealed.

Wales and Monmouthshire.

On the following day, 19 November, the King carried out an almost equally arduous tour. At a housing estate at Pontypool he said: 'You may be sure that all I can do for you I will; we certainly want better times brought to your valley.' And at Blaenavon he told the chairman of the Unemployed Men's Committee, 'Something will be done about unemployment.'

When the King left South Wales he left hope behind him, and by his outspoken comments he probably did, as *The Times* put it the next day, 'greatly help to concentrate attention on the state of the distressed areas and the failure of the industrial revival to penetrate the economic backwaters that are particularly affected'. He had given a demonstration of his capacity for sympathy, of his genuine distress at the misery which surrounded him and he had brought something very like happiness (however fleeting) to men who for so long had known only despair. He had spoken words that have ensured him a place in history and which have led many people to jump to the conclusion that he had some real affinity with the left-wing political parties. More than anything else, he is remembered for the simple reaction: 'Something must be done.'

Yet how many people remember that these words and those which followed them – 'You may be sure that all I can do for you I will' – were spoken a bare three weeks before he left England for good? And how many people have ever known that when he spoke them he had already told the Prime Minister, his mother and his three brothers of his intention to abdicate the throne?

The King arrived at Paddington at seven o'clock in the evening of the second day of his tour. That night he dined with Sir Henry Channon. He was in good spirits and Chips later wrote: 'At once I saw that he was in a gay mood – no doubt a reaction from his depressing Welsh tour, two dreadfully sad days in the distressed areas. . . . The King was jolly, gay and full of cracks. He returned only tonight . . . and must have felt as elated as I do after two or three days in my constituency.'

13

The Morganatic Marriage Proposal

Baldwin, who had been in Scotland while the King had been in Wales, returned on the same day, and on going down to Chequers the following day he found a letter from Walter Monckton:

You will find his decision unchanged on the main question. And he is facing the rest and considering all that is involved, with a real appreciation of the interests which you would wish him to have in mind. I think he will want to see you about Tuesday or Wednesday. I shall no doubt see him before then and I will let you know anything worth reporting. At present his ideas are a little fluid, but I shall remember what you said to me and do my best. He will not do anything precipitate or selfish, saving *il gran refiuto*.

And on the same day Hardinge recorded that he had seen Monckton after he had had an interview with the King, and that Monckton looked on HM's decision to marry and abdicate as irrevocable, although he added that Duff Cooper's influence had not helped. Monckton said that he was urging the King to get it over quickly and go out of the country.

The King was nevertheless undecided. He gave the impression that, although he had made up his mind on the main issue and was at peace with himself, he had neither come to a decision as to procedure, nor even entirely given up hope of finding backing for his belief that he might marry Mrs Simpson and also remain on the throne. A lack of decision on the first of these things seemed natural at this early stage, but his reasons for not abandoning hope soon became apparent.

The *Daily Mail* had given great publicity to the King's visit to Wales, and on Monday 23 November it appeared with a leader under the headline THE KING EDWARD TOUCH. This leader, having said that the magic of personal leadership had never been better shown than by the King's visit to South Wales, continued:

The King was openly disturbed and afflicted by his survey. The lot of the humblest people has always been his nearest anxiety and continual pre-occupation – and the people of South Wales realized that here was a man who cares supremely for their well-being. He has started a fresh chapter of endeavour for the distressed areas. The King does not consider his mission fulfilled by the pilgrimage to derelict mines, extinct forges and forlorn villages. Already he has talked to his Ministers and prompted them into real activity.... The King has called for action. He will want to review the Government's plans and to be kept posted of their progress.

The royal technique repays study. In the first place he approached the difficulties of South Wales resolute to find a remedy however novel the methods of treatment might be. He went to see for himself, personal investigation being the basis for every job of work the King touches. Then, once he had settled in his own mind the extent and urgency of the dilemma, he called for all the evidence available....

The contrast to the way in which national questions are customarily approached can escape nobody. There is consultation, committees are appointed and conference takes place in the solemn apartments of Whitehall, but how often does a Minister as a preface to this consecrated and lengthy procedure go boldly forth to see for himself and measure the problem by independent judgment, following this with action.

If only Ministers would say in the House of Commons: 'I am going to see for myself and act forthwith' instead of 'The matter is receiving attention', at what a refreshing pace the nation's affairs would move! Even such deadweight lethargy as surrounds Britain's most vital need – rearmament – would yield to the King Edward touch.

This leader made it plain that an attempt to form a King's party would be made, and its effect cannot be properly appreciated unless it is remembered that it did incidentally express a general attitude towards government held by increasing numbers of people. These were the days of the Popular Front, of the Spanish Civil War, of a growing awareness of what was happening in Germany and Italy: this was the generation of the thirties, who above everything were tired of the complacency and lethargy exemplarized by the National Government. King Edward VIII could hardly have retained the reputation for championing the cause of the unemployed against the government if it had not been for the growing belief of his subjects that a champion was needed to counter the apathy shown in the face of the appalling conditions in the distressed areas.

The *Daily Mail* leader was immediately countered by a leader in *The Times*:

It is right that the King's contribution to this awakening should be applauded. But it is a wholly mischievous suggestion and one altogether alien to the spirit of the Constitution, which would set his well-known sympathy with the distressed areas against the measures taken by the Government, and which by implication would drive a wedge between the Monarch and his Ministers. The King's Ministers are His Majesty's advisers, and to contrast his personal and representative concern for the well-being of a section of the people with the administrative steps of his advisers is a constitutionally dangerous proceeding and would threaten, if continued, to entangle the throne in politics.... The King's constitutional position is above and apart from party politics, and those who cherish the institution of the Monarchy will always strive to keep it so.

The *Daily Mail* leader was clearly inspired by its owner, Lord Rothermere, whose son Esmond Harmsworth had visited the King at Balmoral and who had joined Lord Beaverbrook in arranging the discretion of the press over Mrs Simpson's divorce suit. In the absence of Lord Beaverbrook on his way to America, these two formed the spearhead of the King's party, and they now made themselves felt in an unexpected way.

Mr Esmond Harmsworth invited Mrs Simpson to lunch with him at Claridge's. His purpose in doing so was to ask whether she had ever considered the possibility of marrying the King morganatically. He explained that a morganatic marriage was one between a member of the Royal House and a woman not of equal birth, in which the wife does not take the husband's rank, and her children are without rights of succession, while their claim on their father's estate is restricted to his personal property. Harmsworth asked Mrs Simpson whether she would be willing to marry the King under these conditions. 'Wallis', the Duke of Windsor tells us, 'replied that the matter was hardly one upon which she could with propriety comment.'

However, in spite of this and one or two other improbable remarks, Mrs Simpson almost certainly favoured this idea as a compromise way out of a situation into which she and the King had so light-heartedly drifted. She immediately explained it to the King, who, although he was not at once attracted to it, nevertheless sent for Mr Harmsworth. He also asked Walter Monckton to look into the legal precedents. Monckton advised him that even in the unlikely event of the Cabinet approving a morganatic marriage, special legislation would be required and there was little prospect of such a bill passing parliament. It is symptomatic of the King's state of mind that in spite of this advice he sent Esmond Harmsworth off to expound the idea to the Prime Minister.

Baldwin agreed with Monckton that parliament would not pass the necessary legislation and he felt sure that 'the British people would never agree to it'. However, he did promise to refer the plan to the Cabinet. Two days later, having heard nothing from the Prime Minister, the King asked him to come and see him. He asked at once what Baldwin thought of this new proposition, and Baldwin replied that he 'had not considered it'. He explained that by this he did not mean that he had given it no thought, but that he had not considered it officially. If, however, the King wanted 'a horseback opinion', he thought that parliament would never pass the necessary legislation. He then explained that if the morganatic marriage proposal was to be 'considered' it would have to be submitted not merely to the British Cabinet but to the Dominion Cabinets as well. He asked the King if he wished him to do that, and the King replied that he did.

On the following day Lord Beaverbrook landed at Southampton and motored straight to the Fort. He was horrified to hear of the morganatic proposal. 'Mrs Simpson', the King said, 'preferred the morganatic marriage to any other solution of the problem.' He also told Beaverbrook that Harmsworth had already laid the morganatic proposal before the Prime Minister. 'In speaking of Mr Harmsworth, the King confessed to some embarrassment. Harmsworth had asked him if I was returning home, and the King had not told him that he himself had recalled me. He asked me to protect him on this point.'

Lord Beaverbrook's dislike of the morganatic marriage proposal was a result of his belief that the politicians had no status at all in the main issue of marriage. The King was free to marry whom he chose and the government had no power in law or in precedent to forbid the banns. But he was not free to make a morganatic marriage because this would require legislation. If the Prime Minister refused time for the necessary bill (or presumably if parliament refused to pass such a bill) the King must accept open humiliation or dismiss his ministers and seek new advisers in the House of Commons. Lord Beaverbrook then gave the King his recommendations, which were: (1) to withdraw the proposal for a morganatic marriage; (2) to find some friend in the Cabinet who would represent his case; (3) not to let the Cabinet reach any decision on any issue until he had measured the strength on either side. He then went off, saying that he would discuss these suggestions with Monckton and also that he would see Sir Samuel Hoare, hoping to persuade him to be the advocate for the King. He found that Monckton agreed with his views and that Hoare could not be persuaded to represent the King, even in the limited role of an advocate who did not necessarily approve of his intentions.

That night, when Lord Beaverbrook at last got to bed after his labours, he was woken at two o'clock in the morning by a telephone call from the King, who was anxious to hear the outcome of his talk with Hoare. 'A conversation took place that greatly embarrassed me. The King spoke with such freedom that I was positively alarmed, and he, in turn, was impatient of the guarded nature of my replies.'

The King then told Beaverbrook once more that, although he approved of his plans and endorsed his recommendations, 'Mrs Simpson preferred the morganatic marriage to any other solution.' 'When he made this statement I knew that the agreement between us was null and void. Whatever he might assent to in his mind, it would not have the agreement of his heart.... A morganatic marriage was what Mrs Simpson wanted, and what Mrs Simpson wanted was what the King wanted.'

Baldwin seems on this occasion to have agreed with Beaverbrook, and told Tom Jones:

The King agreed to go out quietly and he afterwards told this to his Mother and his brothers. But he has clearly now gone back on that. Mrs S. was down at Fort Belvedere over the weekend and has talked him out of it, because on Friday he was where I left him. Walter Monckton wrote telling me that, with the King's knowledge. At our interview the King said he could do nothing without the woman.... There is a 'set' which is backing the marriage. I don't know but I suspect the Beaverbrook-Rothermere Press will take that line.

In fact there was never any chance that the Cabinet would endorse the proposal but, according to Baldwin's biographers Middlemas and Barnes, because of his own dislike of the idea, the Prime Minister was genuinely anxious to see that it was fairly considered. Sir Donald Somervell put the main objection to the idea succinctly if rather cruelly:

I confirmed what of course he knew that the wife of the King is Queen, that it would require an Act of Parliament to prevent this result. I remember adding that it would have been an odd act. If it had been an honest recital it would start, Whereas the wife of the King is Queen & whereas the present King desires to marry a woman unfit to be Queen – be it hereby enacted etc.

And later on, when all this became public, *The Times* put it in rather the same way: 'The constitution is to be amended in order that she may carry in solitary prominence the brand of unfitness for the Queen's Throne.'

Even before he saw the King on 25 November Baldwin had taken the precaution of calling Attlee and Sir Archibald Sinclair (the two leaders of the opposition parties) and Winston Churchill together, and putting to them the question: 'Would they be for or against the government if it came to resignation?' Attlee and Sinclair replied without equivocation that they would refuse to form an alternative government if asked, and Churchill that although his attitude was a little different he would certainly support the government. And in fact Baldwin would have been prepared to resign on this issue. 'Is this the sort of thing I've stood for in public life?' he exclaimed to Tom Jones. 'If I have to go out, as go I must, then I'd be quite ready to go out on this.'

On 27 November Baldwin told his colleagues what had taken place between himself and the King, and explained that, although the King might himself have consulted the Dominion governments through the Governor-Generals on the spot, he was, in Montgomery Hyde's words, 'loath to employ this channel, since he felt that the matter was much too personal, too delicate to be handled by the King himself'. Baldwin said that he was not asking for a decision, but that his colleagues should think it over before the next regular Cabinet meeting on 2 December. Meanwhile telegrams would be sent to the Dominions asking them for their views. The Dominions were asked to choose between three possible courses: (1) that the King should marry Mrs Simpson and she should be recognized as Queen; (2) that he should marry her and she should not become Queen (the morganatic proposal); (3) that the King should abdicate in favour of the Duke of York.

Baldwin was later to be accused, by Beaverbrook and others, and in effect by the Duke of Windsor, of slanting the telegrams against the King. In fact, although he signed them, they were drafted in the Dominions Office, as were all subsequent cables between Whitehall and the Dominions, by Malcolm MacDonald, the Secretary of State, and Sir Henry Batterbee, the Permanent Secretary, with some help from Neville Chamberlain and Sir John Simon.

However, Baldwin was perfectly entitled to make it known that the feeling of the British parliament would in all probability be against the morganatic proposal, and he was also in the position of having to get answers from the Dominions which were not merely unequivocal but could be seen to be so. If by 'impartial' it is meant that he did nothing to influence the Dominion prime ministers on the matter which he believed to be fundamental to the future of the monarchy and which was extremely urgent, then he was not impartial, and it surely would be unproductive to expect any politician in his position to be so.

If the replies which were returned were not in fact unequivocal, it seems to have been more because of an element of the 'backwoods' in their composition, than because of any great difference of view. Thus we are told that Savage of New Zealand, who replied that 'his country would not quarrel with anything the King did, nor with anything his Government did to restrain him', had never before heard of Mrs Simpson and had had to go to the Governor-General for enlightenment. In India, which enjoyed a more limited measure of self-government than the other Dominions, opinion was divided on religious grounds, the Muslims being in favour of the King-Emperor's marriage and the Hindus against it.

However, Canada, Australia and South Africa were perfectly definite, although the Canadian Mackenzie King merely backed Baldwin in whatever decisions he chose to make. The strongest reply came from Lyons, the Prime Minister of Australia, who said that 'in his view His Majesty could not now re-establish his prestige or command confidence as King', while the proposal that Mrs Simpson should become Queen would 'provoke widespread condemnation, and the alternative proposal, or something in the nature of a specially sanctioned morganatic marriage, would run counter to the best popular conception of the Royal Family'. Hertzog of South Africa was almost equally strong, replying that, while abdication would be a 'great shock', a morganatic marriage would be 'a permanent wound'.

Baldwin once more sounded out Attlee, who replied that, while Labour people had no objection at all to an American becoming Queen, he was certain that they would not approve of Mrs Simpson for that position and would object to a morganatic marriage.

Baldwin also sent Sir Samuel Hoare to explain to Lord Beaverbrook the government's attitude. No breach existed, he said; all the ministers stood with Mr Baldwin. And he added that the Prime Minister hoped that when the publicity broke, as it soon must, the press would also present an undivided front. To which the press lord replied in his usual picturesque way that he had taken the 'King's shilling' and was a King's man.

The Cabinet met on 2 December and a general discussion took place. Duff Cooper, alone and in vain, pleaded for delay, suggesting, as he had to the King, that the whole thing might be dropped until after the Coronation and raised again in a year's time. The rest of the Cabinet were unanimous that the morganatic plan was both impracticable and undesirable.

When Baldwin went to see the King on the evening of Thursday 4 December it was therefore to report to him in this sense. By then, however, the whole situation had changed because the British press had at last broken silence on the King's marriage. It is true, nevertheless, as Brian Inglis has remarked, that 'the abdication of King Edward VIII was virtually settled before millions of people in Britain were aware that it was even contemplated, or that there was a crisis of any kind.'

14

The Press Breaks Silence

By the end of November, although the silence of the press was still unbroken, Mrs Simpson's presence in the King's life and physically at Cumberland Terrace began to be very widely known. She could not go about the streets without people turning to stare, strangers loitered about peering at her house, and she even began to receive letters, some of them anonymous.

In other countries, particularly in America and France, the King's Abdication and marriage to Mrs Simpson have often been presented as a 'great romance' – 'the love story of the century'. In England very few people have at any time taken that view. Those who were in favour of allowing the King to marry her and remain on the throne were more inclined to take up a modern and democratic attitude to the monarchy – 'Let him marry whom he pleases' – than any idealized or exalted view of the relationship. Most people saw the Abdication as an incomprehensible and shabby dereliction of duty. 'There are circumstances in the present proposal which freeze the very pulse of Romance,' a writer in the *Daily Telegraph* remarked.

For Mrs Simpson, therefore, the cheers which had so much warmed her heart in Yugoslavia had given way, like the Mediterranean sun, to England's chillier climate. She felt a mounting menace in the air, and many of the letters she received were openly threatening. She was an exceptionally nervous woman and the King was exceptionally nervous for her. When he heard a rumour of a plot to blow up her house, although he believed it to be ridiculous, he arranged for her and her aunt, Mrs Merryman, to join him at the Fort, where they would automatically be guarded. Thus the King and Mrs Simpson were together when the press broke its long silence.

This came about in a manner which had all the by-now-recognizable hallmarks of the Abdication crisis – that is to say, it was not the result of a co-ordinated plan, but happened because in a long period of drift so much steam had been built up that almost any movement of air would be bound to blow the lid off.

On the morning of 1 December the Bishop of Bradford, Dr A. W. F. Blunt, delivered an address to his diocesan conference. According to his later statements, all he intended was a rebuke to Bishop Barnes of Birmingham (a churchman who constantly upset his colleagues by his unorthodoxy and who had suggested that the Coronation should be secularized) and a lament that King Edward was not a more regular churchgoer. What he managed to do, after a dissertation on the religious nature of the Coronation ceremony – 'it is a solemn Sacramental rite, linked up as an integral part in a service

Wallis Simpson and her aunt, Mrs Bessie Merryman, photographed in the grounds of Fort Belvedere in late November by Edward (whose shadow falls across the picture).

of Holy Communion' – was to make some highly equivocal remarks about the chief participant in it:

The benefit of the King's Coronation depends under God upon two elements – firstly on the faith, prayer and self-dedication of the King himself. On that it would be improper for me to say anything except to commend him and ask others to commend him to God's grace, which he will so abundantly need – for the King is a man like any other – if he is to do his duty properly.... We hope that he is aware of this need. Some of us wish that he gave more positive signs of such awareness.

The following morning, 2 December, these remarks of a provincial bishop passed unnoticed in the London newspapers but the *Yorkshire Post* had a leader comment on it. Several other provincial papers likewise commented, while the *Manchester Guardian* published a selection of these comments. The *Yorkshire Post* said:

Dr Blunt must have had good reason for so pointed a remark. Most people by this time are aware that a good deal of rumour regarding the King has been published of late in the more sensational American newspapers. It is proper to treat with contempt mere gossip such as is frequently associated with the names of European royal persons. The Bishop of Bradford would certainly not have condescended to recognize it. But certain statements which have appeared in reputable United States journals, and even we believe in some Dominions newspapers, cannot be treated with quite so much indifference. They are too circumstantial and plainly have a foundation in fact.

For this reason an increasing number of responsible people is led to fear lest the King may not yet have perceived how complete in our day must be that self-dedication of which Dr Blunt spoke if the Coronation is to bring a blessing to all the peoples and is not, on the contrary, to prove a stumbling block....

One other great event had taken place on 1 December – in London the

Crystal Palace had burned down, and once more people were not slow to
see this as an omen. Thus the *Nottingham Journal*, commenting on the
Bishop of Bradford's words, said: 'They seem all the more emphasized by
being uttered on the day when a great monument of Victorian tradition lies
shattered in a smoking ruin.'

On the morning of 2 December the Cabinet had taken the formal, and
with the exception of Duff Cooper, unanimous decision to reject the morganatic proposal on the grounds that it was both impracticable and undesirable. Lord Beaverbrook, lunching immediately afterwards with a member
of the Cabinet, learned without difficulty of this decision, and hurried to
the Palace in a state of agitation which surprised the King. He told him
that he had placed his head on the execution block, leaving Baldwin with
nothing to do but swing the axe.

Lord Beaverbrook asked the King if he had seen the cables to the
Dominions, and hearing that he had not, he told him that they had been
sent to all the Dominions and that they had been framed in the same rigid
way as Baldwin had presented the case to the Cabinet, in effect, 'Do you
recommend the King's marrying morganatically? Or, if the King insists on
marrying, do you recommend abdication?' Beaverbrook then begged the
King to stop them, saying that as a Canadian he knew the Dominions, and
their answer would certainly and swiftly be no. (Apparently neither Lord
Beaverbrook nor the Duke of Windsor appreciated the significance of this
opinion.)

The King also learned of the Cabinet decision from Walter Monckton,
who had been informed by Baldwin. During the day he saw the provincial
papers and in the afternoon Lord Beaverbrook telephoned to warn him to
expect sensational disclosures in the metropolitan morning papers and an
attack in *The Times* from Geoffrey Dawson's fluent and pitiless pen. And
he begged to be allowed to lift the restrictions imposed on the newspapers
friendly to the King, saying that there were many besides himself who held
that there was nothing wrong in the King marrying a woman who had
divorced her husband, and that a strong case could be made. But the King
could not see it that way and in his own account he makes it plain that he
did not desire the responsibility of dividing the nation and was determined
to protect Mrs Simpson from the kind of publicity a newspaper campaign
of this kind would be sure to provoke.

When Baldwin called on the King at six o'clock that evening he found
him very anxious to hear the replies from the Dominion governments, and
he told him that, although these were not yet complete, they had gone far
enough to show that neither in the Dominions nor at home would there
be any prospect of such legislation being accepted. And he showed him
Lyons' telegram.

'What about parliament?' Edward asked.

'The answer would, I am sure, be the same.'

When the King persisted that parliament had not been consulted, Baldwin
replied that he had caused inquiries to be set on foot in the usual manner
and the response had been such as to convince 'my colleagues and myself'
that the people would not approve of a marriage to Mrs Simpson. He then
summed up for the King the three choices before him: (1) he could give
up the idea of marriage; (2) he could marry against the advice of his
ministers; (3) he could marry and abdicate. The Prime Minister prayed that
he would take the first course of action. The second course he described
as 'manifestly impossible', and he explained that, if the King married in

face of the advice of his ministers, he could not remain on the throne. If he would not abandon his project, there was really no choice before him but to go.

The King then said that he seemed in reality to be left with only one choice, and to this Baldwin replied with obvious sincerity that both he and his colleagues hoped he would remain as King. Edward then said explicitly that he would marry Mrs Simpson, even if he had to abdicate to do so.

At this interview Baldwin made the first of several appeals to the King to consider his duty, and that evening he told his wife: 'To all arguments based on responsibility towards his people, the King did not react, not feeling any responsibility which should dictate or influence his conduct.' And he said that the King had said again and again, 'Wallis is the most wonderful woman in the world', and that he could not live without her.

There is no doubt, however, that both the King and Mrs Simpson were shattered by the comments of the British press. The tone of even the most scurrilous articles appearing in America and elsewhere had always been friendly, even at times admiring. They had counted absolutely on his popularity, and they had never imagined a situation in which neither his power and position, nor the deference and love of his people, would be strong enough to shield them from criticism.

The King had that almost pathological dislike of the press which, not unknown in other members of the Royal Family, is the result of being of perpetual interest to it. He had been particularly upset by Beaverbrook's suggestion that there would be a critical leader in *The Times* the following morning, and he had convinced himself that Dawson would attack Mrs Simpson. At this interview with Baldwin he had been insistent that the Prime Minister must prevent this. Dawson recorded:

> In the late evening, as I was struggling with the paper, he [Baldwin] rang me up twice himself ... to say that His Majesty was worrying him to find out, and if necessary to stop, what was going to appear in *The Times*.... In vain S.B. had explained [to the King] that the Press in England was free, and that he had no control over *The Times* or over any other newspaper. When he spoke to me, full of apologies, the second time, it was to say that the King would now be satisfied, and leave the Prime Minister alone, if the latter would read the leading article for him. Could I possibly let him see it for the sake of peace?

Dawson sent a proof of the leader round to Downing Street, where, by the time it arrived, the Prime Minister was in bed and asleep.

But the King need not have worried because, although *The Times* devoted a column and a half to a leader on the crisis, it said very little and did not mention Mrs Simpson by name. 'The storm breaks,' Sir Harold Nicolson wrote in his diary. 'A fine leading article in the *Telegraph* and a confused muddled jumble in *The Times*. I suspect that when Geoffrey Dawson sees a vital crisis he writes the leader himself, and the result is an amalgam of tortuous and pompous nothings. The other papers write in sorrow rather than in anger.' Indeed it was the *Daily Telegraph*, not *The Times*, which emerged with most credit from the crisis, but on 3 December it was the *News Chronicle* which attracted most attention because it was the only paper to mention the morganatic proposal.

The press comments had had an even greater effect on Mrs Simpson than on the King, and had convinced her, as Hardinge's letter had failed to do, that she must leave the country. The King, who had been worried by threats of danger to her, was also anxious for her to leave.

After some discussion it was agreed that she should go to the Villa Lou

Vieie at Cannes, the house of her old friends the Herman Rogers, and the King arranged for his chauffeur to drive her there, and for his friend and Lord-in-Waiting, Lord Brownlow, and his personal detective to accompany her.

They left England on the evening of 3 December, followed by the 'hounds of the Press'. These gentlemen did their level best to live up to the Duchess' description of them and she has told in detail of the extraordinary chase across France, which had all the ingredients of a film sequence but must in reality have been an unpleasant experience. Lord Brownlow fitted admirably into the scenario since he turned out to be present in the role of 'double agent'. At a meeting at Lord Beaverbrook's house the evening before, at which Walter Monckton and Mr Allen, the King's solicitor, were present, it had been agreed that the best, if not the only, method of keeping the King on the throne was to persuade Mrs Simpson to make an act of renunciation. Lord Brownlow was the chosen agent and his task was to urge her to leave the country. Consequently, he was considerably taken aback to be asked by the King the following morning to escort her to France.

Then, as a result of a conversation he had with the King before leaving, Lord Brownlow realized for the first time how far things had already gone, and he changed his tactics. On the journey to Newhaven, instead of persuading Mrs Simpson to leave the country, he urged her to stay and go with him to Belton, his country house, on the grounds that if she left England the King would follow her. But Mrs Simpson replied that she could not see how going to Lincolnshire instead of to Cannes could affect the situation:

At the beginning of December the British press broke silence and, although at first they did not mention Mrs Simpson by name, she decided she must leave England. She arranged to stay with the Herman Rogers in Cannes, and left on 3 December, accompanied by a detective and Lord Brownlow (in the doorway), and followed by the 'hounds of the Press'.

My separation from David would be nearly absolute, whether the actual distance between us was one hundred miles or seven hundred. Knowing David as I did I was more than doubtful that anyone, including me, could change his mind. If I stayed and my pleas failed, I should always be accused of secretly urging him to give up the throne. I told Perry, therefore, that I did not see how his plan could work. If I were to go to Belton . . . and if, in the end, the King should decide to abdicate, the blame attaching to me would be even more bitter than was already the case. It would be said that I was afraid of losing the King; that, having left him at the Fort, I had lost heart and run back in order to hold him.

'You must remember', I said, 'that until this morning I was an utter stranger to all but a handful of people in Great Britain. There is no one to speak for me. I am sure there is only one solution: that is for me to remove myself from the King's life. That is what I am doing now.'

When the Duchess of Windsor wrote these words in her memoirs, she used them as a literary flourish, a statement which did justice to her feelings as she travelled with Lord Brownlow towards Newhaven on that memorable night. She did not, of course, intend to be believed.

All through France at every stopping place she telephoned to the King and, as soon as she reached the Rogers' home at Cannes, began lengthy daily telephone conversations with him. Only a few days later she explained to Lord Brownlow why it would be wrong for her even to attempt to leave the King, and in the meantime she had left him behind at work on a scheme for an appeal against the verdict of his Prime Minister – the only one for which he ever appeared to have much personal relish. A few days before he had said to her that, if there were only some way of making his position known to his people, their decent and loyal sentiments would be felt and the situation reversed, and she had suggested that he should deliver a broadcast in the manner of President Roosevelt's 'fireside chats'. The King adopted her idea with enthusiasm and began to work on a speech. He seems to have been fired by a project that gave him both scope for his special talents and something to do.

The Duke of Windsor says that he sought no special privileges, merely something that the fundamental laws of his realm allowed to his subjects but that the Prime Minister proposed to deny him. He would tell his people that he was determined to marry Mrs Simpson but he did not insist that his wife should be Queen. All that he asked was that 'our married happiness should carry with it a proper title and dignity for her, befitting my wife'. He then made the naïve and unconsidered suggestion that he should leave England for a while so that the country could reflect 'calmly and quietly, but without undue delay' on this matter, and he wrote later that he had tentatively fixed on Belgium as a convenient place to await his people's verdict. This proposal had the two insuperable disadvantages that to ask his subjects to make this decision over the heads of his ministers would have been unconstitutional, and that it required them to arrive at a majority decision by some unspecified means. Although astonishment at the extraordinary lack of judgment the King revealed was tempered by the knowledge of his psychological and emotional state, fifteen years later the Duke of Windsor was still showing the same confidence in the propriety and practical possibility of this scheme.

As soon as he had finished the draft, the King left Fort Belvedere and drove straight to Buckingham Palace to receive Baldwin who had been summoned to hear his new proposal. The King was dead tired and without wasting words he thrust the draft of his speech into the astonished Prime Minister's hands. Baldwin read it and said he would consult his colleagues, but added that he had no doubt what their opinion would be. And he told the King that an appeal to the people over the head of the government would be unconstitutional. The King's answer was rather confused. 'You want me to go, don't you?' he said. 'And before I go, I think it is right for her sake and mine that I should speak.'

To this Baldwin replied:

What I want, Sir, is what you told me you wanted: to go with dignity, not dividing the country, and making things as smooth as possible for your successor. To broadcast would be to go over the heads of your Ministers and speak to the people. You will be telling millions throughout the world – among them a vast number of women – that you are determined to marry one who has a husband living. They will want to know all about her, and the Press will ring with gossip, the very thing you want to avoid. You may, by speaking, divide opinion; but you will certainly harden it.

Baldwin then tried to explain to the King the danger of the King's Proctor intervening before the Simpson divorce was made absolute. He left, having promised to call a special Cabinet meeting to consider the broadcast and, because he did not wish to provoke the King, having agreed that he might consult Winston Churchill. (The following morning he told his colleagues that he thought this was his first mistake.)

When he had gone, the King sent for Walter Monckton and Mr Allen, who were in the Palace, and asked them to take a copy of his broadcast to Lord Beaverbrook and ask for his comments and advice, with a message that he would also like Mr Churchill to see it. (Both these men returned the opinion that his idea would almost certainly be resisted as 'an appeal by the King to the people over the heads of the Executive'.)

Then, tired as he was, the King drove to Marlborough House to see his mother. She told him she had found the newspapers somewhat upsetting, particularly as she had not seen him for ten days. To this he replied that his aloofness had been due to a desire to spare his family from being involved in a matter which he must handle alone, a bland explanation which could not disguise the enveloping egotism and total lack of concern for his family which was characteristic of the King at the time. Although the decision he would finally make would affect the life of his brother as much as his own, and although his mother still mourned his father, all his family were excluded from his councils and even denied access to him except when he chose on rare occasions to see them. The Duke of York seems never to have been consulted about his willingness to take up the duties his brother threw down. The following record in the Duke of York's diary speaks for itself:

The Prime Minister went to see him at 9.0 p.m. that evening and later (in Mary's and my presence) David said to Queen Mary that he could not live alone as King & must marry Mrs— When David left after making this dreadful announcement to his mother he told me to come & see him at the Fort the next morning [Friday 4 December]. I rang him up but he would not see me and put me off till Saturday. I told him I would be at Royal Lodge on Saturday by 12.30 p.m. 'Come & see me on Sunday' was his answer. 'I will see you & tell you my decision when I have made up my mind.' Sunday evening I rang up. 'The King has a conference & will speak to you later' was the answer. But he did not ring up. Monday morning, December 7, came. I rang up at 1.0 p.m. and my brother told me he might be able to see me that evening.... My brother rang me up at 10 minutes to 7.0 p.m. to say 'Come & see me after dinner.' I said 'No, I will come & see you at once.' I was with him at 7.0 p.m. The awful & ghastly suspense of waiting was over. I found him pacing up & down & he told me his decision that he would go.

The truth is that at this time the King's family found him a little mad. After the Abdication was over Queen Mary told more than one person that to all her appeals he had answered: 'All that matters is our happiness', and repeated this over and over again.

On the evening of 3 December, when the King has returned to Buckingham Palace, he announced to Walter Monckton his intention of going to the Fort, and Monckton, horrified that he should be alone, so tired and so late, went with him. The King left Buckingham Palace that night never to enter it again as King, and he remained at the Fort until the crisis ended. He was by now completely out of touch with the Household, owing to his estrangement from his Private Secretary, and Monckton used the Windham Club as an unofficial London headquarters for the King's business, a room being set aside for him. Monckton and Sir Ulick Alexander, the Keeper of the Privy Purse, slept at the Fort, as did Mr Allen sometimes, and they were often joined by Sir Edward Peacock, the Receiver General of the Duchy of Cornwall, who had a house nearby. Monckton and Peacock made notes of the events of those days, and have left us a picture of the all-male society at Fort Belvedere in the last days of the King's reign. All four men worked for the King, none of them approved of his decision, all believed that he failed in his duty, but they made no appeals to him, nor did they question his right to do as he pleased. They served him faithfully and willingly and felt affection and concern for him. In the seclusion of his chosen group he was as charming as ever; on every issue except the main one he behaved impeccably and he clearly suffered an appalling strain.

He almost certainly gave up any serious intention of retaining the throne on the morning of 4 December after Baldwin had warned him that the Cabinet would not consent to his broadcast. On that day Monckton informed Lord Beaverbrook that he could see him no more. 'He was engaging in

Edward sat up late into the night of 10 December at Fort Belvedere, when this photo was taken, writing the speech he was to broadcast to the nation the following evening.

Winston Churchill, who encouraged Edward to resist pressures to abdicate, believing that the King's popularity would prove the overriding factor in the crisis.

negotiations with the Government on the terms of abdication and must dissociate himself with those who were in the other camp. He did not wish to endanger the financial conditions of the Abdication by maintaining contacts of which Baldwin disapproved.' And, although Lord Beaverbrook then appealed to the King for an interview, his appeal was firmly rejected.

Yet on the same day the King said to Sir Lionel Halsey, with whom he was discussing some matters concerning the Duchy of Cornwall: 'I am by no means sure that I am going but wish to clear these points just in case.' And Sir Edward Peacock noted: 'Winston C had seen His Majesty that day and urged him to fight for the morganatic marriage, and assured him that he would get strong support. This had, I think, momentarily unsettled His Majesty ... but, as soon appeared, this hesitation was short-lived.'

Churchill himself had been unsettled by the events of the night before. He had been the chief speaker at a rally at the Albert Hall, the purpose of which was to attack the government for its failure to re-arm, and he announced beforehand that he would incorporate in his speech an appeal on behalf of the King. Beaverbrook warned him not to do this and Citrine said he would leave the platform if he did, and, although he gave the text of his speech in *The Gathering Storm*, he did not actually make it. Nevertheless, he was much inspired by the fervour with which the crowd sang 'God Save the King' at the end of the meeting, and the next day he issued the text of his speech to the press.

The rally at the Albert Hall has been taken by several historians to be the starting point of what they have seen as a movement of support for the King and a moment of real danger of a constitutional crisis. It is extremely difficult to assess what actually occurred. Monckton, for instance, says: 'Between Thursday and Sunday 6th there was a great wave of sympathy for the King and a desire in many quarters to retain him at all cost.' Yet on the night that Churchill was so moved by the singing of 'God Save the King' at the Albert Hall, Sir Harold Nicolson, speaking of an address which he gave in a chapel in Islington, wrote:

At the end Paxton asked them to sing the National Anthem 'as a hymn'. They all stand up and there are no protests, but only about ten out of 400 join in the singing. Poor Paxton is much upset. 'I never dreamt', he said afterwards, 'that I should live to see the day when my congregation refused to sing "God Save the King".'

And Nicolson added: 'I do not find people angry with Mrs Simpson. But I do find a deep and enraged fury against the King himself. In eight months he has destroyed the great structure of popularity which he had raised.'

Crowds formed outside Buckingham Palace, Downing Street and St James's Palace, and people carried boards announcing that they wished the King to stay or Baldwin to go. However, the Duke of Windsor himself says, 'the crowds were not large or particularly demonstrative', although he adds that their sympathies were unmistakably with the King. Finally Oswald Mosley declared for the King: a circumstance which Keith Middlemas and John Barnes believe had some influence on Edward's decision – 'Especially he would not put himself at the disposal of Mosley's Blackshirts' – and one which would certainly not have worried the government.

Whatever the real division of opinion it was certainly at this time that the King's supporters made some kind of a bid. The text of Churchill's speech for the Albert Hall meeting, that was now released to the press, was in essence an appeal for patience, but it accused the government of having solicited assurances from the Leader of the Opposition that he would not form an alternative administration in the event of their resignation (Attlee promptly denied this) and thus confronted the King with an ultimatum. And all this week the Beaverbrook–Rothermere press and the *Daily Mirror* spoke for the King directly and published articles presenting Mrs Simpson in an attractive light. (The American press, delighted at being proved right, devoted more space than ever to the story.) The *News Chronicle*, strongly non-conformist in character, surprised everyone by supporting the King, but the *Daily Herald* supported Baldwin and the constitutional argument,

British newspaper headlines at the time of the crisis.

THE CHOICE

This highly serious cartoon appeared in Punch. It shows Baldwin saying to Edward: 'All the peoples of your Empire, sir, sympathise with you most deeply, but they all know, as you yourself must, that the throne is greater than the man.'

as did *The Times, Telegraph, Morning Post, Manchester Guardian, Sunday Times, Observer* and virtually all the provincial papers.

On the morning of 4 December Baldwin called a Cabinet meeting to discuss the King's request to broadcast, at which it was unanimously decided that it would be impossible, while he was King, to allow him either to broadcast or make any other public utterance which had not been approved by his ministers, since constitutionally they must be responsible for his words. Then the Cabinet attempted to induce Baldwin to deliver an ultimatum warning the King that the matter could not drag on and saying that they must have an answer by midnight, but Baldwin rejected their advice.

At four o'clock on the same day, immediately before the House of Commons adjourned for the weekend, in response to 'widely circulated suggestions as to certain possibilities in the event of the King's marriage', the Prime Minister made a statement on the morganatic proposal. Having explained to the House that there was no such thing as a morganatic marriage in English law and that the Royal Marriages Act of 1772 had no application to the King himself, he went on to point out that 'the lady whom he marries ... necessarily becomes Queen'. This, he explained, would mean that she would enjoy all the status, rights and privileges which attach to that position and that her children would be in the direct line of succession to the throne. 'The only possible way in which this result could be avoided would be by legislation dealing with a particular case. His Majesty's Government are not prepared to introduce such legislation.' When he said these words cheering broke out all over the House and, according to the political correspondent of the *Daily Telegraph*, 'rose to a striking demonstration so prolonged that, for a little while, Mr Baldwin could not continue'.

When the House adjourned for the weekend, Baldwin, accompanied by Major Dugdale, his Parliamentary Private Secretary, drove to Fort Belvedere to inform the King of the Cabinet decision on the question of his broadcast. After the King had heard it, he dropped the matter and never mentioned it again, but it was the turning point after which he decided to abdicate. He wished now to bring the audience to an end, but Baldwin went on to warn him that the sooner he came to a definite decision the better because of a danger of a constitutional crisis, but he added that it was the prayer of himself and his colleagues that the King would change his mind. After he had gone, the King reflected that for him to change his mind would mean publicly renouncing the woman he had asked to marry him, a surrender that would cause the Crown, 'that noble ornament', to 'rest upon a head forever bowed in shame'.

At the time he merely said that he would let the Prime Minister know as soon as possible. Baldwin did not press him further because, as he afterwards told the Cabinet, 'However great the inconveniences and even risk, the decision when taken must be the spontaneous decision of the King.'

Two things temporarily weakened the King's resolution to end the crisis. The first, as we have seen, was the influence of Winston Churchill, who dined at the Fort on the Friday and urged the King to ask for time 'in order to see what measure of support he received'. But both Monckton and Peacock are agreed that his influence was only temporary, and Peacock says that two days later the King said Winston had been very amusing but was quite wrong in what he suggested, and that such a course would be inexcusable. Peacock added: 'He spoke with gratitude of Stanley Baldwin's kindness and help.'

The second and more important influence was that of Mrs Simpson on

the telephone from Cannes. Walter Monckton says that the King spoke to her every day, sometimes twice a day. 'These telephone calls, with a bad line at a long distance, will never be forgotten by any of us. The house is so shaped that if a voice is raised in any room on the ground floor it can be heard more or less distinctly in the whole house.' And Sir Edward Peacock said, more explicitly:

Reporters wait outside the gates of Fort Belvedere for news of any developments.

There was evidently a certain wavering in the King's mind for a short time after Winston's call, based upon the hope inspired by Winston that something could be done, and also, as I know, upon the insistence over the telephone of the lady that he should fight for his rights. She kept up that line until near the end, maintaining that he was King and his popularity would carry everything, etc. With him this lasted only a very short time; then he realized the falsity of the position, and put it definitely aside, saying that under no circumstances would he be a party to a constitutional crisis, or any other move that would weaken the constitution or cause trouble between the Crown and its Ministers.

Mrs Simpson, misled for so long by the King himself, could not fail to be influenced by the views of Lord Beaverbrook and Winston Churchill, and undoubtedly believed that, if the King would only fight, he would win.

Churchill had also endeavoured to put some heart back into Lord Beaverbrook. He drove straight from dinner with the King to Stornoway House. The King telephoned himself to Beaverbrook to tell him of Churchill's coming and Beaverbrook concluded 'that he had changed his mind and was ready to fight for his Throne after all'. But on the morning of 5 December Beaverbrook received news that the King had sent Walter Monckton to London to tell the Prime Minister of his formal intention to abdicate. Beaverbrook wrote later:

The responsibility was the King's. Throughout all the days of public controversy he shackled the Press that was favourable to himself. He would allow us no liberty in expressing our views or in arguing for his cause. His chief desire was to secure a minimum of publicity for Mrs Simpson. He was also anxious to avoid any suggestion of conflict with Baldwin. As a result, the pro-Baldwin Press had the field all to itself.

Reluctantly he was forced to admit to Churchill: 'Our cock won't fight.'

15

The Last Days

Lord Beaverbrook's information was correct and on Saturday afternoon, 5 December, Monckton formally told Baldwin of the King's decision to abdicate. Thus the crisis was over. On Monday 7 December it could be seen to be over, the King and his subjects having separately reached a decision which coincided too closely for any further disruption or interruption of their intentions to be possible. When members of parliament returned from their constituencies after the weekend, they were in a mood of solid agreement. Whether or not there had been any real danger of a constitutional crisis the week before, it quickly became clear that, once the situation was fully understood, the country as a whole felt quite strongly that the King could not marry and remain on the throne.

The House of Commons showed their solidarity by turning on Winston Churchill. His press release had made him unpopular, and when he attempted to ask the Prime Minister for an assurance that no irrevocable step would be taken, he was actually howled down. It is an appalling thing to have several hundred men unexpectedly turn and yell at one, and Churchill was horrified and suitably chastened.

A new diarist had now appeared on the scene, Blanche Dugdale, who gives us an unsurpassable account of the King's mood on the same day:

Lunched at the Club with Walter [Elliot] who explains the King's *one* idea is Mrs Simpson. Nothing that stands between him and her will meet his approval. The Crown is only valuable if it would interest *her*. He must have marriage because then she can be with him always. Therefore he has no wish to form a 'Party' who would keep him on the Throne and let her be his mistress. Therefore he has no animosity against Ministers who are not opposing his abdication.... He is very upset by the newspapers, never having seen anything but fulsome adulation in all his forty years!

The last week of the King's reign was not uneventful. Both his own advisers and the government had for some time been increasingly worried by his vulnerability, if he abdicated, to an intervention by the King's Proctor in Mrs Simpson's divorce suit. Monckton says: 'I was desperately afraid that the King might give up his throne and yet be deprived of his chance to marry Mrs Simpson.' On Saturday 5 December he suggested a solution to Baldwin when the Prime Minister visited the King at the Fort. His proposal was that there should be two bills – one giving effect to the King's wish to renounce the throne and the other making Mrs Simpson's decree nisi absolute immediately. And he wrote: 'This would finally have cleared up a grave constitutional position affecting the whole world and have left no ragged ends or possibilities of further scandal.'

Describing the scene at Fort Belvedere when Monckton made his suggestion to Baldwin, the Duke of Windsor wrote that Baldwin himself thought it a just accommodation but said that some opposition must be expected from his colleagues. He promised his own support and then said that in the event of the Cabinet refusing the second bill he would resign.

On Sunday morning there was a meeting of senior ministers at which Baldwin did what he could to urge his colleagues to accept Monckton's suggestion. However, the others feared an outcry of one law for the rich and one law for the poor, and thought that to rush the decree through would publicly confirm the worst about Mrs Simpson and give the appearance of a bargain. Neville Chamberlain put the reasons against it as follows: (1) it could not be denied that the King regarded the bill as a condition of abdication, and it would therefore be denounced as an unholy bargain; (2) it would irretrievably damage the moral authority of the government at home and in the Empire; (3) it would be looked on as an injury to the marriage law in general; (4) it would injure the respect for the monarchy.

By this time, too, the Cabinet were anxious to get the whole matter wound up. It was hurting the Christmas trade (incredibly this seems to have been true), 'holding up business' and 'paralysing our foreign policy'. And Chamberlain at least was also tired of the continued opportunity given to the 'Simpson Press' to misrepresent what was happening. He complained:

> The public is being told that we are engaged in a fight with the King, because we have advised him to abdicate and he has refused. That is quite untrue, and we must say so. He asked us to examine the morganatic marriage proposal, we told him we could have nothing to do with it, and he has accepted that view. The public is also being told that we are trying to rush the King into a decision that he has not time to think over. That is equally untrue. He has been thinking it over for weeks, though he has been unwilling to face up to realities.

When Monckton was called in to be told that the Cabinet could not agree to the second bill he said that the decision would greatly disappoint the King who, in the light of it, would undoubtedly ask for additional time for thought. But Monckton's response had come from the depths of his deep disappointment, for at Fort Belvedere preparations for the Abdication went on. (When asked directly by the 3rd Earl Baldwin whether his father had promised to resign if he could not persuade the Cabinet, but had not kept his word, Monckton made it plain that the Prime Minister had offered his resignation but he had assured him that 'he was perfectly certain that the King would permit no such action, and persuaded S.B. not to consider it further.' And he said he confirmed this with the King immediately after.)

The events of Monday 7 December are obscure and likely to remain so because everyone gives a different account.

In Cannes, under the influence of Lord Brownlow, Mrs Simpson prepared a statement for the press, which read: 'Mrs Simpson, throughout the last few weeks, has invariably wished to avoid any action or proposal which would hurt or damage His Majesty or the Throne. Today her attitude is unchanged, and she is willing, if such action would solve the problem, to withdraw from a situation that has been rendered both unhappy and untenable.' Lord Brownlow doubted that this statement was sufficiently strong, and wished for a forthright declaration that Mrs Simpson had no intention of marrying the King. But she shrank from dealing him so cruel a blow. She also telephoned the King to tell him of her decision and to read him the statement. 'After I finished there was a long silence. I thought that David in his anger had hung up. Then he said slowly, "Go ahead, if you wish; it won't make any difference."'

The Duke of Windsor's account is not very different, although he leaves out the anger. 'It did not occur to me that she was asking to be released. Yet that was what she meant. And others read into her statement the same thing.'

However, according to both Monckton and Sir Edward Peacock, the King was a party to this statement and it was given to the press with his approval. Monckton says:

Meantime he was most anxious that Mrs Simpson's position should be improved in the eyes of the public, and it was with his full approval that she made her statement on Tuesday, December 8, from Cannes that she was willing to give up a position that had become both unhappy and untenable. This, when published, was looked upon as being perhaps the end of the crisis, but we at the Fort knew of the statement before its publication, and that his intention was quite unchanged.

And Sir Edward Peacock commented: 'She apparently began to think of her own unpopularity, and a statement was suggested, which she issued from Cannes. The King approved, well realizing that this would to some extent divert criticism from her to him, the very thing he wanted.'

On the same day that this statement was circulated to the press, Theodore Goddard learned that another affidavit was about to be served on the King's Proctor by a private individual, to the effect that the intervener was in a position to show why the decree should not be made absolute 'by reason of material facts not having been brought before the court and/or by reason of the divorce having been obtained by collusion'. Goddard felt that he ought to see his client (some say because of the intervention, others because she had begun to issue statements to the press) and he told Monckton that he proposed to go to Cannes. However, when Monckton told the King, he sent for Goddard and forbade him to go. On hearing this, Baldwin then also sent for Goddard and encouraged him to go. His reasons for wanting Goddard to go to see Mrs Simpson are obscure and have been given different interpretations. His biographers believe that he 'made a last and almost certainly genuine attempt to get Mrs Simpson to give up the King' by withdrawing her divorce action. Other motives have been attributed to him, although only Lord Beaverbrook managed to think of one that was discreditable. (He believed that Baldwin did it because, if Mrs Simpson could have been persuaded to withdraw, he would have been absolved without shame from his promise to resign – a likely motive for someone who, according to Beaverbrook, had been plotting for weeks to bring about the Abdication of the King.)

Another solution which has had quite a wide circulation is that when Mrs Simpson left England she took with her the emeralds which Queen Alexandra brought from Denmark at the time of her marriage, and Goddard was sent over simply to get them back. For obvious reasons it is not possible to find corroboration for this. All one can say is that Lord Davidson believed it, and told it to more than one person.

And certainly without some explanation of this kind Baldwin's action seems incomprehensible. When, after weeks of negotiation, he had reached an agreement which, even if it was not entirely satisfactory, brought a much-needed end to the crisis, and done this without putting pressure on the King or dividing the country, why should he try to re-open the whole thing by sending Goddard on this errand? Two things give weight to the idea that this was, nevertheless, what he did. The first is that the Duchess of Windsor's account confirms it. The other is the rest of Baldwin's conduct at the time.

In many ways a humorous man, Baldwin had great areas of unsophistication, one might even say insensitivity, and he invariably over-rated his influence with the King. On the day Goddard left for Cannes he decided that Edward must consult his conscience and that he was the man to make him do it. 'He must wrestle with himself in a way he has never done before,' he is reported to have said, 'and, if he will let me, I will help him. We may even have to see the night through together.' And packing his bag and accompanied by Dugdale, he set off for Fort Belvedere.

The King was surprised when Monckton told him of the Prime Minister's proposed visit, remarking that he thought everything had already been said, but he agreed to receive him.

On arrival at Fort Belvedere, Walter Monckton, who travelled down with the Prime Minister, saw at once that the King was in a state of utter exhaustion and 'seemed worn out'. He also showed obvious signs of distress at the sight of Baldwin's suitcase. Monckton then went to Sir Edward Peacock, who was in the house, and arranged for him to ask the Prime Minister to stay with him at his own house, Bodens Ride, nearby. However, as soon as this suggestion was made to Baldwin, he said it would be better for him to return to London.

In recounting this episode in *A King's Story*, the Duke of Windsor is at his most hostile to Baldwin, charging him with paying this visit merely because it would make his own part in the crisis sound better if he could claim to have made a 'humble and sincere' effort to get the King to change his mind. And he goes on to say that he went to Sir Edward Peacock and asked him to take Baldwin away. This account gives a good deal of interest to the notes Sir Edward made at the time:

He [the King] said to me that at the moment he felt unable to have people about & seemed completely done. I suggested that I take the Prime Minister & Dugdale away & give them dinner at Bodens Ride, but he said immediately: 'I could not do that. The Prime Minister has been so kind as to come here to help me, I could not let him leave without giving him dinner. He must stay.' I finally secured his assent to arrange with the Prime Minister that he & Dugdale should go home after dinner, but he was urgent that I should not do so unless I was sure that it would not hurt the PM's feelings.

Here is Monckton's account of the interview that took place between Baldwin and the King:

Once again when the audience took place I was present with the Prime Minister and the King. The Prime Minister was a little deaf when he was tired, and on this occasion it had a curious result, as when the Prime Minister had urged once again all that he could do to dissuade the King, for the sake of the country and all that the King stood for, from his decision to marry, the King wearily said that his mind was made up and he asked to be spared any more advice on the subject. To my astonishment, Mr Baldwin returned to the charge with renewed vigour and, I thought, put the position even better than before. He asked me immediately afterwards if I thought he had said all that he could, and when I explained that I thought he had done even more, it was plain that he had not heard the King's request to him to desist.

The audience took place in the drawing-room.... I can see them sitting there now, the King in his chair in front of the fire, Mr Baldwin at right angles to him on the sofa, and myself on a chair between them. It was the room in which the Abdication was to be signed in three days' time.

The grim faces of Edward and his brother Albert, Duke of York, not long before the Abdication announcement.

That night there were nine to dinner, the King, the Dukes of York and Kent, Monckton, Peacock, Allen, Ulick Alexander, Baldwin and Dugdale. The King was as jolly as a lark. Monckton wrote:

This dinner party was, I think, his *tour de force*. In that quiet pannelled room he sat at the head of the table with his boyish face and smile, with a good fresh colour while the rest of us were pale as sheets, rippling over with bright conversation, and with a careful eye to see that his guests were being looked after.... As the dinner went on the Duke [of York] turned to me and said: 'Look at him. We simply cannot let him go.' But we both knew there was nothing we could say or do to stop him.

In the meantime in Cannes it seems likely that Mrs Simpson understood for the first time the inevitable end of this affair and did indeed agree to do anything that might prevent the King from abdicating. She was ready to surrender everything, even to withdraw her divorce petition. Goddard telephoned to Baldwin the following message:

I have today discussed the whole position with Mrs Simpson – her own, the position of the King, the country, the Empire. Mrs Simpson tells me she was, and still is, perfectly willing to instruct me to withdraw her petition for divorce and willing to do anything to prevent the King from abdicating. I am satisfied that this is Mrs Simpson's genuine and honest desire. I read this note over to Mrs Simpson who in every way confirmed it.

(signed) Theodore Goddard
(counter-signed) Brownlow

But this whole absurd adventure had been begun days, even weeks, too late, and, if it had been successful, could only have resulted in the King losing both the throne and his future wife. By now the King was absolutely determined, and surely he was right to believe that, if he had given up Mrs Simpson for the Crown at this juncture, it would have rested on a head 'forever bowed in shame'. No one could alter his decision.

However, now it was the turn of the Cabinet, previously so anxious for an ultimatum, to have second thoughts, although this may have been the result of a wish to safeguard themselves. A formal message was sent to the King: 'Ministers are reluctant to believe that Your Majesty's resolve is irrevocable and still venture to hope that before Your Majesty pronounces any formal decision, Your Majesty may be pleased to reconsider an intention which must so deeply distress and so vitally affect all Your Majesty's subjects.' The King replied: 'His Majesty has given the matter his further consideration but regrets he is unable to alter his decision.'

Nothing remained but the formalities and the arrangements for the King's future rank and finance.

On 9 December Monckton and Peacock went to see the Duke of York and 'secured his assent to His Majesty retaining Royal Rank & that if and when he is allowed to come to England he should have the Fort to live in. The Duke of York authorized Monckton to tell this to the King.'

Later on the same day Monckton and Simon drafted the King's Message to Parliament. And later still Monckton went back to Downing Street where arrangements were made for the Instrument of Abdication and the Messages to be distributed throughout the Empire at the right time and place. He also had an interview with Queen Mary who said to him: 'To give up all this for that!'

Monckton arrived at Fort Belvedere with the draft Message and the draft Instrument of Abdication at 1 a.m. the next morning. Sir Edward Peacock was already there and had told the King of a Cabinet decision that he should stay out of England for a period of not less than two years.

On Thursday morning, 10 December, the Instrument of Abdication was signed and witnessed by the King's three brothers, as was the King's Message to the House of Commons. That afternoon the Speaker to the House of Commons read the King's Message to a packed House and, speaking from notes, Baldwin then made one of the most famous speeches of his whole career. Here is Sir Harold Nicolson's account of it:

The Prime Minister then rises. He tells the whole story.... His papers are in a confused state ... and he hesitates somewhat. He confuses dates and turns to Simon, 'It was Monday, was it not, the 27th?' The artifice of such asides is so effective that one imagines it to be deliberate. There is no moment when he overstates emotion or indulges in oratory. There is intense silence broken only by reporters in the gallery scuttling away to telephone the speech paragraph by paragraph. I suppose that in after-centuries men will read the words of that speech and exclaim. 'What an opportunity wasted!' They will never know the tragic force of its simplicity. 'I said to the King....' 'The King told me....' It was Sophoclean and almost unbearable.

When *A King's Story* appeared it became clear nevertheless that the speech left the King with a grievance. That morning Baldwin had asked Walter Monckton whether there were any special points the King would like him to mention, and the King sent him two notes: one asking him to say that he and the Duke of York had always been on the best of terms as brothers and 'the King is confident the Duke deserves and will receive

the support of the whole Empire'; the other asking him to say that 'the other
person most intimately concerned had consistently tried to the last to dissuade the King from the decision which he had taken'. Baldwin read out
the first note but he did not mention the second. In the same way the first
note was found among his papers, the second was not. To anyone who has
studied what Baldwin felt, it seems obvious that, whereas the King would
undoubtedly have sent such a request, Baldwin would have found it impossible to comply with it. How easy, if that were so, to crumple it up in one's
pocket.

The financial arrangements for the future Duke of Windsor were initially
discussed by the Cabinet, and Hardinge pressed the Prime Minister through
Walter Monckton to combine in the Instrument of Abdication the provision
for an income of £25,000 a year with an undertaking on the ex-King's part
not to return to the country without the consent of the Monarch and the
government of the day. And Monckton makes it plain that he believed that
if the King had made up his mind earlier he would have negotiated from
greater strength.

However, in the end the financial arrangements were made not with the
government but with the Duke of York. Probably the chief reason for this
was that any settlement had to take into account the peculiar position of
Balmoral and Sandringham, of which, under the wills of Queen Victoria
and King George V, Edward VIII was a life tenant. Any satisfactory financial
settlement had to be based on the transfer of those to his brother. Naturally
no one but their financial and legal advisers was a party to the settlement,
but informed guesses put the figure for Sandringham and Balmoral at one
million pounds and the yearly income paid by George VI to his brother at
£60,000. Over and beyond this the Duke of Windsor is believed to have
taken substantial sums out of the country from other sources.

At Fort Belvedere only one thing seriously upset the King. This was a
message from Sir John Simon saying that in the changed circumstances he
would feel bound to withdraw the detective who had been guarding Mrs
Simpson at Cannes. The King was so greatly distressed that Monckton pro-
tested to Simon who, possibly as a result of this, decided to bear the brunt
of any criticism himself, and reversed the order.

The day ended with what Lord Birkenhead has described as 'an emotional
and somewhat embarrassing evening'. Mr and Mrs Hunter, who were
friends of the King's, had been invited to dinner and Monckton, who was
not present, received from Peacock the following account of what happened:

In a short time the butler came in to say that Mrs Hunter was of the party
at the Fort and wanted very much to see me. So I drove over and saw Kitty Hunter,
who burst into tears and explained to me how Mrs S. had fooled her to the last,
declaring that she would never marry the King. Her account of the dinner suggests
that the poor King must have had a pretty difficult time, because apparently Kitty
and George wept into their soup and everything else during the meal, in spite
of the King's heroic efforts to carry off the dinner cheerfully.

Once he had decided to abdicate, the King determined to fulfil his desire
to broadcast to the nation. He tasted at once the joys of being a subject of
the King because the government could no longer restrain him. However,
he instructed Walter Monckton to inform Baldwin that as a matter of courtesy he would allow the Cabinet to see in advance what he intended to say.
On the evening of 10 December he worked late into the night and he was
up early the next day to finish his speech. Then he invited Winston Churchill
to luncheon to wish him goodbye and to show him the draft. (During this

luncheon he ceased to be King.) The Duke of Windsor has said that it is
not true that Churchill wrote his broadcast speech – he wrote it himself
– but he was responsible for one or two phrases which the student of Chur-
chilliana should be able to spot.

As Churchill stood on the doorstep saying goodbye to the ex-monarch
there were tears in his eyes and he gave a fresh association to Marvell's
famous lines on the beheading of Charles I:

> He nothing common did or mean
> Upon that memorable scene.

The ex-King's decision to broadcast to the nation made urgent the question of his future rank and titles. 'The pundits were confounded,' Sir John
Wheeler-Bennett writes, and they sought the counsel of the new King. In
a memorandum annexed to his record of the Abdication crisis, George VI
gives an account of an interview with Lord Wigram and Sir Claud Schuster
(as representative of the Lord Chancellor), who came to ask his view on
the matter. The question, the King was told, was urgent because Sir John
Reith, the Director-General of the BBC, was proposing to introduce the ex-
King on the air as Mr Edward Windsor. The King said that this would
be quite wrong but that before going any further it was necessary to know
what his brother had given up by the Abdication. Upon Schuster replying
that he was not quite sure, King George, who is normally represented as
being completely bowled over at this time by his sense of his own inadequacy, gave a convincing exhibition of regal testiness as well as the solution
to the problem:

> I said, it would be quite a good thing to find out before coming to me. Now
> as to his name. I suggest HRH D[uke] of W[indsor]. He cannot be Mr E.W. as
> he was born the son of a Duke. That makes him L[or]d E.W. anyhow. If he ever
> comes back to this country, he can stand and be elected to the H. of C. Would
> you like that? S replied No. As D of W he can sit and vote in the H. of L. Would
> you like that? S replied No. Well if he becomes a Royal Duke he cannot speak
> or vote in the H. of L. and he is not being deprived of his rank in the Navy, Army
> or R. Air Force. This gave Schuster a new lease of life and he went off quite happy.

King George also gave instructions as to how his brother should be described on the radio that night, and it was on his specific command that
the ex-King was introduced as His Royal Highness Prince Edward. That
evening King George visited his brother to tell him that he had decided
to create him a Duke as the first act of his reign. 'How about the family
name of Windsor?' And the following morning at his Accession Council
he announced his intention to create him the Duke of Windsor, although
it was not until after the Coronation that the style and title were given legal
form.

During the day the ex-King received what he has described as 'a hint'
from the Prime Minister that he would be gratified if he would stress that
he had at all times received every possible consideration from him; a hint
about which the Duke of Windsor writes bitterly, after brooding for years
on the fact that Baldwin had refused his own request to do justice to Mrs
Simpson. And during the day it was arranged, through Mrs Simpson on
the telephone, that he should go to Baron Eugene de Rothschild's house,
Schloss Enzesfeld, near Vienna – the last stages of the Abdication having
been conducted at such speed that not until now had any consideration been
given to the ex-King's future.

That evening he dined with his assembled family at Royal Lodge, and

Introduced by Sir John Reith as 'His Royal Highness Prince Edward', the former king makes his Abdication speech. Without referring to Mrs Simpson by name, he confessed his inability 'to carry the heavy burden of responsibility ...without the help and support of the woman' he loved.

Edward leaves for Portsmouth after his broadcast, to sail immediately for France. It was the beginning of a self-imposed exile that lasted thirty-five years.

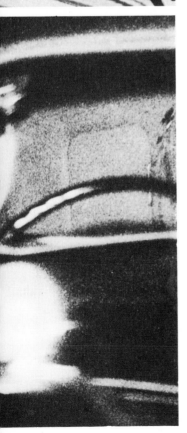

after dinner Walter Monckton fetched him and drove him to Windsor Castle from where he was to broadcast. Mounting the Gothic staircase to a room in the Augusta Tower, he was met by Sir John Reith. So that his voice might be tested, he read a newspaper report of a reference to the fact that the new King was an ardent tennis player. Then Sir John Reith announced: 'This is Windsor Castle, His Royal Highness Prince Edward,' and he spoke to the listening world in a voice which, gradually gaining confidence, ended on a high note of courage:

At long last I am able to say a few words of my own.

I have never wanted to withhold anything, but until now it has been not constitutionally possible for me to speak.

A few hours ago I discharged my last duty as King and Emperor, and now that I have been succeeded by my brother, the Duke of York, my first words must be to declare my allegiance to him. This I do with all my heart.

You all know the reasons which have impelled me to renounce the throne. But I want you to understand that in making up my mind I did not forget the country or the Empire which as Prince of Wales, and lately as King, I have for twenty-five years tried to serve. But you must believe me when I tell you that I have found it impossible to carry the heavy burden of responsibility and to discharge my duties as King as I would wish to do without the help and support of the woman I love.

And I want you to know that the decision I have made has been mine and mine alone. This was a thing I had to judge entirely for myself. The other person most concerned has tried up to the last to persuade me to take a different course. I have made this, the most serious decision of my life, upon a single thought of what would in the end be the best for all.

This decision has been made less difficult for me by the sure knowledge that my brother, with his long training in the public affairs of this country and with his fine qualities, will be able to take my place forthwith, without interruption or injury to the life and progress of the Empire. And he has one matchless blessing, enjoyed by so many of you and not bestowed on me – a happy home with his wife and children.

During these hard days I have been comforted by my Mother and by my Family. The Ministers of the Crown, and in particular Mr Baldwin, the Prime Minister, have always treated me with full consideration. There has never been any constitutional difference between me and them and between me and Parliament. Bred in the constitutional tradition by my Father, I should never have allowed any such issue to arise.

Ever since I was Prince of Wales, and later on when I occupied the Throne, I have been treated with the greatest kindness by all classes, wherever I have lived or journeyed throughout the Empire. For that I am very grateful.

I now quit altogether public affairs, and I lay down my burden. It may be some time before I return to my native land, but I shall always follow the fortunes of the British race and Empire with profound interest, and if at any time in the future I can be found of service to His Majesty in a private station I shall not fail. And now we all have a new King, I wish him, and you, his people, happiness and prosperity with all my heart. God bless you all. God Save the King.

After the broadcast he returned to Royal Lodge to say goodbye to his family. It was late and his mother and his sister Mary left quite soon, but the four brothers and Walter Monckton sat on until midnight when the Duke of Windsor and Monckton left to drive to Portsmouth. As he took his leave of his brothers he bowed to the new King, a gesture which led the Duke of Kent to cry out: 'It isn't possible. It isn't happening.'

All the way down he talked quietly and composedly to Walter Monckton about their early friendship at Oxford and about the First World War.

At Portsmouth the ex-King had been expected for hours before he arrived, and a naval guard with rifles and fixed bayonets had been paraded, while the *Fury* waited alongside, ready for sea. On the dockside friends and members of his household waited to say goodbye. Admiral Sir William Fisher, Commander-in-Chief Portsmouth, was there to say goodbye for the Navy. There were tears in his eyes as he did so. The King seemed in the same good spirits he had shown all week, and, if he felt any emotion appropriate to the enormity of the occasion, he gave no sign of it. His friends escorted him down to his cabin to say goodbye. 'Godfrey Thomas had served him for 17 years,' Monckton wrote, 'and felt that in some way he had failed in his duty, and that what was virtually his life's work had been shipwrecked.'

Fury sailed immediately and anchored in St Helen's Roads for the night, proceeding in time to cross the Channel and arrive in France in the morning.

16

After the Abdication

The immediate aftermath of the Abdication is chiefly remembered for three things: the indelicate speed with which the erstwhile friends of the ex-King and Mrs Simpson scuttled; the broadcast of the Archbishop of Canterbury; and the placidity with which the British people accepted the event.

Of the first there is unhappily no doubt. No defence can disguise the fact, vouched for by dozens of witnesses, that in the weeks following the Abdication almost no one could be found who had ever been on terms of intimate friendship with the ex-King or Mrs Simpson. All eyes were turned longingly to the new occupant of the throne. Osbert Sitwell commemorated this sad state of affairs in a poem which has never been published and of which the title 'Rat Week' is perhaps the best part. The only thing that can be said in extenuation of this exhibition of human weakness is that not many of the King's friends had understood that he meant to marry Mrs Simpson and would abdicate if necessary to do so: and, of the few who had ever asked the direct question, none had received a truthful reply.

The Archbishop's intervention is no easier to defend. Lang had suffered from his inability to give any guidance during the course of the Abdication and he now felt that he could not merely say 'kind, and of course true things about the late King's charms and manifold services' and that he was bound to refer to the surrender of a great trust. On Sunday 13 December, he broadcast to the nation in words which gave offence to very many people:

What pathos, nay what tragedy, surrounds the central figure of these swiftly moving scenes! On the 11th day of December, 248 years ago, King James fled from Whitehall. By a strange coincidence, on the 11th day of December last week King Edward VIII, after speaking his last words to his people, left Windsor Castle, the scene of all the splendid traditions of his ancestors and his Throne, and went out an exile. In the darkness he left these shores....

From God he had received a high and sacred trust. Yet by his own will he has abdicated – he has surrendered the trust. With characteristic frankness he has told us the motive. It was a craving for private happiness. Strange and sad it must be that for such a motive, however strongly it pressed upon his heart, he should have disappointed hopes so high and abandoned a trust so great.

Even more strange and sad it is that he should have sought his happiness in a manner inconsistent with the Christian principles of marriage, and within a social circle whose standards and way of life are alien to all the best instincts and traditions of his people. Let those who belong to this circle know that today they stand rebuked by the judgment of the nation which had loved King Edward.

Daily Herald

No. 6498   FRIDAY, DECEMBER 11, 1936   ONE PENNY

THE KING ABDICATES: WILL BROADCAST TO-NIGHT

LEAVING COUNTRY: MAY GO TO ROME

Duke Of York Succeeds To The Throne	∗	**Will Be Known As King George the Sixth**

NEW RULER VISITS MOTHER

THE DUKE OF YORK, who succeeds King Edward on the Throne, photographed late last night when he arrived at 145, Piccadilly, his London home, from Windsor Lodge.

KING EDWARD VIII ABDICATED YESTERDAY. HE WILL BROADCAST TO THE NATION TO-NIGHT— "AS A PRIVATE INDIVIDUAL, OWING ALLEGIANCE TO THE NEW KING."

The broadcast will, it is expected, be made at 10 p.m., probably from Fort Belvedere. But there is a suggestion that it may be made from abroad, for it is known that the King wishes to leave the country at once.

It was stated last night that he might go to Rome—possibly by plane.

The new King is the Duke of York, who will almost certainly take the title of King George VI. Ten-year-old Princess Elizabeth becomes next in the line of succession.

Relinquishes

All His Titles

King Edward's last act as Monarch will be to sign a commission enabling the Royal Assent to be given to the Abdication Law which Parliament is rushing through all its stages to-day.

With the renunciation of the Throne the King relinquishes all his titles except that of Prince Edward, but it was rumoured last night that he might prefer to be known as plain "Mr. Windsor."

The new reign will be formally inaugurated by a Grand Accession Privy Council at Buckingham Palace to-night, and the new Monarch will be proclaimed, with all the heraldic pageantry of old, to-morrow.

Later in the day, both Houses of Parliament will meet so that M.P.s and Peers can take the oath of allegiance to the new King. The sitting is expected to last late into the evening.

Coronation Day, fixed for May 12, may not be postponed. Even if it is, the delay will be for only a few weeks.

"I Am Going to

Marry Mrs. Simpson"

Mr. Baldwin made the dramatic announcement of King Edward's abdication in a hushed House of Commons yesterday afternoon, and explained how the King had told him, three weeks ago:—

"I AM GOING TO MARRY MRS. SIMPSON, AND I AM PREPARED TO GO."

It is significant that the Abdication Bill, by subsection 3 of Clause I, specially exempts the King from the operation of the Royal Marriages Act, so that he will be left as free as any ordinary citizen to marry whom he pleases.

The Abdication Paper was signed at Fort Belvedere at 10 o'clock yesterday morning, in the presence of the Duke of York, the Duke of Kent and the Duke of Gloucester. They all signed the document as witnesses of their brother's act.

The Duke of York went to Fort Belvedere, by car from London last night, for a final dinner with the King before he embarks on his exile. After dinner, the Duke returned to London and, early this morning, visited his mother at Marlborough House.

News Taken

Calmly

Nothing is yet known of the arrangements that will be made for King Edward's future income. The new Civil List, by which it will be governed, will not be drawn up till after Christmas.

CROWDS CHEER DUKE

Police Have To Clear Way For Car

A GREAT CROWD packing Piccadilly last night, broke into wave upon wave of cheers, when the new King returned to his home there last night.

Motor horns shrieked in salute as thousands of people swarmed round his car.

All traffic in Piccadilly was disorganised. Buses and taxis blocked the roadway and extra police were raced to the spot to control the crowd.

It was ten minutes before the royal car could drive the few yards into the forecourt of the house.

The new King smiled to women who jumped on the running-board and peered in.

ON RAILINGS

At last he was able to step from his car. As he did so he turned to the crowd and raised his hat several times.

Men and women climbed the railings and every other vantage point to catch a glimpse of him. Scores clambered on the roofs of taxis.

As he went inside the House the crowd sang the National Anthem.

A few minutes after midnight the new King left the house again and drove to Marlborough House to see Queen Mary.

AT PALACE

A crowd of several thousands assembled traffic outside Buckingham Palace and remained police vote on the decision to clear them from the Palace railings.

In each the police assured the crowd that neither King Edward nor the new King was inside.

A number of young men and women shouted "We want Edward," but others sang the National Anthem.

Shortly before midnight extra police were called from Scotland Yard to deal with a crowd of a few hundred people who had assembled in Whitehall, opposite Downing-street. The police shepherded them to Trafalgar-square. As they moved off shouts of "We want Edward" mingled with cheers and cries of "God Save the King."

Earlier in the evening a cordon of 26 police was thrown across the Whitehall entrance to Downing-street when Blackshirts tried to demonstrate.

Six people arrested during the demonstration in Whitehall will appear at Bow-street police court this morning.

NO COINS OF KING EDWARD

RUSH TO BUY STAMPS

No King Edward VIII coins will ever be in circulation.

No coins could have been made before a royal proclamation, announcing the date on which the coinage would come into circulation.

Such a proclamation was expected this month. It would have described the design for the King's head and the designs of the reverse sides for the different denominations.

The existing King Edward stamps will be issued until the stocks are exhausted.

Within a quarter of an hour of the abdication announcement, post offices at Southampton were rushed yesterday by individuals who purchased all King Edward stamps of the higher denominations.

ONE WIRELESS PROGRAMME TO-DAY

The B.B.C. announced late last night that a single programme only would be broadcast to-day from all transmitters.

All transmissions will cease after King Edward has spoken.

(See Page 17.)

A torrent of abuse fell upon the Archbishop from all sides, and the broadcast seems to have had only one beneficial effect. It added to the literature of the Abdication, not very strong in wit, the following neat little squib:

(*Opposite*) *A typical newspaper headline of Friday, 11 December 1936.*

> My Lord Archbishop, what a scold you are!
> And when your man is down, how bold you are!
> Of charity how oddly scant you are!
> How Lang, O Lord, how full of Cantuar!

Most memorable of all, however, was the speed at which the British forgot the ex-King and turned to the new one (and, although this is the complaint against the ex-King's friends, in the unambitious public it seemed a virtue). There were several reasons for it, of which the most important, essentially in normal times forgotten, is that it is the institution itself which enslaves the mind. It would not be correct to say that one king is as good as another, because there are very large limits to this, and because, although it may be true that no human being could in his own person sustain the weight of idolization, it is also true that, for all the rich paraphernalia, the solemn and bolstering pageantry, the ramifications of the king's business, the monarchy remains only as strong as its hold on men's imaginations. It is a question of faith. HRH Prince Edward had disturbed this faith a little, and the public, longing for reassurance, turned eagerly to his successor.

The English are usually represented as being passionately involved in the crisis, and some indeed were. Speaking for one section of these, an officer in the Royal Scots Fusiliers, of which the Prince of Wales had been Colonel-in-Chief, said: 'We loved him. We would have drawn our swords for him. And then, by God, *didn't he let us down!*'

Others simply felt sad. But the emotions of the majority of British people may have been summed up in a cartoon which appeared soon after in a British newspaper. In this a workman throws down his tools and turns to his mate with the question: 'How can I do my work without the help and support of the woman I love?'

In any case the people of England forgot King Edward VIII until in the summer of 1972 his body was brought home for burial.

There will always be room for speculation about the Abdication. The Duchess of Windsor has told us that when she and the Duke were first married only one thing marred their happiness:

> After the first burst of joy in rediscovering each other and being together we found our minds turning back in interminable post-mortems concerning the events leading up to the Abdication ... this endless re-hashing of the lost past became almost an obsession with us until one evening David said despairingly, 'Darling, if we keep this up we are never going to agree, so let's drop it for good.' Then and there we vowed we never would discuss the Abdication again, and to this day we never have.

If the two principals could not agree, it is unlikely that any writer will ever be allowed the last word on the subject. Nevertheless, there are one or two aspects of the Abdication which have received little attention.

It is always taken for granted that Edward VIII was in character and temperament ill-equipped for the role of monarch. *Capax imperii nisi imperasset* runs the tag from Tacitus used about the Abdication. 'Had he never been emperor, no one would have doubted his ability to reign.' And it is almost inevitable that this will be the final verdict on him, for on what is he to be judged if not on his actual performance?

Yet during the whole of his reign he was under maximum strain and at times near the edge of a breakdown. He was not in a mental state to be judged, and, while it may be true that under his particular stars his character made him unsuitable for the throne of England, it might nevertheless be argued that under a happier configuration he could have made a good king.

One of the main complaints against him was that he was incapable of the sustained work which is required of a monarch, a complaint which must seem extraordinary to anyone who has knowledge of the immense programmes he undertook as a young man, of the eagerness to serve which he exhibited in all his contacts with the unemployed and the working men of Britain, of the trouble he took over his speeches, both as Prince of Wales and later, after the Abdication, as Governor of the Bahamas.

It may be true that he had no taste for paperwork and could never have spent the necessary hours on the eternal red boxes. But surely some means could have been found to alter the procedure so that he was presented with précis of only the most important documents. His grandfather, King Edward VII, disliked formal audiences with his ministers and by 1905 had almost ceased to give them to anyone, 'with the exception of the Prime Minister, the Foreign Secretary and Arnold Foster occasionally – when he forced himself upon him'. A committee of seven, which included Mrs Keppel, was formed to perform for the King 'the kind of service which the Prince Consort had performed for Queen Victoria'. Surely in different circumstances it would not have been beyond the wits of Edward VIII's secretaries to supplement his good qualities and overcome his bad ones.

But to make a good king it is necessary to have the will for it. From the earliest age the Prince showed a lethal inability to find attraction in anyone but a married woman, and, when he finally met the woman to whom he was to devote the rest of his life, she had two husbands living and, because she was American, no natural understanding of the limits of the King's power, or of the discretion and devotion to duty required of the woman whose fate is linked with his, either as Queen or in any other relationship.

From the moment he fell in love with Mrs Simpson he proceeded wilfully and entirely unnecessarily to compromise both her and his own position. If one can imagine a man secretly but determinedly intent on the unlikely task of making a divorced commoner Queen, or if not Queen a morganatic consort, how would one expect him to behave? Surely with the greatest possible discretion and a considered attempt to gather a band of serious and experienced advisers around him. Yet it was not so much that the Prince drifted on to his fate, as that he went out of his way to feed the world press with gossip and scandal, covering his loved one with jewellery, flaunting her everywhere he went, showing a reckless disregard for conventions and a complete indifference to the feelings of his family, above all to any chance of gaining sympathy for his project.

How then is it possible to explain that, when the crisis broke, until his anger with Hardinge induced him to employ the service of Walter Monckton, without either advisers or a plan of campaign, almost the only thing he could think of to do was to send for Lord Beaverbrook?

Again, we have been told so much of his desire to democratize and modernize the monarchy, and, if not to confront the establishment, at least to reform it. Yet during the course of his reign there is almost no evidence that he had given any real thought to these exceedingly interesting and in many ways necessary projects. He succeeded, through impatience and more or less by accident, in suggesting one or two reforms which have since been

12 December: Edward's brother Albert, who took the title of George VI, leaves for St James's Palace to take the Oath of Allegiance before the Accession Council.

The new Royal Family – the shy, stuttering new king, who was to prove a popular and effective monarch, with his wife Elizabeth, their two daughters Elizabeth and Margaret, and members of the court. His father, George V, was reputed to have said, a few weeks before his own death, 'I pray to God that ... nothing will come between Bertie and Lilibet and the throne'.

thought desirable, and he effected some economies which had become necessary, although in doing this he showed what to some observers seemed a lack of consideration for old and loyal servants and an unacceptable meanness. These were the sum total of his achievements.

The truth seems to be that his mind was never given to the task that by inheritance and years of training was his. There is no indication that the mental strain from which he suffered during the crisis was due to a prolonged struggle between his conscience and his inclinations. Indeed, rather the reverse, he seemed to fear only that something might hurt Mrs Simpson or separate her from his side. Here is what Stanley Baldwin said about him to his niece:

He is an abnormal being, half-child, half-genius. It is almost as though two or three cells in his brain had remained entirely undeveloped while the rest of him is a mature man. He is not a *thinker*. He takes his ideas from the daily press instead of thinking things out for himself. He never reads – except, of course, the papers.

He is *reasonable*: that is to say, when he really *sees* a thing, he does it. You might say he is amenable to reason – except of course, on that one subject....

The last days before the Abdication were thrilling and terrible. He would *never* listen to reason about Mrs Simpson. From the very first he insisted that he would marry her. He had *no* spiritual conflict *at all*. There was no battle in his will. I tell you this and it is true. He is extraordinary in the way he has no spiritual sense; no idea of sacrifice for duty. *That* point of view never came before his mind.

I set it all before him. I appealed to one thing after another. Nothing made the least impression. It was almost uncanny: like talking to a child of ten years old. He did not seem to grasp the issues at stake. He seemed bewitched....

He has no religious sense. I have never in my life met anyone so completely lacking in any sense of the – the – well, what is *beyond*. And he kept on repeating over and over again: 'I can't do my job without her – I am going to marry her, and I will *go*.' There was simply no moral struggle. It appalled me.

Yet the King had been reared to an understanding of the constitutional position. Subconsciously he must have known, as everyone else did, that there was no question of his marrying Mrs Simpson and remaining on the throne. ('The real puzzle', Sir Colin Coote was to write, 'was how anybody could ever have thought it possible for her to become Queen of England, and of seven British Dominions as well.') For a week or two he appeared to be negotiating with the Prime Minister. However, the docility with which he accepted a negative answer to every proposal can only be explained if one believes that he was instinctively aware when he first decided to marry Mrs Simpson that this would involve giving up the Crown; and that his unprecedented, completely unexpected and otherwise inexplicable decision to marry her was partly inspired by a deep longing to escape the terrible responsibilities of the role he had inherited: a role to which he was in some ways temperamentally unsuited, and for which he had from his earliest youth shown some distaste, as well as the conviction that it was not inescapable.

Walter Monckton has asserted that the King had a religious side to his nature but adds: 'One sometimes felt that the God in whom he believed was a God who dealt him trumps all the time and put no inhibitions on his main desires.' And he also says: 'Once his mind was made up one felt he was like the deaf adder "that stoppeth her ears; which refuseth to hear the voice of the charmer".'

Both at the time of the Abdication and for the rest of his life the King would always show the most extraordinary obtuseness in relation to the facts. He believed that his abdication of his duty would be seen as the honourable course in the situation in which he found himself; and he held to this view forever after. Yet to people reared to the moral concept which inspired the poet Lovelace to write 'I could not love thee (Dear) so much, Lov'd I not honour more', and who were between two wars in which, when necessary, they would die for it, his conduct could never seem anything but contemptible. It was this profound difference in understanding which would bedevil his relations with his country and his family for the rest of his life.

The belief that the pressures of the King's life had built up an instinctive desire to escape the throne – and it must be remembered that he managed to increase immensely the burden he had to carry because of his temperamental inability to be guided by his courtiers down safe, traditional paths – will naturally run into objections. One of these is that, according to Lord Beaverbrook, on the night he left England he said to one of his companions: 'I always thought I could get away with the morganatic marriage.' Yet there is no way in which the morganatic marriage proposal can be shown to have had an important bearing on the King's conduct, more particularly on his subconscious motives; it was suggested to him for the first time by Esmond Harmsworth less than three weeks before the end, and he understood almost immediately that it was unlikely to be accepted. As we have seen, he persisted in it merely because 'I've got to do something. At the very least I'll get my head in a more comfortable position on the block'; a statement which, if we can believe it, might reasonably be given in evidence of the view expressed here.

But if the King simply bowed out, what of the plot? And what of Baldwin's great skill? If the first was non-existent, perhaps the second has been overrated. In 1965 Sir Ulick Alexander, who, it will be remembered, was one of the small staff who resided at Fort Belvedere during the crisis, wrote a letter to *The Times* in which he said:

I was of course not present at the private discussions between the Prime Minister and the King during this period, but what was said was always discussed afterwards by the King with the three of us and I found it, and I know at least one of my colleagues found it, extremely difficult to decide on what line Mr Baldwin was proceeding.

And in truth Baldwin never seems to have been quite certain what he should do. He was forced into action in the first place by Hardinge and the party at Cumberland Lodge; on almost every occasion it was the King who sent for him and initiated the next stage of the negotiations (although he always dealt admirably with the suggestions made to him); and at the very last he was apparently willing to endanger the agreement which had been reached, by sending Goddard to Cannes and going himself to reason with the King at Fort Belvedere. Sir Harold Nicolson saw artistry in the fact that he dropped his notes and asked for confirmation of dates during his speech to the House of Commons, but he was in a very nervous and exhausted state and earlier he had left his notes behind and had had to send Dugdale back to fetch them. It is so easy with hindsight to think of the Abdication in the context of the smoothness with which it passed and with which the new King commanded the loyalty of his subjects, and to see Baldwin as manœuvring skilfully in the background. But at the time those most intimately concerned with it greatly exaggerated the danger to the monarchy and had no feeling of manipulative power. It seems far more likely that Baldwin behaved as most politicians do in a crisis and followed his nose; and that his success was due to a happy combination of his best and his worst qualities. He emerges as a man of large character, kind, devoted to the

POST OFFICE TELEGRAM

Charges to pay				No.	OFFICE STAMP
RECEIVED	s.	d.			

Prefix. Time handed in. Office of Origin and Service Instructions. Words.

m 13 8 27 Leicester Sq 24

From (Admiralty) To

Mrs Baldwin 10 Downing St

Sincere thanks for kind letter so much appreciated yours and Mr Baldwin great understanding at this difficult time

Edward

For free repetition of doubtful words telephone "TELEGRAMS ENQUIRY" or call, with this form at office of delivery. Other enquiries should be accompanied by this form and, if possible, the envelope.   B or C

The friendly telegram that Edward sent to the Baldwins on his departure from England. It was only in later years that the Duke of Windsor came to believe in Baldwin's involvement in a 'plot' against him.

monarchy and fond of the King. He also had a tendency to inertia in face of a crisis. This forced the King to lead again and again, and since he had made up his mind to marry Mrs Simpson, and was a man of determined bad judgment, virtually all Baldwin needed to do was to show the patience and lack of aggression which came naturally to him. Against this view there can be put one or two remarks he made at the time, but history is at its most misleading when pinning down the small change of everyday life, particularly when this is between men who share some common experience but are otherwise strangers to each other.

When the Duke of Windsor left England he sent Baldwin a friendly personal message and it was only after many months of the influences of exile that he began to believe in the existence of a plot against himself. Nevertheless, since the charge has been made, it is as well to point out that it could only have had substance if Baldwin had represented a minority view. In fact, his view was shared by the Cabinet, by the leaders and almost all members of all political parties, by everyone except a handful of MPs, by the vast majority of his countrymen and of the populations of the Dominions.

In his long exile the Duke went very near to falling into the trap his father had warned him about so long ago, confusing his person with his position. It was to the last that the loyalties of the Prime Minister and the government belonged. Once they despaired of saving the monarch, it was their duty to save the monarchy.

17

The Duke and Duchess

In June 1937 the ex-King and Mrs Simpson were married at the Château de Candé, near Tours. A small group of friends witnessed the ceremony but none of the bridegroom's family attended. The Duchess of Windsor later wrote: 'David longed to have his sister and his brother, and most of all his mother, near him at his marriage. . . . But . . . the unspoken order had gone out: Buckingham Palace would ignore our wedding.'

Indeed it would have been hard for any member of the Royal Family to attend the wedding because the religion of their country did not recognize divorce. It was not part of their duty to flout this religion, still less in so public a manner as by attending the Duke's wedding.

The day before the wedding Walter Monckton had arrived from London with a letter from the King, in which he informed his brother that he had been pleased by Letters Patent 'to declare that the Duke of Windsor shall, notwithstanding his act of Abdication . . . be entitled to hold and enjoy for himself only the title, style or attribute of Royal Highness, so however that his wife and descendants, if any, shall not hold the same title or attribute.' The Duke of Windsor was to be HRH: his wife was not.

The Duke received the news as he would have a wound in battle. It struck at his deepest emotion and it altered him as gunshot might have done. From now on he would live with this fact and never forget it, any more than a man who lives in pain can forget it, although for short periods he may sometimes feel it less. He had so secured himself from within that he was more than ordinarily vulnerable to blows from without. So obdurately was he armed against any understanding of the magnitude of his dereliction of duty, that the actions of his family and the government of his country were to him incomprehensible and completely unexpected. As time went on he suffered blow after blow, but nothing ever hit him like this hideous discourtesy to his wife.

The explanation for what, unexplained, seems so incredibly mean, is that, as George VI reminded Baldwin at the time, 'once a person has become a Royal Highness there is no means of depriving her of the title', and neither the King and Queen nor anyone near to them understood this couple well enough to be sure that the marriage would last. They knew little of Mrs Simpson except that this was her third marriage. And they knew little of him. They had always exaggerated his passing affairs and underestimated his essential faithfulness. Now he had shown himself completely unpredictable. Baldwin told his niece: 'His family are all wondering what will become

of him when at last he opens his eyes and sees the sort she really is.' And what would become of her? Where would Her Royal Highness go? Would there be marriage and re-marriage? More than one Royal Highness? Was there no limit to the possible damage to the throne?

From the beginning, the matter of the title caused trouble. Who would bow to the Duchess and who would not? Walter Monckton said he found that his head 'bowed easily' but some of the Windsors' friends felt genuinely unable to extend this courtesy to her. Nevertheless, in their own household it was made known that the Duke wished his wife to be referred to as Her Royal Highness.

In his farewell broadcast Edward had said: 'I now quit altogether public affairs', but almost in the next sentence: 'If at any time in the future I can be found of service to His Majesty in a private station, I shall not fail.' There is no doubt that, although at the time he gave no great thought to his future career, he never questioned that after a short period abroad he would return and be given some post which made use of his talents and training. It might be too much to say that he saw himself as merely changing places with the Duke of York, but he certainly envisaged a situation far nearer to that than to what was actually in store for him.

Yet while the Duke longed for useful employment, his public actions did not inspire confidence. In October 1937 the Duke and Duchess announced that they intended to visit Germany and, despite the urgent pleas of friends including Lord Beaverbrook, the visit went ahead. They met Hitler, Goering, Himmler and other leading Nazis and were welcomed by enthusiastic crowds wherever they went. The visit caused considerable comment everywhere and in England impatience that the ex-King would not retire in peace. It would be some years before, accepting his situation although still not understanding it, he would give up hope of a public life.

(Opposite) Edward and Mrs Simpson on their wedding day in June 1937, at the Château de Candé, near Tours, France.

The Duke and Duchess of Windsor visited Nazi Germany in October 1937, despite strong advice from friends.

At the outbreak of the Second World War he returned to England where he expected suitable employment. He was made Liaison Officer with the British Mission to France, a post which carried little responsibility; but he showed aptitude for military duties and performed them successfully. In May 1940 he left Paris to join the Duchess in Biarritz. From there they went to their villa in the South of France, leaving it to cross the border into Spain when the situation became obviously dangerous. From Spain they went on to Portugal.

In Portugal, the Duke refused to go to England unless he received assurances that his wife would be accorded equality with the wives of his brothers, and until he knew what his job would be. In June and July 1940, Winston Churchill had therefore to spare time to deal with the affairs of the Duke of Windsor. He offered him the Governorship of the Bahamas, an appointment which the Duke accepted but seemed in no hurry to take up. The German Foreign Office papers showed (when they were published after the war) that the Germans plotted at this time to get him to return to Spain, a neutral country friendly to Germany. Although the details of this plot were not known in England at the time, it was known that the Duke was in constant touch with Spaniards of known German sympathies. Finally, Walter Monckton was sent out to persuade him to leave for the Bahamas.

He was in some ways a good Governor and carried out much of his duty efficiently. But, in an island where most of the population is of mixed race, he made no secret of his colour prejudice and he involved himself, quite unnecessarily, in a controversial trial for the murder of Sir Harry Oakes. The Duchess was unpopular because she made no secret of her chagrin at the appointment, which she regarded as petty and provincial, and spoke of herself as an exile.

The Duke tendered his resignation as Governor of the Bahamas in March 1945, five months before his term was up, and after the war the Duke and Duchess went back to France. They had some difficulty in deciding where to live, not only because they still retained the hope of eventually returning to England, but also because he preferred the country, she the town. Eventually they were offered a house in the Bois de Boulogne by the French government and later they bought an old mill about forty-five miles outside Paris.

There is a widespread belief, which persisted throughout the Duke's life, that he was prevented from returning to England. This is not true. After the war no one objected to his return, but he made it absolutely conditional on his wife being received by his family and being given the same rank and status as the wives of his two younger brothers. Once this had been refused, it was most unlikely that he would ever have weakened on a matter about which he felt so deeply. Soon, however, his resolve was much strengthened by the great generosity of the French government. He was given the house in the Bois de Boulogne at a nominal rent, and also a special status which meant that he paid no income tax. It would have cost him a fortune to live in England.

Another idea, which is prevalent but equally without foundation, is that the British denied the Duke any opportunity to work. It is true that they would not offer him employment in those spheres which he thought suitable to his rank and talents. It may even be true, as the Duchess states, that the 'silent ban' extended to any form of public work in which the British government was concerned. Beyond this they had neither interest nor power, and the ex-King of England, with his vast fortune, his undoubted status, his unrivalled contacts, could surely have had for the asking a position at the

head of half the organizations in the world – those for the relief of poverty and suffering, for the promotion of the arts or international relations, for the preservation of the environment or wildlife, for all the myriad other things which occupy the minds of men and women of imagination and good-will.

The Duke and Duchess with guests at the old French mill they bought some forty-five miles from Paris. They also had a house, given to them by the French government, in the Bois de Boulogne.

Yet the fact that he did not avail himself of these opportunities was his misfortune as well as his fault. He wanted not so much work as status, not so much to give, as to receive recognition, for himself and for his wife. All these things which were his by right of birth and which in his youth were so little regarded were now denied him, and denied, he believed, through the ill-will of a few powerful people. So it was true, as his wife recorded, that he was left with a haunting sense of waste and that it took courage for him to take up the small burdens that were all that were left to him. Yet there was never any doubt that between him and despair or regrets there remained his complete and continuing happiness with his wife.

If one asks why Edward VIII gave up his throne for Wallis Simpson, one must look for the answer in himself. But if one wants to know how she succeeded in making him happy, it was very largely through her domesticity. Towards the end of her life one of her few close friends said of her: 'The only thing that could be said against Wallis is that in all her life she never did anything except keep house.'

The beauty and splendour of her houses is well known. All Paris contributed to their furnishing. The interior decoration, in the hands of a famous firm, was supervised in every detail by the Duchess. For months she visited antique shops, searching for furniture, chandeliers, candelabra, pictures, china and glass. She was not easily satisfied and rooms that did not please her were repainted, while the antique dealers came and went so that she might try the effect of their goods in her house. No trouble was too much for her, no expense too great.

She spent hours, too, in the salons of the great Parisian dressmakers, and the clothes she wore were as much a result of art as the furnishing of her rooms. And she went nearly every day to the hairdresser or to have her face done.

The Duke still played golf and, once they acquired the mill, resumed his interest in gardening. But he also shared in his wife's interests. Sometimes he went shopping with her, sometimes not, but they discussed endlessly the colour schemes and the arrangement of rooms. Both were meticulous, perhaps too meticulous to be much loved – the curtains must fall just so, the chairs, the lamps, the pepper pot stand, not here or here, but here. He shared, too, her love of clothes, and he never tired of adding to her jewels. Most of all he loved her authority.

One of their secretaries, Diana Wells Hood, has given us a picture of the Duke's happiness with his wife which is absolutely convincing.

His wife was constantly in his thoughts. If he went out alone he looked for her the moment he returned home. If she went out without him and remained away for any length of time, he became nervous and pre-occupied.

He never made any attempt to conceal his feelings. He was frankly demonstrative. More than once I saw him take her impulsively in his arms and kiss her tenderly. . . .

He bought her exquisite jewellery and other beautiful gifts. Nothing was too good for her. He sought in every way to make her happy. He himself was happy and light-hearted in her presence.

If she called him from some other part of the house he would leave what he was doing and go to her immediately. Once he got up and ran to his wife in the middle of a haircut.

Fruity Metcalfe, who had ample opportunity to observe their relationship, said in a letter to his wife, written in 1940 after the Duke had returned from a visit to England, 'It was really delightful to see how pleased he & W. were to get together again. It is *very true* & deep stuff.'

But, although the Duke seemed content to submerge his life in hers, it would be a mistake to think that this humility had any counterpart in his relations with anyone else. To the end of his life he carried about him the aura of his royal birth, he never outgrew the habits and expectations of his youth, and, to everyone but his wife, he could be formidable. Always moody, he could still make or mar a dinner party, and people who attempted to give him advice he did not wish to hear were made instantly aware of the royal displeasure. 'The Duchess has already said she is not interested in that,' he would say sharply, and finally.

People who served them seemed, nevertheless, to have liked and respected them. Englishmen travelling to Paris on their business were treated with kindness and hospitality, often asked to stay in the house, even to bring their wives. Everyone was impressed by the skill with which the Windsors put people at their ease, and, contrary to rumour, the servants seemed fond of them and proud to be in their employ.

The Windsors spent a large part of every year in New York and they seemed to be forever travelling. When they boarded a boat or a train there were always reporters to record the fact and to count the luggage. They seldom travelled with less than thirty-odd pieces, as well as valets, chauffeurs, secretaries, maids and dogs. In the winter they went to Palm Beach and in the summer to Biarritz or to Venice or to some other place in southern Europe. They presented to the world a fantasy of wealth and luxury and

The Duchess took endless pains over the interior decoration of her homes, and over her own appearance. She and the Duke are seen here on their twelfth wedding anniversary in their Paris house.

elegance, like a couple invented by *Vogue* or *Harper's Bazaar*. Reporters counted avidly how many times she went to the hairdresser, the number of dresses she bought and how many times she wore them, while one famous newspaper columnist called her the best-dressed woman in the world.

After the war the Duke returned to London at fairly long intervals and stayed with his mother at Marlborough House. He would almost always pay a call on the King as well. Occasionally, the Duchess accompanied him and then they stayed either at Claridge's or with friends. Those who still retained an interest in the doings of the Windsors wondered about the relationship of this man with the mother and brother who were so relentless in their determination not to meet his wife.

The Windsors en route to New York, where they spent a large part of every year.

Some time in the late forties the Duke found a new and very profitable career. *Life* magazine published a series of articles based on his memoirs, which later appeared as *A King's Story*. He earned a great fortune from books and articles but he had a more compelling reason for breaking the rule of reticence which in a constitutional society is binding on kings and princes. He wished to put history straight. He believed himself to have been deprived of his ordinary rights ever since he left the throne, for reasons which were completely unworthy and totally unexpected. 'I played fair in 1936,' he said to the late James Pope-Hennessy, 'but I was bloody shabbily treated.' As he looked back on the long history of personal slights to himself and his wife, how easy for him to believe, as she had always believed, that he had been the victim of men who, because of his intractable independence and the influence his popularity gave him, were glad to replace him by his brother. Neither he nor the Duchess, who later also published her memoirs, were ever able to see the bold outlines of the plot or to explain how the trick was done; they simply felt that they had been outplayed, and that honesty, chivalry, goodwill and decency in human relations had been beaten by cunning.

The Duke's book is never really explicit, but he achieves his effect by the dark tone of his musings and an overt hostility to men who, until then, had believed that the negotiations at the time of the Abdication had been carried out with patience on their side and goodwill on both.

A King's Story sold hundreds of thousands of copies all over the world and was later made into a film. Behind the scenes the book caused unrestrained anger and concern. Those who had taken part in the events the Duke described were often astonished to read a version of them which bore no relation to their own memories. Many people would have liked to make some public protest. All were restrained from further publicity at the time out of consideration for King George.

For the world at large the Duke's decision to publish had many benefits. In the first place no other writer could have told us so much about his character and mentality, as both consciously and unconsciously he revealed. In the second, by making a case which sooner or later others were bound to answer, he ensured that all the details of his reign were made public years before they might otherwise have been. In the twenty years after the publication of *A King's Story* everyone who had any part in the Abdication crisis had his say, yet one of the strangest aspects of the case is that the Windsors seem never to have understood the licence they were giving others to publish, and continued to resent any revelations or criticism about themselves.

In February 1952, when George VI died, the Duke of Windsor travelled immediately to England and took his place alongside the other royal dukes in the funeral procession. In March 1953 he was already in London when

(*Opposite, top*) *February 1952: on one of his brief visits home, this time to attend the funeral of his brother, George VI, Edward sits next to his mother Queen Mary, who herself died the following month. His strained expression is reminiscent of that caught by the photographer as he left for Portsmouth, and exile, fifteen years earlier.*

A signed portrait of the Windsors.

Queen Mary's illness took a serious turn and he was able to visit her bedside until the end. Once more he took his place with the rest of the family in the ceremonial which followed her death. On both these occasions he came to England alone. In 1967, however, at the ceremony of unveiling a plaque to Queen Mary at Marlborough House, Queen Elizabeth decided to extend the courtesy of an invitation, not merely to the Duke, but also to his wife. They were cheered and clapped as they arrived for the ceremony and afterwards they were seen chatting with the Queen and the Queen Mother. This was the first public recognition of the Duchess by the sovereign of England.

Nothing now remained but to grow old gracefully, and this, after their own fashion, the Windsors undoubtedly did, the Duchess never scorning aids to the process. In her old age she became more beautiful and more refined, and when she was recognized on her occasional visits to London it was usually because someone's attention had been attracted at first by her elegance. To the end she dominated the Duke and to the end he adored her.

In May 1972, during a state visit to France, Queen Elizabeth went to see her uncle, the Duke of Windsor. The Duke was within a few days of his seventy-eighth birthday and it had been rumoured for some time that he was not well. In informed circles it was known that he had cancer of the

(Opposite, bottom) Queen Elizabeth II, the Duke's niece, broke the royal boycott of the Duchess when, in 1967, she invited both the Windsors to a ceremony commemorating Queen Mary. Here, the Duke kisses his sister-in-law, the Queen Mother, as Wallis looks on.

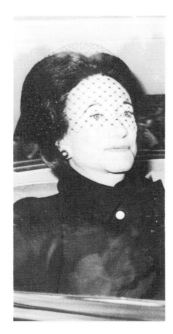

Elegant to the last, at the age of seventy-five the Duchess of Windsor drives through the gates of Buckingham Palace after Edward's death in 1972 and the return of his body to the country of his birth.

throat and could not live for more than a few weeks.

On 29 May, within a few days of the Queen's return to England, the Duke of Windsor died. It was announced immediately that his body would be interred in the royal burial ground at Frogmore. The Queen expressed her heartfelt sympathy with the Duchess and tributes were paid to the dead man by the leading statesmen of the world.

In death the Duke received the pomp and ceremony he had foregone in life. His coffin lay in state for two days in St George's Chapel, Windsor, and flags were flown at half-mast on public buildings all over the country.

The initial announcements of the death and homecoming of the Duke had been made comparatively quietly. As the week went on, however, it became apparent that there was taking place one of those large expressions of public opinion which occur as if by spontaneous combustion. The press, which had not initiated this, was, nevertheless, extremely sensitive to it, and more and more columns of print and more and more photographs of the Duke and Duchess filled the newspapers. The obituary columns concentrated very largely on the dead man's achievements as Prince of Wales or the details of the story of the Abdication. In the *Daily Telegraph*, Sir Colin Coote exhorted history to remember the 'vivid lively Prince Charming' rather than 'the weary, wayward, wandering ghost' of later years, and he concluded: 'It was very largely due to him that his going was not cataclysmic. His determination that what he did should not be politically upsetting was as strong as his resolve to do it.'

In this he voiced the most generally held belief. For, as the week went on, it became clear that the British were determined that, in death, they would honour this man. Most striking of all were the crowds that flocked to Windsor and stood in a queue at times a mile long to pay their respects. It was estimated that 57,000 people filed past the coffin. There seem to have been three reasons for this demonstration of respect for the dead man, who had seemed so long forgotten in England. The first, the usual appeal of every event touching the Royal Family; the second, the genuine affection older people felt for the memory of the Prince who had shown so much concern for simple folk. The third reason was more unexpected. There was no doubt that many of the people in the crowd were there to give expression to a feeling that the dead man had been shabbily treated.

On Friday 2 June the Duchess of Windsor arrived in an aeroplane of the Queen's Flight to be met at Heathrow by Earl Mountbatten of Burma. At the Queen's request, she stayed the weekend at Buckingham Palace but, distressed and unwell, she did not attend the ceremony of Trooping the Colour the following day which at the Queen's wish included a tribute to the Duke. That day was the thirty-fifth anniversary of her wedding day.

The funeral service in St George's Chapel took place the following Monday, and afterwards the body of the Duke of Windsor was buried at Frogmore near the garden where he had played as a child.

(Opposite) The small figure of the Duchess, boarding the aeroplane at Heathrow to return to France.

Immediately after the service the Duchess returned to France. All through the week the newspapers had been full of photographs of her with members of the Royal Family, of the Duke's coffin, and of the crowds that gathered to see it. The most dramatic photograph, which appeared the day after the funeral, showed the Duchess boarding the aeroplane at Heathrow the afternoon before – a small, black-clothed figure climbing determinedly up the steps. She would not turn again, one felt, for a last look at the land her husband had given up for her, and this was the ending of an episode – an episode in the history of England and in the long life of its leading family.

Appendix

The Message from King Edward VIII to the two Houses of Parliament announcing his Abdication.

Members of the House of Commons [Lords]

After long and anxious consideration, I have determined to renounce the Throne to which I succeeded on the death of My father, and I am now communicating this, My final and irrevocable decision. Realizing as I do the gravity of this step, I can only hope that I shall have the understanding of My peoples in the decision I have taken and the reasons which have led Me to take it. I will not enter now into My private feelings, but I would beg that it should be remembered that the burden which constantly rests upon the shoulders of a Sovereign is so heavy that it can only be borne in circumstances different from those in which I now find Myself. I conceive that I am not overlooking the duty that rests on Me to place in the forefront the public interest, when I declare that I am conscious that I can no longer discharge this heavy task with efficiency or with satisfaction to Myself.

I have accordingly this morning executed an Instrument of Abdication in the terms following:

I, Edward VIII, of Great Britain, Ireland, and the British Dominions beyond the Seas, King, Emperor of India, do hereby declare My irrevocable determination to renounce the Throne for Myself and for My descendants, and My desire that effect should be given to this Instrument of Abdication immediately.

In token whereof I have hereunto set My hand this tenth day of December, nineteen hundred and thirty-six, in the presence of the witnesses whose signatures are subscribed.

(Signed) EDWARD R.I.

My execution of this Instrument has been witnessed by my three brothers, Their Royal Highnesses the Duke of York, the Duke of Gloucester and the Duke of Kent.

I deeply appreciate the spirit which has actuated the appeals which have been made to Me to take a different decision, and I have, before reaching My final determination, most fully pondered over them. But My mind is made up. Moreover, further delay cannot but be most injurious to the peoples whom I have tried to serve as Prince of Wales and as King and whose future happiness and prosperity are the constant wish of My heart.

I take My leave of them in the confident hope that the course which I have thought it right to follow is that which is best for the stability of the Throne and Empire and the happiness of My peoples. I am deeply sensible of the consideration which they have always extended to Me both before and after My accession to the Throne and which I know they will extend in full measure to My successor.

I am most anxious that there should be no delay of any kind in giving effect to the instrument which I have executed and that all necessary steps should be taken immediately to secure that My lawful successor, My brother, His Royal Highness the Duke of York, should ascend the Throne.

EDWARD R.I.

Genealogical Table

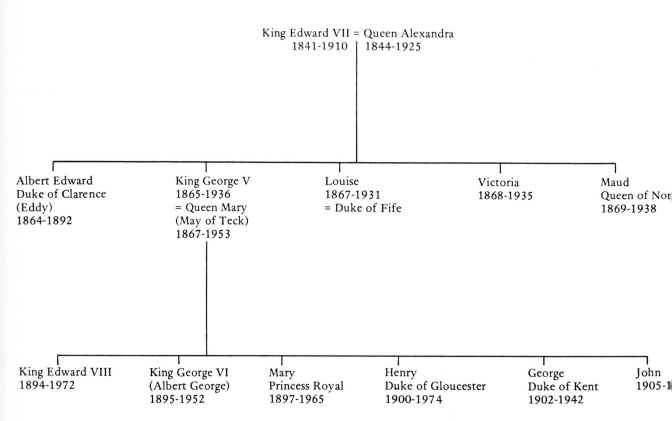

King Edward VII = Queen Alexandra
1841-1910 | 1844-1925

Albert Edward
Duke of Clarence
(Eddy)
1864-1892

King George V
1865-1936
= Queen Mary
(May of Teck)
1867-1953

Louise
1867-1931
= Duke of Fife

Victoria
1868-1935

Maud
Queen of Nor
1869-1938

King Edward VIII
1894-1972

King George VI
(Albert George)
1895-1952

Mary
Princess Royal
1897-1965

Henry
Duke of Gloucester
1900-1974

George
Duke of Kent
1902-1942

John
1905-1

Bibliography

Airlie, Countess of, *Thatched with Gold*, Hutchinson, 1962.

Asquith, Lady Cynthia, *Diaries 1915–18*, Hutchinson, 1968.

Beaverbrook, Lord, *The Abdication of Edward VIII*, Hamish Hamilton, 1966.

Birkenhead, F. W., *Walter Monckton*, Weidenfeld & Nicolson, 1969.

Bolitho, Hector, *Edward VIII*, Eyre and Spottiswoode, 1937.

Channon, Sir Henry, *Chips, the Diaries of Sir Henry Channon*, edited by Robert Rhodes James, Weidenfeld & Nicolson, 1967.

Cooper, A. Duff, *Old Men Forget*, Rupert Hart-Davis, 1953.

Cooper, Lady Diana, *The Light of Common Day*, Rupert Hart-Davis, 1959.

Dugdale, Blanche, *Baffy, the Diaries of Blanche Dugdale 1936–37*, Valentine Mitchell, 1973.

Esher, Viscount, *Journals and Letters of Reginald, Viscount Esher*, Vol. 2, Nicolson & Watson, 1934.

Feiling, Keith, *Neville Chamberlain*, Macmillan, 1946.

Furness, Lady Thelma, and Vanderbilt, Gloria, *Double Exposure*, Frederick Muller, 1959.

Gardiner, A. G., *Certain People of Importance*, Jonathan Cape, 1926.

Gore, John, *King George V, A Personal Memoir*, John Murray, 1941.

Hardinge, Helen, *Loyal to Three Kings*, William Kimber, 1967.

Harris, Kenneth, *Kenneth Harris Talking To*, Weidenfeld & Nicolson, 1971.

Hood, Diana, *Working for the Windsors*, Allan Wingate, 1957.

Hyde, H. Montgomery, *Baldwin, the Unexpected Prime Minister*, Hart-Davis MacGibbon, 1973.

Inglis, Brian, *Abdication*, Hodder & Stoughton, 1966.

Jones, Thomas, *A Diary with Letters*, Oxford University Press, 1954.
Whitehall Diary, Vol. 2, Oxford University Press, 1969.

Lockhart, J. G., *Cosmo Gordon Lang*, Hodder & Stoughton, 1949.

Lowndes, Marie Belloc, *Diaries and Letters of Marie Belloc Lowndes*, Chatto & Windus, 1971.

Lyttelton, Oliver, *The Memoirs of Viscount Chandos*, The Bodley Head, 1962.

Mackenzie, Compton, *The Windsor Tapestry*, Rich and Cowan, 1938.

Magnus, Philip, *King Edward the Seventh*, John Murray, 1964.

Middlemas, Keith, and Barnes, John, *Baldwin*, Weidenfeld & Nicolson, 1969.

Nicolson, Harold, *Diaries and Letters, 1930–39*, Collins, 1961.
Diaries and Letters, 1945–62, Collins, 1966.
King George V, His Life and Reign, Constable, 1952.

Pope-Hennessy, James, *Queen Mary*, George Allen & Unwin, 1959.

Sencourt, Robert, *The Reign of Edward the Eighth*, Anthony Gibbs & Phillips, 1962.

Stevenson, Frances, *Lloyd George, A Diary*, Hutchinson, 1970.

Templewood, Viscount, *Nine Troubled Years*, Collins, 1954.

Wheeler-Bennett, John, *King George VI*, Macmillan, 1958.

Windsor, the Duchess of, *The Heart Has Its Reasons*, Michael Joseph, 1956.

Windsor, HRH the Duke of, *A King's Story*, Cassell, 1960.
A Family Album, Cassell, 1966.

Wrench, J. E., *Geoffrey Dawson and Our Times*, Hutchinson, 1955.

Young, G. M., *Baldwin*, Rupert Hart-Davis, 1952.

Index